The Gospel and Islam:

A Compendium

Abridged Edition

Don M. McCurry, Editor

MARC
919 West Huntington Drive, Monrovia, California 91016
A Ministry of World Vision International

The Gospel and Islam:

A Compendium

Abridged Edition

Library of Congress Number 78-78291

Copyright © 1979 by
MISSIONS ADVANCED RESEARCH AND
COMMUNICATION CENTER
A Ministry of World Vision International

ISBN 0-912552-26-3

Printed in the United States of America

PREFACE

The task of sharing the good news of Jesus Christ with Muslims
has always been one of the greatest challenges facing the
Christian Church. Today that challenge is even more apparent as
political events call attention to Muslim lands, and as a new
openness to consider the claims of Christ is reported among a
number of Muslim peoples.

So it was with eager anticipation that the North American
members of the Lausanne Committee for World Evangelization
received a proposal for a North American Conference for Muslim
Evangelization. The proposal was initiated by Dr. Peter Wagner
of the Fuller School of World Mission and presented by the
Reverend Don M. McCurry, a veteran missionary and a student at
that school. The Lausanne Committee members warmly agreed to
co-sponsor such a conference with World Vision in the Fall of
1978.

Don McCurry had worked since the late 1950's as a missionary
to Muslims in Pakistan. He came to study at the Fuller School
of World Mission convinced that one of the greatest obstacles
to Muslim evangelization was the lack of culturally congenial
churches for Muslim converts. His broad experience and his
personal warmth and sensitivity made him ideally suited to be
director of this strategic conference. World Vision, through
its MARC center, kindly provided office space, staff help and
generous financial support to help make this project possible.

LINCOLN CHRISTIAN COLLEGE AND SEMINARY

From the first the organizers were committed to the concept of a "working" conference where participants would be carefully selected and thus highly motivated. Forty foundation papers were distributed to prospective participants at one-week intervals. The quality of the person's written response to these papers determined whether or not he or she would be finally chosen as one of the 150 participants at the conference itself!

A very special group of people, therefore, arrived at the conference on October 15, 1978. This was undoubtedly the first time that so many people representing so many different constituencies and types of ministries aimed at Muslims had gathered together to pool their resources and learn from one another. The boldness and creativity of the foundation papers had already set the mood for a new freedom to grapple with the issues head on and to make honest evaluations of past and present efforts. The presence of various categories of people (missionaries, mission executives, anthropologists, Islamicists, communicators and third world consultants) allowed for a balanced and realistic discussion of new strategies and approaches.

Testimonies by missionaries to Muslims indicated clearly that the mission to Muslims cannot be a mechanical or calculated enterprise, but rather must be a ministry of service inspired by the Holy Spirit with power.

This compendium is one tool which it is hoped will be of practical help to all who minister among Muslims. The conference also pointed out the acute need for a central "nerve center," a research and training institute for Muslim evangelization. This institute has now been formed at the Samuel Zwemer Institute in Southern California with Don McCurry as its director.

The conference ended with a note of hope and encouragement. There was a new commitment to reaching the 720 million Muslims with the good news of Jesus Christ, a new determination to pool resources and work together for this end, and a confidence that culturally congenial churches could be established for and by Muslim converts. Above all, there was a new assurance that "the God who is the Saviour of all men," (I Timothy 4:10) wills to give to multiplied thousands of Muslims a living and saving faith in Jesus Christ who is Lord of all!

Leighton Ford
Charlotte, North Carolina
February 14, 1979

FOREWORD

Some conferences "debate, declare and depart." Other
conferences change history. The 1978 North American Conference
on Muslim Evangelization has become one of those history-
changing conferences.

In the tradition of Edinburgh, Berlin and Lausanne, the Glen
Eyrie conference is already influencing the shape and direction
of world evangelism. More than 150 representatives from many
nations, church traditions, backgrounds, and experiences came
together with a single purpose--to seek God's direction for
more effectively proclaiming Jesus Christ to the 720 million
followers of Islam. With repentance, new insight and a sense
of unity, the participants left believing that God is doing a
new work among Muslim peoples and that the Church must move
quickly if it is to be a faithful instrument in his hands.

The conference foundation papers, speakers, task force reports
and conference report describe the needs of Muslims, the failings
of the Church, and the exciting opportunities for evangelization
that face churches and missions today. The Muslim world is
undergoing social and political disruption. There is new openness of heart and mind among many Muslims. There is also a
closing of access to some Islamic nations. The Church must turn
from ineffective methods and seek culturally appropriate ways to
present Jesus Christ faithfully and powerfully.

The tasks before the Church are many. The gospel must reach
hundreds of millions of Muslims. Missions and missionaries must
repent of their lack of sensitivity, of their indifference, of

their unwillingness to break with tradition. National churches must come out of isolation and move into their cultures with renewed vigor. National Christians and foreign missionaries must work together in a spirit of true interdependence.

This conference has shown us something of what the future of Muslim evangelization may hold. A multi-purpose training institute and research center is being planned to help coordinate efforts and to share knowledge. Aptly named for one of the most famous of all Christian servants to Islam, Samuel Zwemer, this institute will reflect his words when he said that the Church in its ministry to Islam "was called to a deeper study of the problem, as well as a more thorough preparation of its missionaries and a bolder faith in God."

There is more. Task forces have been proposed to explore the theological issues that affect evangelization of Muslims and to publish studies that will aid the Christian witness to them. Programs have been described that will encourage training, church growth and witness to Muslims on all continents, including North America. And these are but a few of the exciting results of this historic meeting.

This conference has given the Church renewed vision and hope for evangelism in the Muslim world. The Church must now respond to that vision and to that hope.

Now is the time to expect a growing harvest among Muslim peoples.

Now is the time for hard work and financial commitments.

Now is the time for believing prayer, for faithful dedication, for courageous witness.

Now is the time to truly believe that God will bring his glory to all the Muslim world.

Now is the time of salvation for the world of Islam. The harvest field is ripening. The Lord of the harvest calls. Where are the workers? The Church must delay no longer.

W. Stanley Mooneyham
President
World Vision International

ACKNOWLEDGMENTS

My first thanks are to God for his sustaining grace through the conference experience and the work of this compendium.

Secondly, I must thank those who prayed and still are praying: for those who have faithfully prayed for us throughout our work both in Pakistan and now here; for Vonette Bright and the Campus Crusade prayer partners; for Jack McAllister and the prayer people of the World Literature Crusade; for Gerald Swank and the friends of Sudan Interior Mission who set aside days of prayer and fasting; for the International Intercessors of World Vision; for all of the un-named friends who have prayed for us.

Special acknowledgments must go to the staff of Fuller School of World Mission. Ralph Winter first suggested a research program on new approaches to Muslims. Arthur Glasser gave a special invitation to come and join in inaugurating a year of Muslim studies. Charles Kraft arranged for the conference and the compendium work to feed into the dissertation program. Peter Wagner and Edward Dayton accepted the proposal Robert Douglas and I drafted as a term paper in their class on "Strategy of Missions."

Peter Wagner took the initiative in gaining the sponsorship of the North American Lausanne Committee on World Evangelization for the conference. Again, a special word of thanks to the members of that committee who launched us in this venture.

Stanley Mooneyham and World Vision deserve special recognition for their great generosity in funding both the conference and the compendium as well as providing the project management staff for the former and the office staff for the compiling of this volume. Burt Singleton, who served as the starting project manager for the conference, has performed a tremendous service in the same capacity in overseeing the various aspects of the workload in putting this book together. Carol Glasser, who stepped into the project management position for the conference, and whose extraordinary dedication made the conference what it was, brought the same high quality of work with her into the proof-reading of this entire text. Dan Brewster served as assistant editor on the foundation papers prior to the conference and has done a great service for us all in summarizing the participant's responses for this volume. Special thanks are due to each of those who shared in the typing load: Carol Kocherhans, Valerie Tinley, Susie Mabee, Moye Loya, Betty Lou Williams, all of World Vision, as well as Linda Myers. Thanks to other World Vision employees James Griffith and Gloria Luna who provided invaluable assistance in procurement of materials and the art work, and Mary Janss-Clary who came to our rescue as we approached our publication deadline. Thanks also to David Cashin of the Samuel Zwemer Institute.

To each of the 17 authors who contributed to this volume a profound expression of gratitude for their invaluable articles and their rejoinders to the participants' responses. It should be noted that two of the authors have asked to remain anonymous.

And finally, a word of thanks to the hundreds of respondents who have added immeasurably to the cause of Muslim evangelization by their enthusiastic interaction with the ideas expressed in the papers that formed the bases of the conference issues.

Don M. McCurry

CONTENTS

A TIME FOR NEW BEGINNINGS

Don M. McCurry

Resurgent Islam, with its 720 million adherents, is gaining a prominence it has not had for centuries. The Arab-Israeli conflict has been the perennial issue in world politics ever since the end of World War II. Oil, the life-blood of the industrial West, is now the key to world economics. Muslims are not only at the heart of the above affairs, but continent by continent, their concerns are at the root of many major issues. Cases in point are: the insurgency of the Moro Liberation Front in southern Philippines; the recent civil war in Pakistan resulting in the creation of Bangladesh; the war on Cyprus between Muslim Turks and Christian Greeks; the unresolved civil war in Lebanon; Ethiopia's problems with Somalia; Libyan-fomented guerilla movements in many parts of the world, and Iranian student riots in the United States. Added to these, are the headline catching struggles between traditional Islam and secular trends. Egypt barely averted the imposition of Shariah Law. Iran is in shambles as the mullahs battle the army. Pakistan as of March 1979 will be under Islamic law for the first time in its history.

While all of the above mentioned trends were developing, new currents were flowing in the Christian movement. At the Lausanne Congress on World Evangelization in 1974, an awakened and alert leadership of Protestant missions made us aware that Muslims may constitute the largest single block of unreached people in the world. Of the three billion unreached, 24 percent were Muslims. This represents one out of every six human beings. As startling as this information was, it was overshadowed by far more stunning data. Only two percent of the North American Protestant missionary force was actually engaged in trying to win

Muslims to Christ.

It is true that one-third of the Protestant missionary force of the world is non-North American, and some of them are engaged in Muslim evangelization. And it also must be noted that churches exist already in many Muslim lands. While thanking God for these historic churches, it should be noted that long-standing bitter rivalries and worse, even wars, with Muslims have left both ancient scars and fresh wounds. These have enervated the commitment of these churches to evangelize their oppressors.

With the exceptions of Indonesia, a small segment of the Anglican church in southern Iran, and new groups in Bangladesh and Tunisia, existing churches in Muslim lands are from non-Muslim backgrounds. Recent surveys reveal that virtually no missionary societies have arisen from these churches for the purpose of evangelizing Muslims.

It is not unfair to say that, whether we are talking about local churches in Muslim lands, or ex-patriate missionaries, there is a formidable cultural distance between the evangelizers and the unreached Muslim people groups.

I. COMMUNICATOR AND CULTURE

Traditionally, missions to Muslims have rejected the culture of the converts and imposed that of the missionary or evangelist. This pattern of extractionism and insistence on a double conversion, that is, first to Christ, and then to the culture of the missionary or evangelist, may well be the single most important reason for a greater lack of results in work among Muslims. To say this is not to minimize the grave theological misunderstandings Muslim have about Christian doctrine, or to ignore the possibility of any unrepentant human, Muslim or otherwise, to resist the Lordship of Christ. Assuming that a Muslim does choose to follow Christ, it does not follow that that person will automatically embrace the cultural forms or the Christian practices of the evangelist.

In looking back over the account of the birth and growth of the church in New Testament days, we note that both Jesus and Paul came up with radically new approaches. Jesus, you will recall, said that new wine must be put in new wineskins. He constantly challenged the Jewish leaders at every point where they tried to absolutize their cultural forms that were contrary to the intent of Scripture. He spiritualized the meaning of the Kingdom of God and freed it from the cultural-boundness of Jewish politics and religious forms. To the Samaritans he said, "neither here nor in Jerusalem." Worship must be in "spirit and in truth."

With Paul, the issue burst the bounds of Palestinian Judaism
and spilled into the vast cultural melange of the Mediterranean
basin. His lot was to poineer in the whole area of establishing
the essence of the gospel, universally applicable, over against
the rich diversity of its cultural expressions. In essentials,
he stressed the universality of salvation to all believers,
whether barbarian, Scythian, Greek, Jew, slave, master, male or
female. But in cultural expressions, he became as a Greek to
Greeks, as a Jew to Jews, as without law to those without law,
as under the law to those under the law. What he wrestled with,
he knew, was more than just his personal approach in missions;
the leaders of the Church must face these issues and come up
with a solution that would allow it to grow anywhere. His
insights and courage set the stage for the early phenomenal expansion of the Church. The clues to his thinking are directly
traceable to their sources in Christ's own approach.

II. CHRIST AND CULTURE

What were the principles and assumptions upon which Jesus
operated with regard to humankind and their cultures? First,
we notice that he did not ignore the fallenness of human nature.
He spoke directly about sin, error and disobedience. His
opening word was, "Repent, for the Kingdom of God has come."
That word alone implies something is wrong with the old order
and a new one has to be established. To admit this is to confess that culture - all cultures - being man made, are flawed.
Hence, the need for judgment.

At the same time, we read that we were made in God's image.
Jesus constantly appealed to this, for instance, in saying that
to sin against the poor and needy is to sin against him. He
commended what was praiseworthy in human culture and behavior.
Nevertheless, he knew what we needed. We needed to be re-made -
to be born again. He didn't pray that we be taken out of the
world, only that we be kept from the Evil One. His goal was to
bring into existence a transformed humanity which would be one
with him. When he used the illustrations of believers being salt
and light and leaven, it implied that through us cultures would
be leavened - transformed.

As we watch Christ relate to persons of different cultures:
Samaritans, Greeks, Syo-Phoenicians, we learn that he never
sought to impose Jewish patterns on them. He allowed them to
remain what they were - only transformed by their encounters
with him. In searching for the basis of Jesus' tolerance with
those of other cultures, we need to range throughout the
Scriptures. In the very beginning, in Genesis, we read that

God himself, to save man from becoming totally unrecoverable, generated the multiplicity of languages and ethnic varieties of humankind (Genesis 11). Paul gives significance to this in his sermon on Mars Hill, when he points out that God set the bounds of the nations - that they might seek after him (Acts 17). And finally, in Jesus' final revelation to John, he shows him people of every tongue and tribe and nation - redeemed and living in the presence of the Lord (Revelation 5). In so doing, he affirmed the reality and validity of all cultures - transformed and redeemed.

In brief, the work of Christ was to both judge and redeem, to prune and transform. He never sought to enforce structural uniformity. He sought to forgive and transform both individuals and their societies - their cultures.

III. CHRIST AND ISLAMIC CULTURES

When we seek to apply the above precepts to evangelizing Muslims, we are moving into uncharted waters. The weight of the history of churches and missions is in favor of "extractionism." By this we mean taking the Muslim convert completely out of his cultural environment. The basic assumption behind this method is that Islamic cultures are totally evil. Nothing is redeemable. All must be condemned. Accompanying this judgmental attitude toward Islamic cultures, was a notable lack of critical thinking on the part of the evangelist about his own culture. The result of this combination of assumptions usually resulted in what we have now come to label "cultural shock" for the new convert. In addition to the legitimate conversion to Christ, he or she was then forced to accept the cultural forms of the evangelist or missionary. In either case, it was unfamiliar and strange and frequently repugnant.

Islam, from its side, contributed to this unfortunate pattern by promulgating the "law of apostasy." This was based on a quranic passage that originally applied to pagan Arabs who became Muslim and then reverted back to paganism. In the course of time, it came to be applied to any Muslim who became any kind of non-Muslim, including converts to Christ. If the death sentence was not carried out physically, it almost always was socially and culturally. The former Muslim was expelled. With the Muslim society thus expelling such converts, and the missionary/evangelist unwittingly cooperating by receiving him and welcoming him into his own cultural forms of faith, the practice of extractionism was established and unchallenged for centuries. The result has been that the new convert was cut off from the very milieu where he could be the most effective, that is, from the people of his own culture.

In Pakistan, I watched this pattern repeated over and over again, and with the same heart-wrenching results. Casualties and heartaches. Of the 700 conversions discussed with colleages, 350 have been lost track of. Of the 350 still known to profess faith in Christ, only 10 percent still identify with the existing church. And of those 35, not one feels emotionally welcome or at home in the existing churches. The reasons are not hard to identify. The structure and the flavor of these churches are both Western and Hindu-ish. Approximately 95 percent of the members were won from Hindu backgrounds, before the birth of Pakistan, by western missionaries. The question that has arisen out of this Pakistan situation, and it is not unlike that dozens of other countries, is, "Does a convert from Islam to Christ have to necessarily join one of these churches?" Could a church be formed for those who have come out of Islamic backgrounds that would be culturally congenial to them? To begin to ask this kind of question led to the birth of a cluster of "new" questions.

How much of his culture can a Muslim retain and say with integrity, "Jesus is Lord of my life?" Out of this came further refinements: "Is there anything in Islamic culture that is acceptable and should be retained?" "Are there customs that are relatively neutral - practices that are not necessarily relevant to religious issues?" And finally, "Can we identify those practices and beliefs that are positively evil that must be either replaced with functional substitutes or done away with altogether?"

These questions were a cause of deep consternation. Theologically, the question arose as to whether or not this would lead to syncretism and heresy. With regard to the existing church, would this lead to a schismatic spirit and further divisions. Up until recently the prevailing attitude was that we should stick with the old patterns. But the questions wouldn't die. How would Christ relate to living Islamic cultures today? The answer that has come is that he relates to Islamic cultures the same way he relates to any other culture, namely, he both judges and transforms; he never sets out to obliterate. Out of this ferment has grown the effort to apply the best of our thinking to the discipling of the Muslim nations.

IV. A TIME FOR NEW BEGINNINGS

While the above kind of thinking was developing in missionary circles, God, evidently, had been preparing people in several other lines of thought, too. Anthropologists, both Christian and non-Christian, had been giving a lot of attention to Islamic cultures. They looked at Muslims where they were and began to describe the dynamics of what was going on. Terms like "folk

Islam" and "popular Islam" cropped up in the literature and opened up hundreds of new vistas on Islamic cultures that did not fit the older traditional picture of classical Islam. With these descriptions also came the knowledge that none of these cultures were static; frequently, at least three strands of movement could be identified: the older cultural and religious heritage, pre-dating Islam, was very much in evidence, and often more dominant than the Islamic forms that had been imposed or embraced later, and these two could be seen interacting with the strand of secular influences from the West and from communism.

Other scholars began sharing their insights on how social change takes place, the role of innovators, and how old forms give way to new ones. Along with this came valuable findings from communication experts. At first, these insights were only germane to phenomena inside of a given culture, but soon they were applied to cross-cultural problems. Bible translators, both those who advocated "dynamic equivalence" translations and those who wanted the more literal approach, get involved in the discussions on how the communicator and receptor perceive.

In theological circles, "contextualization" became the latest concept to occupy our minds, especially as we grappled with the implications of this approach in cross-cultural situations. What is the essence of the gospel? How is it best communicated in strange new cultural contexts? What will this mean in Islamic milieus?

It didn't take long for some of those concerned with missions to Muslims to realize that the time was most opportune for making new beginnings. In doing so, it became apparant that scholars from several disciplines needed to meet and interact with one another in developing more effective approaches in evangelizing Muslims.

The idea for holding a conference to bring all of these concerns and insights together came out of a "Strategy of Missions" class at the Fuller School of World Mission. From here it went to the North American Lausanne Committee on World Evangelization. This Committee took the initiative in sponsoring this conference along with World Vision assisting with funding and planning.

Taking into consideration all of the above developments, the design of this conference would have to be different from any of its antecedents. The question was how to bring together the skills, experience, and insights of those people who could help us become more effective in discipling Muslims.

V.   THE DYNAMICS OF AN UNUSUAL TYPE CONFERENCE

Several concerns faced us as we asked ourselves what needed
to be done. Our first concern was to get highly motivated
people involved who could make a difference in Muslim evangelization. The second was to identify the major issues that needed
to be raised and discussed. And the third was the design of the
process that would insure maximum participation before the
conference, bring prepared participants to the conference proper,
and issue in ongoing activities after the actual meetings were
held.

Based on issues identified, in the first instance, at a mini-
consultation in Grand Rapids, a further effort was made to
solicit experienced workers for their ideas. Out of this correspondence a list of 17 subjects emerged. These became the foundation paper titles. Authors were recruited for each of these
and their names and bio-data are included in this volume. The
process of sending out papers and eliciting responses on a
weekly basis actually worked! Author after author has
commented on how valuable those responses have been. The key
issues raised in these responses have been summarized and along
with the author's rejoinders (when obtainable) are included with
the original articles.

With regard to the selection process, participants were
chosen based upon their level of response to the 40 foundation
papers that would be sent them during the six months preceding
the conference. This was to insure a high level of preparedness.

The design of the week together at Glen Eyrie, in Colorado
Springs, was a major concern. Several assumptions influenced
that design. One was that people of various disciplines and
roles needed one another if they were ever going to come up
with adequate strategies for reaching the unreached Muslims of
our world. We believe that God honored this concern for a full
expression of "body life" by giving us executives, missionaries,
professors, Islamicists, anthropologists, theologians, media
experts, and overseas national consultants to participate in the
events at the conference.

Another major assumption was that our faith would be
strengthened by the testimonies of those who were having fruit
in their work. And God, indeed, used this to rekindle the
flame in many a discouraged heart. God is going to do "great
and mighty things." The prayers that went up during the last
48 hours of the conference, I am sure, opened up the portals of
heaven for God to pour out his blessings - harvest blessings
throughout the Muslim world.

20

But there has to be a practical side, too. And one of our assumptions in this area was that work goes better when you plan for it. So, built into the design were some very demanding activities on planning strategies against field situations. Not unexpectedly, there was much resistance to this on the part of those for whom it was a new experience. Nevertheless, men and women, North Americans and overseas nationals, listened to one another and worked together. By the third day of the conference, real enthusiasm was evidenced in tackling the field situation set before them.

The final major assumption was that the conference was not an end in itself; it was merely a one-week segment in an ongoing process. Task forces were formed toward the end of the week that set in motion activities and relationships that will continue until we see Muslims coming to Christ from every tongue and nation.

The gist of these task force reports are highlighted in the Conference Report included in this volume. Because of the sensitive nature of material contained in them, they will not be published. But various responsible persons are taking up the actions advocated. Several of these activities will be facilitated by a newly forming institute described below.

VI. THE FORMATION OF THE SAMUEL ZWEMER INSTITUTE

Following the conference, and taking its cues from task force recommendations, a local steering committee was set up in Southern California to bring into being a "nerve center/coordinating hub" that would conduct research, train people for working with Muslims, and in general, promote the cause of Muslim evangelization. This steering committee, brought into existence the executive committee and subsequently the full board of what is going to be called The Samuel Zwemer Institute. This Institute will seek to carry out a large number of the ideas suggested at the conference. It sees itself as a servant organization to the whole Christian movement as pertaining to reaching unreached Muslims for Christ.

VII. THE UNFINISHED TASK

The 17 foundation papers included in this volume by no means exhaust the number of issues that need to be taken up if we are to take seriously our Lord's command to disciple the nations, and in our case, all of the approximately 3500 Muslim ethnic groups in the world. They open up a wide variety of subjects with which we all must grapple if we are going to be more effective in our work. The reader is invited to become part of the ongoing process. Most of these essays were initiatory.

Many of the ideas have not yet been tested in the fires of
field experiences. It is a time of new beginnings. Your
participation is essential. The insights you already have or
will gain in the days ahead need to be shared. We encourage you
to stay in touch. Let us join hands in our common task of
reaching unreached Muslims for Christ.

VIII. THE PLACE OF PRAYER

The conference that led to the publishing of these papers was
conceived in prayer. All throughout the preparation and the
proceedings themselves, a mighty volume of prayer was ascending
to our Heavenly Father. Without prayer now the things being
advocated will not happen. It is most fitting that this essay
concludes with an appeal for your prayers. This volume is not
an intellectual exercise; it is an expression of deep concern,
finding its source in the heart of God for reaching unreached
Muslims for Christ. He invites us to join with him in that
wonderful activity.

Two verses that have burned within my heart during these
months of preparation are the following: "Call unto me and I
will answer thee, and show thee great and mighty things that
thou knowest not" (Jeremiah 33:3). And, "Ask of Me and I shall
give thee the nations for thine inheritance" (Psalms 2:8). Let
us offer ourselves in prayer and practice as God's instruments
for the coming harvest in the Muslim world.

THE GOSPEL AND CULTURE

Paul G. Hiebert

Can an illiterate peasant become a Christian after hearing
the gospel only once? And if so, what do we mean by his
conversion?

   Imagine, for a moment, a Pakistani peasant returning to
his village after a hard day's work in the fields. His wife
is still preparing the evening meal, so, to pass the time,
he wanders over to the village square. There he notices a
stranger surrounded by a few curiosity seekers. Tired and
hungry, he sits down to hear what the man is saying. For
an hour he listens to a message of a new God, and something
in him moves him deeply. Later he asks the stranger about
the new way, and then, almost as if by impulse, he bows
his head and prays to this God who is said to have appeared
to men in the form of Jesus. He doesn't quite understand
it all. As a Muslim he knows that there is only one God,
and to worship any other is idolatry, but how can God have
a son without a wife? It is all so foreign to him.

   The man turns to go home, and a new set of questions
flood his mind. Can he still go to the mosque in order to
pray, for it is dedicated to the worship of the one God?
Should he tell his family about his new faith? And how can
he learn more about Jesus--he cannot read the few papers
the stranger gave him, and there are no other Christians
within a day's walk. Who knows when the stranger will
come again?

THE PROBLEM

How do we bring the gospel to Muslims in Arabia, or Pakistan, or India or Indonesia? Suddenly, in the last few years, we are confronted by a great many new words and theories which are supposed to answer our question: dynamic equivalent Bible translations, church growth, missiology, cross-cultural communication, contextualization of the gospel, and on and on. What can we make of all of this?

Actually, the problems we face in missions are not new, nor are many of the insights advanced by modern mission theory. In fact, many of them are found in Acts 15, the first Church conference, because this was really a mission conference called because the Church had been too successful in planting churches in other cultures.

At the outset, the Christians had won a fair number of Jews into their fellowship. There had been a few disagreements among them, to be sure. Some of the Jews had taken up Greek customs, and there were a few Gentiles who had become Jewish proselytes in order to join the Church but who had not fully given up their pagan ways. But, in general, they were pretty well agreed on what it meant to be a Christian.

That was until this Paul, the radical, began to preach to the Gentiles and told them that they did not have to become Jews in order to be followers of Jesus. They ate pork, they kept their immodest Grecian dress, and, above all, they did not keep the sabbath and refused to be circumcised--the two central symbols of God's covenant with his people! If they could do this and still be Christians, what did it mean to be a Christian?

So the first Church conference was held to decide the questions what is the gospel--the good news unto salvation, and how does it relate to a people's culture? In order to be Christians do people have to change their dress...their food habits...their marriage practices...their ties to their relatives...their ideas of God...their worship of idols...or what?

Three key principles on the relationship of the gospel[1] to culture emerge from the text.

I. THE GOSPEL VERSUS CULTURE

So long as the Church remained within a single culture, the cultural question did not arise. The Christians could express their beliefs using their language and their cultural symbols, without giving thought to how this language and culture molded their beliefs. Only those areas of a culture that came into direct conflict with the gospel were called into question.

But when the Church crossed into other cultures the Church was forced to face the question of culture. The gospel had to be translated into new languages, and languages often put the world together in radically different ways. For example, in English we have three tenses: past, present, and future--and these seem to be the only logical possibilities to us. But another language may have only two tenses: past and present. In it there is no future, because the future does not really exist--it is only the anticipation of the present. A speaker in that language does not say, "I will go to town tomorrow," as if the future exists and is certain. Rather he says, "I am planning on going to town tomorrow," a statement about the present which does exist. Other languages have four tenses.

Even a word such as "God" does not mean the same thing in different languages. In English, "God" is a being distinct from all other creatures. He has a life that is different from human life, animal life or plant life. In Telugu (South India), there is only one form of life, so the life of God is the same as the life of a human, or an animal or a plant. There is no word in Telugu that speaks of God who is distinct from the rest of creation. So what word do you use for God when you translate the Bible?

Language is only the beginning of the translation problem. It only reflects a much deeper set of assumptions about reality, and a world-view that underlies a culture. When Christianity enters a new culture, it must not only be translated into a new language, but also into the thought forms, symbols and customs of a new culture.

But what do we mean by "culture?" Originally the word was used to describe the behavior of the elite--the rich, the educated, the sophisticated. Anthropologists have broadened its meaning to include all people. By "culture" they mean "the integrated system of learned patterns of behavior, ideas and products characteristic of a society."[2]

There are several parts to this definition. First, note that it refers to patterns of learned behavior--to cultural forms. These run all the way from shaking hands as a form of greeting (or spitting on one another's chest as they do in one South American tribe), to patterns of family organization, and to the most complex international institutions. Second, note that these forms are all linked to meanings. The flag is not simply a stylized piece of cloth. It symbolizes the nation. Finally, note that the definition refers to integration. Culture is not an odd assortment of patterns, these patterns relate to each other and fit into a fundamental set of assumptions about the way the world really is put together, and how it ought to function--namely, to a world-view. It is this integration of cultural traits into the total cultural picture that makes changing cultures so difficult. Patterns cannot simply be taken out, added or replaced without causing cultural disruption on the one hand, and a reinterpretation of the newly introduced patterns on the other.

Different cultures do not simply give different labels to the same world--they create different worlds. This difference gives rise to many of the basic problems facing cross-cultural missions. We are all aware of the culture shock we face when we move into a new culture. This is due not to the dirt, or poverty, for those coming to the West face the same shock. The shock is due to the fact that we are completely illiterate in the new culture--we just do not know how to behave in it. We are also aware of the cultural misunderstandings that arise when we move abroad. For example, some African tribes thought missionaries were witches for only witches kept cats as pets. At night their witches would enter the cats and go around the village "gathering souls" in order to eat them.

A deeper problem created by cultural differences is the fact that each of us has learned that our cultural ways of doing things is the "right way," and the tendency, therefore, when we meet other cultures, of thinking they are "primitive" or "uncivilized." Somehow, to eat with forks and spoons is more "civilized" than eating with one's fingers, even though these forks and spoons have been in a great many other people's mouths.

But for missions the real problem of cultural difference is the fact that any message must be translated into new thought forms, and into new cultural patterns, if it is to be understood in another culture, and in the translation, the meaning changes. It is impossible to translate from one culture to another without a shift in meanings.

How then do we test what new meaning the message has in another culture so that we can make sure it is as close to the original as possible? Our natural tendency is to look for familiar behavior patterns and cultural forms--does the man kneel when he prays, does he go to church regularly. But these are poor indicators of what is really going on in the minds of people. It takes a great deal of careful research based on feedback from the people themselves to discover what they really are thinking. Only then will we know whether the people have understood the heart of the gospel, and be able to correct their misunderstandings. Cultural translation is an ongoing process of communication, feedback, recommunication and more feedback.

If culture is all of our learned thought and behavior patterns, what then is the gospel? And how do we differentiate
it from culture? This is a difficult question and one we must
face every time we bring the gospel into a new cultural
context. The other alternative is to equate the two, and
require that all converts become Americans, or Englishmen, or
whatever the missionary's culture is. However, we must
remember that had the first missionary conference reached
this conclusion, we today would all have to become Jews in
order to become Christians, and realistically speaking how
many of us would have become Christians with all the cultural
changes and restrictions that that would have entailed?

We must recognize that there is a fundamental difference
between the gospel and a culture. Even though it is not always
easy to distinguish between them, we must, with the guidance
of the Holy Spirit, continually do so, for if we do not make
the distinction, we reduce the gospel to a particular culture.

II. THE GOSPEL IN CULTURE

To distinguish between the gospel and culture is difficult
enough, but the first missionary conference found that the
relationship between gospel and culture is more complex than
that. They found that they had to use cultural forms in order
to communicate the gospel. The gospel cannot be thought or
expressed apart from the languages of spoken words, writing,
drama, ritual or the arts. The issue in the conference was
whether the cultural forms of circumcision and keeping the
sabbath were the only ways in which the gospel could be
expressed, and the decision was "no." The elders decided that
Greek and Roman forms could be used to declare the gospel and
to build the church. The reasons they gave were that the
prophets had said the day would come when "all of the rest of
mankind would seek the Lord," and that the Holy Spirit had been
given to Greek and Roman converts as well. In fact, one is
struck by the almost complete freedom of expression permitted
new indigenous forms of Christianity. Converts in other
cultures were only to abstain from meat offered to idols, from
blood, from anything strangled and from fornication. These
are obviously not the core of the gospel, but cultural
practices prohibited in part because these were particularly
offensive to Jewish Christians.[3]

But what is the application of this example to our illiterate
peasant? Which of his own cultural forms can he use in his
Christian life? Is it proper for him to continue to hold up
his hands or to kneel when he prays? Can he still use the term

"Allah," which means "God," when he refers to the God of the
Bible, or what term should he use? Can he use Urdu to declare
his faith, or use drums and local musical forms in his Christian songs? Can he meet with fellow Christians in the mosque?
Does he have to divorce his second and third wives and make
them into prostitutes?

Obviously, there must be some change in the behavior of the
new Christian, for conversion, too, expresses itself in
cultural forms--in a new life as well as a new heart. The
new Pakistani Christian can probably use a great many of his
old cultural forms without undermining his faith. He can
sleep on his old bed, eat his standard foods, and worship
sitting on the floor. Other cultural forms will need to be
reinterpreted in order to convey a Christian message, just
as western Christians adapted Easter, Christmas, or, for that
matter, bridesmaids who were originally intended to confuse
demons who came to carry off the bride. Some of his old
customs will have to be dropped for they are so tied to his
old religious system that to continue them would compromise the
essential nature and uniqueness of the Christian message.
But in this case what new cultural forms can be used to express
the Christian message--forms that people understand so that
they will understand the message? And who is to decide which
cultural forms may be used, which reinterpreted and which
rejected: the local Christians...the missionary...the American
agency or church? The first missionary conference was called
to answer precisely these kinds of questions.

III. THE GOSPEL TO CULTURE

True, culture is the vehicle that carries the message of the
gospel to people. But there is another dimension to the
relationship between gospel and culture. Just as the gospel
calls people to repentance and new life, so it calls for new
lifestyles, and the forsaking of cultural practices and
institutions that foster sin. In Acts, the proscriptions
did not deal with theological beliefs, but with cultural forms.

The gospel always stands in divine judgment on human
cultures. It speaks not only of new birth, but also of righteousness and love. It speaks for strong families and fellowship, and against injustice, hatred, greed and immorality. And
here we must stand alongside our new Pakistani brother and in
all humility admit that our own culture is not Christian. It,
too, must be brought under the Lordship of Christ. The gospel,
not western civilization, is God's good news to mankind.

We have not answered our original question--can an illiterate Muslim become a true Christian after hearing the gospel

only once, and, if so, what does that mean? Yes, it means
accepting Christ Jesus as Lord and Savior. But what must this
mean to him in his thought patterns, and how must it express
itself in his life? The future of Muslim missions and of the
Church in Islamic lands depends in a great measure on how we
answer these questions.

FOOTNOTES

1. Although the precise nature of the gospel is not spelled
out because it is beyond the scope of this paper, it is
taken as a given that there is a unique revelation from God
that is supracultural and this revelation is recorded in
the Bible. Just what constitutes the essential core of the
gospel unto salvation must be discussed in another paper.

2. This definition of culture is obviously very elementary.
On the one hand, it avoids an extreme behavioralist position
through the inclusion of "ideas." On the other hand it
avoids a purely mentalistic position by noting that the
anthropologist derives his or her understanding of cultural
maps by observing behavior. In other words, there is a
linkage between culture and behavior. The key word here
is patterns. No idea, no behavior, no object in itself
constitutes culture. It is the pattern behind sets of
these that we explore. In this sense, the definition tends
towards a more contemporary definition of culture in terms
of sets of shared cognitive maps.

3. It should be obvious by now that, at least in my model, one
cannot treat any cultural trait without dealing with its
theological implications. As Marshall McLuhan and others
have pointed out, we cannot divorce the form from the
meaning, or the media from the message. Every media or
behavior pattern has a structural message in addition to
the message it carries. This, in part, is what it means
for the gospel to be in culture. For this reason I believe
we must move beyond dynamic-equivalent translations, at
least when it comes to cultural practices other than
language that tend to divorce form from meaning completely.
To push dynamic equivalence too far is to overlook the
message in the media, and to overlook the fact that in
future years second and third generation students in a new
church will be reading the Bible in its original languages
and wonder why translations of the Bible in their native
languages diverge from the original texts.

BIBLIOGRAPHY

Geertz, Clifford
    1973   The Interpretation of Cultures. New York: Basic Books.

Guthrie, Donald
    1969   "Galatians," The Century Bible. Thomas Nelson and Sons.

Hiebert, P. G.
    1976   Cultural Anthropology. Philadelphia: J. B. Lippincott.

Kuhn, T. S.
    1970   The Structure of Scientific Revolutions, 2nd edition. Chicago: University of Chicago Press.

Machen, J. Gersham
    1947   Origin of Paul's Religion. Grand Rapids: Eerdman Publishing Company.

SUMMARY OF PARTICIPANT'S RESPONSES

The responses to Dr. Hiebert's paper were lively and thoughtful. By far, the majority were in basic agreement with Dr. Hiebert's positions and felt his paper was an excellent introduction to the conference proceedings. There were, however, an array of questions, comments and criticisms which indicated a high degree of interest and a wide range of opinions which provoked a stimulating cross-fertilization of ideas. This summary and those for each paper will focus on the questions and critiques rather than simply restating the affirmations.

Dr. Hiebert's discussion of the need to translate the gospel into new thought forms provided much interest. The respondents wondered how the meaning of the message would be tested in another culture to make sure it is as close to the original as possible. (Note that the author responded to this question on p. 61.) And, one asked if in fact the <u>meaning</u> of the message would change when it is translated into new thought forms, as Dr. Hiebert suggests, or if the meaning would remain constant while the forms changed.

On the author's treatment of the Acts 15 text, respondents wrote: "Right message, wrong proof text," and argued that "Acts 15 is not really representative of what happens to Muslims;" that Dr. Hiebert presses Acts 15 into the gospel/culture mold; and that the text does not fit because in fact, the Jews were part of the same culture as the Gentiles. "The Acts 15 question," some said, "was not whether the gospel could be expressed other than through circumcision and Sabbath keeping, but rather whether the cultural forms of circumcision and following <u>all</u> of the Jewish customs and ceremonies were the only ways in which the gospel could be expressed."

The debate on the paper's opening question, "Can an illiterate peasant become a Christian after hearing the gospel only once?," was especially notable. Interestingly, the respondents who commented lined up about evenly on both sides of the question. Those answering in the affirmative said:
--"Sure, it happened all the time in the New Testament."
--"There are lots of Ethiopian eunuchs out there."
--"Yes, if the Holy Spirit has prepared his heart."
--"Yes, but it will be, of course, a continuing process."
--"Yes, but like a planted seed, it will not mature without nurture and care. Unless he hears again and again he will probably slip back into his old ways."
--"Yes, provided the gospel message is presented in its pure form; unencumbered with irrelevant cultural appendages."

Those answering the question negatively said:
--"The possibility of effective communication in such a situation
is highly unlikely, and should communication take place, the
fear and shame of praying publicly would inhibit response."
--"No, he won't even recognize it as a Christian message."
--"We must assume that conversion will take place only over a
long period of time."

Other respondents straddled the fence:
--"God could convert the peasant on only one hearing, but he
hasn't chosen to do so."
--"Even having one missionary preach to the peasant is indicative of a problem. How can a Muslim learn about body life
unless he sees it in action?"

Finally, Dr. Hiebert's paper provoked a wide range of response on the general issue of the gospel and culture. One
person felt that the author was off target since "the whole
world is rapidly becoming one culture," and another argued that
"the missionary who adapts may have no more success than the
one who doesn't." Most respondents, however, were much more
sensitive to the importance of the culture question and lauded
Dr. Hiebert's insightful treatment. There was thoughtful interaction on what God calls Muslims out of, whether or not we are in
the same "family" with Islam, if the Muslim, to be converted,
must believe in a new god, and on the nature of the gospel within
its various cultural contexts.

AUTHOR'S REJOINDER TO PARTICIPANT'S RESPONSES

The task of a lead paper is to raise a few relevant questions; not to provide their answers. To attempt the latter would be presumptious, at least in fields so complex as the cross-cultural communication of the gospel. But to ask the right questions is by no means easy or irrelevant for a great many resources, human and other, have been spent on answering the wrong questions.

From the responses it became apparent that the opening question, "can an illiterate person, such as Ahmed, a Pakistani peasant, be 'born again' after hearing the gospel but once," is more than rhetorical. Some believe that he cannot, others that he can. Some raise the issue of realism. Because Muslims rarely, if ever, become Christians upon first hearing the gospel, they felt the story was irrelevant. Others noted that the case was precisely what they had experienced.

Admed's case was not intended to raise the question of reality, although, hopefully, it reminds us that we are dealing with real people in real life situations whose destinies will not depend on our agreement on missiological issues. Rather, Ahmed was used to raise a theological and conceptual question by creating an extreme case that reveals the bare bones of the issue. "Normal cases" are not hard to handle, but they also often cover up the basic issues. It is in the "extreme case," the most difficult to resolve, that we must wrestle with the critical issues--in this case with what it means to be "born again." If we can resolve the case of Ahmed, we should have few difficulties with normal cases.

In raising the question of gospel and culture, the paper does not attempt to draw the line between them. To do so at this stage would bog us down in arguments of detail before we had resolved the overall picture. We must first agree that the question of gospel and culture and the relationship between them is a relevant one. But is this not to ask the obvious? Maybe so, but I think not. First, it is clear that those who are theologically oriented did not take the implications of culture too seriously, just as those who are anthropologically oriented were too cavalier with theology. Second, anthropological research is beginning to show us how deeply cultures mold our thoughts, and this raises profound questions which we must face. To be sure, there are fundamental similarities between all peoples, and these are important. But it is the differences that create many of our problems in missions.

The question of cultural variance is a two-edged sword. We are made painfully aware of the differences of those to whom we go. But we need also to recognize the extent to which our own culture has molded us. A simple example can illustrate this. Westerners, influenced by Aristotelian logic, tend to think in terms of "bounded sets." For instance, they think of the category "Christians" as a group of people who share a minimum set of common characteristics (which are intrinsic to the person, and which are defined in creedal or behavioral terms). Furthermore, all Christians are perceived as "fully Christian" and are distinct from non-Christians. The category is defined primarily in terms of the boundary between Christian and non-Christian, and the maintenance of this boundary becomes essential to preserving the category.

If we think in terms of bounded sets, evangelism means bringing people into the circle of Christians, and conversion means crossing the boundary. Once in, a person is seen as fully a Christian. Growth may be desirable, but it is not an essential part of the structure of the category.

Other cultures seem to use other principles for creating their categories. For example, Hebrew and Arabic thought makes extensive use of "centered sets." In these, things are grouped according to the direction things are moving--according to the centers towards which they are headed. In these terms, a Christian is a person who is headed towards Christ. There are those who are "near Christ" in the sense that they know a great deal about him, but because they do not make him their center or God, they are not Christians. Such were the Pharisees. Others, like Ahmed, may have a minimal knowledge of Christ, but may turn their allegiance towards Christ, and thereby become Christians. If we think in terms of centered sets, conversion is "turning around" and heading towards a new center. But turning is not the end of the matter, for one must continue to move towards the center. Growth is an essential part of the structure of centered sets. On the other hand, while there is a clear boundary between those headed towards and those headed away from Christ, there is no need to preserve and accentuate the boundary in order to maintain the set. What is essential is maintaining the center.

In short, there is an objective reality called "new birth" and the Lord knows who are his. But we who see through a glass darkly, when we seek to make clear what we understand to be Christian, must define it not only in terms of theology, or of cultural meanings and forms, but also in terms of the deep cognitive structures we are using.

THE CROSS-CULTURAL COMMUNICATION OF THE GOSPEL TO MUSLIMS

Donald N. Larson

The North American Conference on Muslim evangelization is being
convened because Christians are not as effective as they would
like to be in evangelizing Muslims and the topic of cross-
cultural communication is on the agenda because leaders believe
that the complex processes underlying communications with
Muslims need special attention. The invitation to contribute an
article on cross-cultural communication to this conference came
as good news and bad news. The bad news is that I probably know
less about Muslims than readers of this paper. The good news is
that Christian/Muslim communication, as a specific case of
cross-cultural communication, is probably no more complex than
other cases and some analysis of the processes may actually
prove useful to the readers. The common purpose of these
articles is to lay a groundwork for discussion in October 1978,
when the conference convenes. My objectives therefore are:
1) to clarify what we mean by cross-cultural communication, 2) to
address a fundamental problem which appears when Christians and
Muslims communicate and 3) make some recommendations.
Hopefully, this will generate discussion leading to greater
effectiveness in communicating with Muslims.

I

No human talks to every other human. Because of his confine-
ment to a relatively small time-space niche, he talks only to a
relatively small number of people during his lifetime. In fact,
he does not even talk with all the co-occupants of his niche.
For the most part, he limits himself to those whom he knows and
who know him; his personal community, including kinsmen, fictive
kinsmen, associates and acquaintances. Here he finds frequent

35

and regular speaking partners. Not many Muslims have Christians in their personal communities, and vice versa.

At first the typical human talks only to his kinsmen. But as time passes, his personal community grows. He talks to more and more people on a regular and frequent basis. Strangers become acquaintances, acquaintances become associates, etc. In fact, although he may never talk with more than a handful of humans, he may come to view all humans as "fictive kinsmen" (Nelson 1971). Not many Christians and Muslims view one another as fictive kinsmen.

The basis of life in the personal community is <u>shared culture</u>, the body of knowledge (including its inventory and organization) that people use to interpret experience and generate behavior (Spradley and McCurdy 1975). Among other things, this shared culture includes the knowledge of conditions under which people talk together. Conditions must be just right if one human is to talk to another. If conditions are not just right, talking does not occur. It is in one's personal community that he develops this set of conditions. Christian and Muslim confront each other in terms of these conditions which they have learned in their personal communities.

Of the many conditions which shape communicative events, those involving <u>belonging</u> seem to be fundamental. Thus when one person recognizes the person approaching him as <u>member</u> or <u>insider</u>, he sets one plan into motion. When he views him as <u>non-member</u>, or <u>outsider</u>, he follows another. Communication between <u>outsiders</u> is often characterized as cross-cultural communication. Christian and Muslim are typically <u>outsiders</u> to one another.

Christian and Muslim share different cultures and it is in the differences between them that collisions originate. Such cultural collisions are exacerbated by differences in the way each uses language to map culture into sound, for because of such differences, each reads the meaning of the other's message in terms of his own system.

In principle, at whatever points the cultures and languages of Christian and Muslim are similar, mutual understanding comes relatively fast. Where differences are many and great, mutual understanding comes slowly and only with great expenditure of effort.

When Christian and Muslim meet, therefore, it is not with clean slates but under conditions established in their respective groups and in terms of what each knows at that point in his life and how it is organized in his mind. They engage each other as outsiders. Well-defined boundaries keep them separate. They may be able to talk freely about the weather, but when it comes to the central issues of life, like their respective worldview and lifestyle, they tend to avoid each other. When they cannot, they tend to collide.

Language provides a scan of one's cultural knowledge. When utterances leave the Christian's or the Muslim's mouth, what he knows and how he organizes it is evident. When Christian utterances enter Muslim ears, the meanings of those utterances are organized on the basis of what is already in the Muslim mind. Likewise, when Muslim utterances enter Christian ears, the meanings are organized by the Christian on the basis of what is already in his mind.

To put it somewhat differently, as a Christian transmits what he knows, the Muslim takes it, compares it with what is already in his mind and processes it accordingly. In the same way, as the Muslim transmits what he knows, the Christian processes it on the basis of what is already in his mind. That is, the Muslim organizes what the Christian sends according to what he knows, and the Christian does the same thing. Each controls his own output. However, neither exercises much control over what the other does with what he transmits. Neither can withdraw what is already in the other's mind. At best he can say things which may supplement or rearrange it.

One's language is ideally suited for talking about his own experience. Using unmatched languages or talking about unmatched sets of experience creates problems for both parties. So collisions between Christians and Muslims tend to originate in mismatched experience (cultural problems) and/or mismatched media (language problems). As they try to communicate, one may say to the other, "I don't know what you mean" or "I don't know what you are saying." These two statements differ. The first suggests that one is having trouble finding a way to plug the other's experience into his own. The second one suggests that one can't extract any meaning at all from what the other is saying. In the one case, he lacks sufficient experience to fully grasp the meaning of the other's message. .In the other, he lacks the ability to extract the other's message from his medium.

So what happens? If one should assume that the other's apparent lack of comprehension arises from language problems, when in fact it arises from common experience, he modifies the form of what he says without providing sufficient background and elaboration for the meaning to crystallize for the other. On the other hand, if he assumes that the other's problem is lack of experience, when in fact it is language, he elaborates endlessly, not realizing that the other is not getting much meaning from what he is saying. Both of these problems are very real.

The Christian may jump to the conclusion that his communication problem with a Muslim lies in the language being used when in fact it may lie in the gap between the Muslim's experience and his own. One's experience is too limited to perceive the meaning in the message which the other is sending.

The general problem boils down to the specific problem of belonging. Christian and Muslim belong to different "tribal" traditions. In their respective groups each comes to know different things, map them into language in different ways, meet others under different conditions and hold different beliefs.

When Christian initiates a conversation with Muslim and tries to persuade him to become a Christian, he undertakes a complex task.

The Christian may not stop to reflect on these processes, but if he hopes to make sense with Muslims, he must understand them and deal forthrightly with the problems that they create. But how shall he deal with them?

II

Christians are divided over ways to view encounters with Muslims. Evangelicals encourage and try to persuade Muslims to become Christians. Others (evangelicals usually refer to them as nominal Christians), leave initiatives to Muslims themselves. Evangelicals themselves are divided over what it means to become a Christian and over what to expect of Muslims by way of response to the gospel.

This matter has grown complex over the centuries. At first "becoming a Christian" referred to a Jew, Samaritan, Ethiopian, etc., who was following Christ as Lord. Terms like Jewish Christian, Ethiopian Christian, etc., referred to someone who had transcended his tribal orientation and boundaries and entered into new transformed relationships with people of mutually exclusive tribes with whom he worshiped, worked and witnessed in ethnically and racially heterogeneous congregations. Even Jews and their Gentiles entered into new and unusual relationships.

In these "supra-tribal" congregations members of mutually exclusive groups passed into one another's worlds as they followed Jesus as Lord in their common faith. A way to say this is that they bi-passed (Larson 1976). Such bi-passing did not

lead them to abandon their respective tribes but to relate to
them in a new way. Here is a way to picture the process:

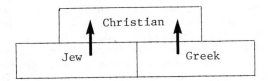

   Bi-passing appeared to violate conditions of belonging, and
indeed it did to some extent. However, the unique service of
the Christian community was to live supra-tribally in diverse
tribal settings.

   In Paul's reference to a "single new humanity" (Eph. 2:15),
he appears to allude to just this kind of relationship.

   As time passed, some Jewish Christians began to insist that
Galatians who wanted to become Christians should bear the marks
by which Jews recognized one another as such. In so doing, they
passed into the Jewish community by meeting new belonging
conditions that Jewish Christians imposed. In such "Judaizing,"
a form of tribalizing, one believed that outsiders could be
admitted to his tribe as members if and only if they met
conditions which insiders imposed. To picture this:

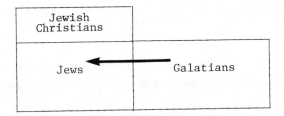

   For those who take Paul's rejection of Judaizing as didactic,
"becoming a Christian" involves a radical transformation of the
tribal point of view, not merely conversion from one tribe to
another.

   Over the centuries Christian congregations have taken on a
variety of tribe-like characteristics and lost some of those
which characterized original "supra-tribal" congregations.

   Today this problem is still with us. Some Christians
("Christian One") call for the Muslim to follow Jesus Christ as
Lord, helping him to identify and meet the belonging conditions
of this supra-tribal community about which Jesus himself spoke.
Their strategy is to develop relationships that transcend

traditional boundaries between Christians and Muslims. They see
the Christian congregation as an ethnically and racially heterogeneous unit in which people from a variety of traditions
belong to one another through faith in Christ in a sense which
transcends the tribe. Through bi-passing, as Jesus Christ
transforms their lives, Christian and Muslim belong to each
other in new ways. Their purpose is realized when the Muslim
belongs to the Christian community and uses it to live
Christianly in the Muslim community. We may picture this as
follows:

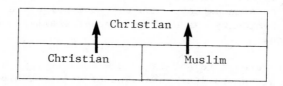

Other Christians ("Christian Two") call for the Muslim to
abandon the community of Islam with its characteristic worldviews and lifestyles and "become Christians" by meeting certain
belonging conditions which they themselves define and impose.
Their strategy is to facilitate the Muslim's passing into the
Christian congregation as they know it. According to "Christian
Two," when the Muslim becomes a Christian, he no longer belongs
to the Islamic community. The purpose of "Christian Two" is
realized when the Muslim renounces his Islamic connections,
meets new belonging conditions and becomes part of a new
network. The outcome is incremental; a gain in the Christian
community and a loss in the Islamic community. The assumption
is that the two communities are mutually exclusive units of the
same level, like two baseball teams playing each other. We can
picture this as follows:

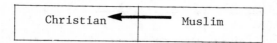

The Muslim is not likely to respond to "Christian Two's"
invitation to become a Christian. Little wonder. The Islamic
community provides him with a sense of belonging and all the
security and satisfaction that it entails. He is not likely to
give it up easily. If he perceives what the Christian is saying
as an invitation to shift from the Muslim community to the
Christian community, he simply rejects it.

Of course, if he is already marginal, he may attempt to meet
the belonging conditions of the Christian community in order to
recapture the security and satisfaction that he needs.

The failure of the Muslim to respond leaves "Christian Two" frustrated. He may blame himself for lack of effectiveness. Or he may blame the results on the Muslim's hard heart. Some keep at it. Some modify their approach. Some give up.

Long ago Judaizing Galatians were condemned. Today Christianizing Muslims is ineffective. To increase effectiveness we must recognize the limitations of passing and commit ourselves to bi-passing instead.

III

According to his belonging conditions, "Christian Two" can describe for the Muslim what he must do to become a member of his congregation. However, these same belonging conditions tend to discourage "Christian Two" from passing into the Muslim's world or even listening seriously to him. Listening politely is necessary but becoming too curious is unnecessary or even unwise, or so he thinks.

The more "Christian Two" thinks of what he knows and the less he thinks of what the Muslim knows, the more he talks and the less he listens. He may just assume that whatever is in the Muslim's mind makes no difference in establishing the point he is trying to make. But he pays a price for this arrogance. As he talks and the Muslim listens, he fails to find out what the Muslim is doing with the knowledge that he is trying to share. The Muslim may be ignoring it or radically reinterpreting it in his own terms or rejecting it totally as "crazy things that Christians say." "Christian Two" will never know until he stops talking. It is risky to talk without listening.

The Christian must know something of what the Muslim knows in order to make effective use of his own knowledge and experience. Likewise, the Muslim cannot transmit much of what he knows without knowing a good deal of what the Christian knows. The less knowledge and experience the Christian and Muslim have in common, the more important it is for them to engage each other in this way if they hope to convey what they know in an effective way.

Only when the Christian can understand and appreciate the Muslim's reality as he does can he talk about his own Christian reality in terms which the Muslim can understand and in ways that enable him to appreciate the Christian's point of view.

Therefore, if the Christian hopes to touch the Muslim at significant points in a significant manner, he must be prepared to talk, but he must also be prepared to listen.

The Christian must talk a little as the Muslim listens. As
the Muslim listens, he comes to know more about what the
Christian knows and how he organizes it. But then they must
reverse roles. As the Christian listens to the Muslim, he comes
to know more about what the Muslim knows and how he organizes
it. As the process continues, understanding grows through
taking turns at talking and listening. Mutual correction
occurs. Elaboration takes place as necessary. Points of agreement and disagreement are identified, clarified, documented,
altered and reinforced.

Such mutual self-discovery begins with a commitment to
bi-passing.

Passing into one another's world takes time. It requires
great attentiveness to differences of language as experiences
are compared. At first each can talk only about what he knows
and has experienced in his own terms. But gradually, as each
begins to sense the way the other experiences things, each is
able to use the other's words to talk about his own experiences.

Solving the problems that arise in bi-passing requires
different strategies. In one situation the Muslim may be unable
to extract the Christian's message from its medium. Failure to
communicate can be traced back to differences in the media, not
in the messages themselves. So the Christian must modify the
form of what he has said. In another, the Christian may be
unable to comprehend the Muslim's experience. Failure to
communicate can be traced back to cultural differences. So the
Muslim will have to provide more background information.

So Christian and Muslim need to learn to use one another's
language in the same way. They also need to listen to one
another much better to determine where their experiences are
different and fill in the gaps accordingly.

IV

A commitment to bi-passing is the sine qua non of increased
effectiveness in communicating with Muslims. In view of what
the Scripture says, this should come as no surprise to
Christians. Unfortunately the gap between "Christian One" and
"Christian Two" appears to be as wide as that between Christians
and Muslims. Humanly speaking, Muslims are not likely to
become Christians until "Christian One" and "Christian Two"
commit themselves to passing into one another's world.

BIBLIOGRAPHY

Anderson, John D. C.
    1976   "The Missionary Approach to Islam: Christian or
              'Cultic'?," Missiology 4:285-300.

Cragg, Kenneth
    1956   The Call of the Minaret. New York: Oxford
              University Press.

Goldsmith, Martin
    1976   "Community and Controversy: Key Causes of Muslim
              Resistance," Missiology 4:317-324.

Gowing, Peter G.
    1978   "Of Different Minds," International Review of
              Missions 67:74-85.

Hall, Edward T.
    1977   Beyond Culture. New York: Doubleday.

Kerr, David
    1976   "Personal Encounters with Muslims and Their Faith,"
              Missiology 4:325-330.

Khair-Ullah, F. S.
    1976   "Linguistic Hang-Ups in Communicating with Muslims,"
              Missiology 4:301-316.

Kimball, Solon T. and James B. Watson
    1972   Crossing Cultural Boundaries. San Francisco:
              Chandler Publishing Company.

Larson, Donald N.
    1976   Bi-passing: Making Sense When Worlds Collide.
              Limited circulation of prepublication edition.

    1977   "Missionary Preparation: Confronting the
              Presuppositional Barrier," Missiology 5:73-82.

Latourette, Kenneth Scott
    1970   A History of the Expansion of Christianity: Advance
              Through the Storm. Grand Rapids: Zondervan.

McCurry, Don M.
    1976   "Cross-Cultural Models for Muslim Evangelism,"
              Missiology 4:267-284.

44

Nelson, J. Robert
   1971   No Man is Alien: Essays on the Unity of Mankind.
          Leiden: E.J. Brill.

Pedersen, Paul, Walter J. Lonner and Juris G. Draguns, editors
   1976   Counseling Across Cultures. Honolulu: University
          of Hawaii Press.

Spradley, James P. and David W. McCurdy
   1971   Conformity and Conflict. Boston: Little, Brown and
          Company.

   1975   Anthropology: The Cultural Perspective. New York:
          Wiley.

SUMMARY OF PARTICIPANT'S RESPONSES

Dr. Larson has inspired many and confused some in this excellent paper. Comments ranged from "excellent," "very perceptive," "a fresh, lively paper," to "confusing--it turns on nothing," "exceedingly clear but simplistic," and "why are the Judaizers always getting picked on?" Many people liked his ideas but wanted more--e.g.: "good as far as it goes," and "sure, we should listen, but to what?" Others clearly disagreed with Dr. Larson, such as the one who said: "The roots of the problem lie in Islam, not in communication principles."

The most interesting comments came in response to three portions of Dr. Larson's paper--his "bi-passing" concept, his "Christian one" and "Christian two," and his diagrams of the conversion process. Most respondents liked the "bi-passing" idea, but this new term was not fully understood. Repeatedly readers complained that it was not adequately defined and that they needed some illustrations. Others remarked that we must beware of Christian nihilism--bi-passing even some of the essentials of the Christian faith in order to "win" the Muslim.

Dr. Larson's "Christian one" and "Christian two" approaches elicited considerable response. A reader wondered what traditional categories they fell into: conservative vs. liberal, persuaders vs. nominals, or what? Another asked what the difference was between demanding conversion into the culture of the Christian witness and demanding conversion into a supra-tribal group called "Christians." Some respondents had their own characterizations of "Christian one" and "Christian two:"
--"'Christian two' does not listen out of conviction, but
   'Christian one' may not listen out of habit."
--"'Christian one' leads to idealism and relativism; 'Christian
   two' leads to bigotry and jargon."

Dr. Larson's diagrams of various conversion approaches also generated a lot of interest, and inspired a number of alternate models representing the ideal process. Many respondents presented new diagrams which they felt more accurately described the conversion-in-culture process. Note the subtle distinctions in examples shown below:

1. "A diagram for 'Christian three'--one who leads Muslims into a position similar to 'Jews for Jesus.'"

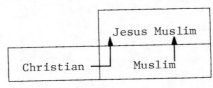

46

2. This one shows that Christians also have to do some "stretching."

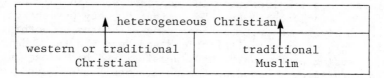

↑ heterogeneous Christian↑	
western or traditional Christian	traditional Muslim

3. One reader preferred this model:

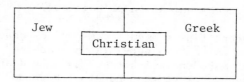

4. Finally, one reader stressed that both Christianity and Islam are supra-tribal and that it ought to be made clear that the Muslim convert is not choosing between being Arab or Christian or between Arab and Western. Rather, from within his culture, whatever it is, he is choosing allegiance to Christ.

Christian	
American/European	Arab/Pakistani/Turks etc.

AUTHOR'S REJOINDER TO PARTICIPANT'S RESPONSES

I am grateful to know that my paper provided inspiration, help and insight to most readers. In this response, I will concentrate on those matters which left some readers confused.

My paper turns on a simple observation: when members of mutually exclusive groups meet, they tend to avoid each other. When they cannot avoid each other, they tend to collide. However, there are times when members of mutually exclusive groups are able to pass into one another's worlds. The fundamental reason for our difficulty in cross-cultural communication is that the groups in which we are reared are ethnocentric, judging other groups and their members in our terms, not by means of a set of transcendent categories that apply equally to themselves and others. In the paper, I have referred to this as "tribalism" and some readers reacted unfavorably to my choice of words. Of course, none of us likes to think of himself as "tribal."

Early Christians exemplify what I have called "bi-passing." In heterogeneous congregations (Jews and their Gentiles) they learned to work, worship and witness together, engaging in the cooperative creation of knowledge that was new to each of them. It was, I believe, the spirit of the living Christ among them that made this possible. They were able to transcend the boundaries which their respective groups maintained.

As with Jews of old who, because Christians sought to help Gentiles to find Christ within their cultural context and then to relate to him as common Lord, the task of Christians with reference to Muslims remains unchanged. Some Christians concur in this assessment; I have called them Christian One. Other Christians see the task differently: to call Muslims out of the community of Islam into the Christian community and then set up boundaries by which they (the Christians) recognize when the Muslim has indeed become a Christian. I have called these Christian Two.

I have also tried to show, from a theoretical point of view, that Christian One's position is likely to be far more attractive, and, I believe, more biblical than that of Christian Two.

Some have reacted to my comments on the communication process as "simplistic," or "obvious." However, the importance of listening to one another is not always recognized, even though it is where all successful cross-cultural communication begins. We evangelicals are much better at talking than at listening. Our talking would be much more effective if it were balanced by serious attempts to listen.

   Some of my critics say that the roots of the problem are in
Islam. This is a simplistic assessment, as far as I am
concerned. The root of the problem lay in the relationships
between Christians and Muslims and the very great and understandable difficulty that members of mutually exclusive
groups have in communicating with one another. Yet, the genius
of the Christian community, viewed over the past two millennia,
is in its capacity to recognize the nature and source of its
own sin, to allow Christ to deal with it redemptively and then
to overcome the limitations of any Christian tribalism which
may have seeped in over time. If there is tribalism in the
Christian, and if the Christian is unable to overcome it, what
does he really have to offer the members of the different
tribes?

   "Bi-passing" is perhaps a new term. However, the concept is
as old as the Christian community itself in which members of
different groups engaged in the cooperative creation of a
contextualized gospel, one after another from one time, place,
setting, to another. New supra-tribal relationships developed
in union with Christ in each context. We need to let the
concept of "bi-passing" judge us. Are we entering into relationships with Muslims which resemble those of the Jews and their
Gentiles in Galatia, Ephesus, Corinth? If not, why not? Have
the rules changed?

THE INCARNATIONAL WITNESS TO THE MUSLIM HEART

Bashir Abdol Massih

Dr. Saeed Khan Kurdistani, an outstanding Iranian Christian, died in 1942. In the 1960's a friend of mine served with the government in Dr. Saeed's area and became acquainted with an old man there. The aged man, when asked if he had known Dr. Saeed, caught his breath and whispered: "Dr. Saeed was Christ himself!"

Surely the desire of every person witnessing to Muslims is that Christ, in all his fullness, may be visible. Western culture, however, often looms so visible that the Muslim has trouble seeing him. Culture is a major factor in the incarnational witness.

UNDER #4.

I. LOVE: THE KEY TO INCARNATIONAL WITNESS

The incarnational witness means more than just the Living Word being clothed in flesh. Jesus became flesh in a specific time-space setting. There were cultural implications. We know that God sent his Son into a Jewish cultural setting. For Jesus, it meant a Jewish expression of his human nature. It meant a Jewish lifestyle in Jewish culture with Jewish customs and a Jewish family setting. Paul sums it up succinctly: "For I tell you that Christ has become a servant of the Jews on behalf of God's truth..." (Romans 15:8). Jesus became the servant of the wayward Jewish nation! How can I be a servant of Muslims?

Jesus intricately involved himself with the Jewish people. His greatest heartache came from them. Finally they crucified him. What caused him to identify so absolutely with them? To

discover the answer, follow him to the mount overlooking
Jerusalem right before the crucifixion. Tears splash on the
dusty ground (Luke 19:41). He weeps, "How often would I have
gathered thy children together, even as a hen gathereth her
chickens...and ye would not" (Matt. 23:37). His heart overflowed with pure love. Nothing less would suffice.

Nassim, a Muslim on the train, listened with open heart as
the missionary spoke of Christ. When asked why he was so open,
he replied with deep emotion, "Years ago, a Muslim friend and I
saw two Catholic sisters holding out their hands to receive
money for a new hospital building. As we passed them, my
friend in contempt spit in the extended hand. Thoughtfully,
the sister pulled out her handkerchief and wiped off the spit,
then smiling at my friend said, 'All right, that was for me.
Now what will you give Jesus?'" Nassim looked at the missionary with tears in his eyes and with a catch in his voice said,
"Can anyone forget love like that?"

The incarnational witness across cultural barriers to the
Muslim demands that it be a witness of love motivated by love.
Nothing less will suffice. The disciples in John 4 were
shocked to discover Jesus bridging the cultural gap between
himself as a Jew and the Samaritans (John 4:9, 27). The
Samaritans held wrong doctrines, had polluted their race with
Gentile blood, and were the enemies of Jews. The Jews called
them dogs. Jesus touched them deeply in love. He completely
identified with them, even to the point of sleeping in their
beds and putting his fingers in the same bowl with them at
mealtime (John 4:40). Could there be a more beautiful example
of an incarnational witness? For us to carry any kind of
western pride or superiority to the Muslim world, must of
necessity cut us off from them. This is the opposite of the
incarnation which bridged the great spiritual and cultural gulf
between "us" and "them."

II. APOSTLE PAUL ON THE MESSENGER AND HIS INCARNATIONAL WITNESS

Paul too said, "I have made myself servant unto all, that I
might gain the more" (I Cor. 9:19). "I am made all things to
all men, that I might by all means save some." "And this I do
for the gospel's sake" (I Cor. 9:22, 23). "Unto the Jews I
became as a Jew, that I might gain the Jews" (I Cor. 9:20).
"To them that are without law, as without law (being not without law to God, but under the law to Christ)" (I Cor. 9:21).
Paul is saying that in respect to culture, the messenger must
change, rather than the hearer of the message. (The only
exception to this principle being where the culture of the
hearer is so linked with sin that it cannot be cleansed by God
(Acts 15:20)). Paul is saying that the living message must be

spelled out in a cultural-time-space setting. Christ must
become incarnate in specific cultural forms.

Is not this the true meaning of Christ's incarnation? The
previous state of Christ's person in glory was brought so completely into subjection in the incarnation that <u>he actually
appeared before men as one of them</u>! Though the divine nature
exuded forth from Jesus, he was distinctly like us. Paul says
in essence that he (Paul) became as a Jew to the Jews, and as a
Gentile to the Gentiles. He made Christ incarnate in Jew-like
form to reach them, and Christ incarnate in Gentile-like form to
reach them. Dare we follow the train of Jesus and Paul and say,
"Christ incarnate in Muslim-like form to reach them?" Do we
find a resistance in our hearts at this point? Surely this
prejudice is not born of Christ's incarnational love, who "being
in the form of God...made himself of no reputation and took upon
him the <u>form</u> of a servant, and was made in the <u>likeness</u> of men,
and being found in fashion as a man, he humbled himself and became obedient unto death?" (Phil. 2:6-8). Paul tells us to be
likeminded! (Phil. 2:15). How far are we willing to go to bring
Christ incarnate in a Muslim context? Could it be that if we
were to wear a turban and a robe, and go into their places of
worship, and even be mistaken for one of them, that we would
indeed be following Christ's model of the incarnation?

III. WHO IS THE INCARNATIONAL WITNESS?

The incarnational witness is one in whom love has worked so
deeply that he seeks in every way possible to become like the
hearer so that he can manifest the gospel in thought, communication, and religio-cultural forms that relate meaningfully to
the hearer. The incarnational witness realizes, of course, the
"offence of the gospel" itself, but he will seek to avoid any
other objectionable factors. North Americans especially should
remember that there is much in their lifestyle that is objectionable to sensitive Easterners which has nothing to do with
the offence of the Cross (Brudick and Federed 1958).

IV. A LOOK AT SOME EVANGELICAL RELIGIOUS FORMS

We evangelicals pride ourselves that we don't have forms and
symbols in our worship, but we do. Elaborate buildings, church
spires and bells, a cross up front, the types of clothing worn
in church or pulpit, the order of worship, the hour of worship,
length of service, day of worship, use of the organ and piano in
worship, men and women sitting together, closing eyes to pray,
benches, choirs, Sunday schools, Wednesday night prayer meeting,
one-man pastor, separation between clergy and laity, keeping of
Christmas and Easter, funeral forms, wedding forms, prayer
before meals, women with heads uncovered in church--all are

forms or symbols that we use in our religious lives. None of them are specifically commanded in the New Testament. Presumably none of them are contrary to Scripture or we wouldn't do them. They usually are very precious to us, and we are quite attached to them, and often react when they are questioned or altered.

It appears from Scripture though that forms are of minor concern to Christ. Jesus tells us to pray. What forms should we use? The one simple instruction in Scripture as to form in praying, lifting up holy hands (I Tim. 2:8), is largely ignored by evangelical Christians, and obeyed by Muslims! When the woman in John 4 inquired where one should worship (John 4:20), Jesus lifted worship above specific forms and places, stating that the time was coming when they would neither worship in the mountain of Samaria nor in Jerusalem. The important thing was to worship God in spirit and in truth (John 4:23). Four things were important in true worshippers: 1) focus of worship ("the Father" through the Messiah), 2) right God-man relationship ("worship the Father," communication with him), 3) inner life pure and right ("worship...in spirit") and 4) accordance with the body of truth ("worship...in truth"). How then were the Samaritans to worship their new-found Messiah? Jesus was really saying, "The outward forms you use in worship are not crucial as long as you hold these four points in focus. The glory of my incarnation is that I delight to be incarnate in varied and different worship forms. So worship in the cultural form you feel most comfortable with as long as you worship the Father in spirit and in truth." Muslim converts who state that their deepest experience of worship to Jesus is in kneeling with their heads to the ground are free to worship just that way, structuring their place of worship accordingly. Jesus frees them from worshipping in western patterns. Have we? Historically we have rejected their style of worship and have built them western-style buildings and had them sit on benches with legs crossed as in evangelical services in the West. How willing are we for Jesus to be incarnate in sanctified Muslim religious cultural forms?

We are commanded to preach. How? Like the Pentecostals? Like the Brethren? Like the Anglicans? The content of our praying and preaching is very clear from Scripture, but the form is left open-ended. We are told to gather together for worship, but the examples and simple instructions we have in Scripture (Acts 2:46, 5:42, I Cor. 14:26-40), are largely ignored by Christians. That we as Westerners could have presumed to take our religious culture halfway around the world and sell it to India, Africa and the Middle East as scriptural truth along with Christ, seems preposterous. But we have usually done it. If these religious forms are so precious and meaningful to us, that

to break them causes deep feelings and reaction, how must a
Muslim, who comes to Christ, feel when we insist on stripping
him of all he ever knew?

V. THE INCARNATIONAL WITNESS RELATIVE TO ISLAM

The record of Jesus and the Apostle Paul says that Jesus
loves to become incarnate in any given culture. He, of course,
will sanctify those elements useful to his purpose and prohibit
sinful practices. Therefore the unbiased messenger of Jesus
Christ to Islam will find much in a Muslim's religious culture
that, after sanctification by Christ, will be a beautiful
vehicle through which Christ can reveal himself.

The five pillars of Islam basically are compatible with
Scripture in most of their forms but not always in their content. Declaring the testimony (shahada) is a scriptural principle. A short, concise shahada seems to have been formulated
by the early Church (I Tim. 3:16). Prayer (salat) is certainly
enjoined in Scripture. Recited prayers are not against
Scripture. We Christians recite or read prayers every Sunday
and often through the week, for we sing written hymns, and many
of them are prayers. Fasting is enjoined in Scripture and so is
giving money to the poor or to God's servants. Many Christians
make pilgrimages to the Holy Land and we often hear testimonies
of the blessing of walking in that sacred land.

Surely the reader is thinking, "But the Muslim does all these
things for merit before God, and that's not compatible with
Christ." True. But what he needs is a change in focus and
perspective rather than a change in forms. Suppose a North
American, who has been trusting for merit before God in his
church membership, in his regular attendance at church and
Sunday school, in his giving money to the poor and to the
church, and in his good works, comes to Christ. Do we tell him
that since he previously was trusting in those things for
salvation, that he must now stop all of them? Of course not!
The important thing is that his purpose and perspective be
corrected, that he sees Christ as his salvation, life and merit
before God.

The mosque has always impressed me as being a spiritual
center in a local community. Its doors are open every day, and
local Muslims enter to pray, and stay to visit a few minutes
afterward. Students come to study for exams within the peace
and quiet of its walls. Theological students often are accommo-
dated, and are seen pursuing their studies and religious duties,
all this, of course, in addition to scheduled meetings there.
Does this not express something of what the early Christians
must have experienced in their religious and social life?

The minaret (manara--center of light or shedder of light), is a symbol of light to men as well as a voice, and is certainly a beautiful concept as meaningful as a church spire or bell. Modest dress of conservative Muslims is not against Scripture, nor is the separation of men and women in worship.

The Persian Muslim wedding is rich with meaningful symbols. The bride and groom sit side by side, facing a mirror, indicating that until that point they did not know each other directly. On a cloth in front of them is placed: 1) a Quran in the center, that it may be the center of their lives, 2) fresh greens, that their marriage may not grow stale, 3) goldfish, that their marriage might be full of life, 4) bread, that their table may never be bare, 5) an egg, that God may make them fruitful, 6) sugar lumps, to be broken over their heads that their lives together may be sweet and 7) a candle, that God may give them light on their new untrodden path. If the Bible were at the center with Christian content and message, could Christ become incarnate in this cultural form? I think he would be delighted.

VI. A CONTEMPORARY INCARNATIONAL WITNESS TO ISLAM

About ten years ago, God quietly brought a born again Orthodox priest into Muslim evangelism in the Middle East. We'll call the priest Rev. Brahim. Two things about his ministry amazed me. Rev. Brahim has been able to baptize literally hundreds of Muslims into Christ in a country where almost no Muslims were being saved. The other was that God chose to use an Orthodox priest to win Muslims in a country where there is a very strong evangelical national church.

In the Thursday night meeting, the hall overflowed into a lower room with closed circuit television. Singing predominated the first hour with a deep sense of the Spirit's presence. Rev. Brahim preached for an hour and 20 minutes, and then opened the meeting for written questions. Finally, after three hours, the meeting broke up.

VII. SOCIO-CULTURAL FORMS IN REV. BRAHIM'S MINISTRY RELATING TO A MUSLIM

1. Time was unhurried and free, making a Muslim feel very much at home, for that is true in Muslim meetings.

2. Loudspeakers blared with the windows wide open, very culturally in step. A battery of tape recorders surrounded Rev. Brahim, again culturally proper. A revival-like excitement filled the meeting, just as in mosque meetings I've attended.

3. The platform was filled with people, and an informality and a strong sense of belonging pervaded. Those present were more like participants than spectators.

4. Rev. Brahim dealt with families as a unit, with focus on the heads of homes, who in Muslim culture are the decision-makers. Older young men tend to carry something of this position also. Baptisms are performed with family units.

5. Thursday night was most appropriate for Muslims to attend.

6. The sexes were segregated on the main floor and the balcony was reserved for women--an excellent place for a Muslim woman not used to the prying eyes of men.

7. Rev. Brahim wore a turban-like cap and a long robe, similar to the dress of Muslim religious men.

VIII.   TEACHING AND COMMUNICATION FORMS IN REV. BRAHIM'S
MINISTRY RELATING TO MUSLIMS

1. Strong, dynamic and lengthy preaching appeals to a Muslim. I've seen long and fervent preaching, with more than one doing the preaching, even at Muslim weddings. Dynamic use of the language, especially Arabic, is very important.

2. The liberal use of stories and illustrations, rather than cold logic, is also important.

3. Repetition of verses in unison often echoed in the hall. How beautiful to see and hear 2000 people quote Scripture along with Rev. Brahim! Also, he taught Scripture to the 400-500 who stayed afterward for the time of questions.

4. Strong and emotional heart appeal--the way to a Muslim's will is not through his head. The meeting was charged with life and emotion, just like mosque meetings.

5. Young men studied in an informal Bible school set up very similarly to the informal religious training of Muslim leaders in the mosque.

6. Miracles were present as a persuasive mover of the Muslim will and as part of his religious logic, for he is a firm believer in the supernatural.

56

IX.   RELIGIO-CULTURAL FORMS IN REV. BRAHIM'S MINISTRY RELATING TO A MUSLIM

1.   Rev. Brahim's preaching was prominent, fervent, and came with the authority to which a Muslim will respond.

2.   The hall was mostly bare except for a few pictures up front.

3.   Rev. Brahim's attire fit in with a Muslim's idea of a religious leader.

4.   Many lifted their hands in prayer, as Muslims do.

5.   The authority in the religious Muslim home is the father, and appeals were made to the heads of homes.

6.   Praying was never done sitting down. Rev. Brahim had the congregation stand, then facing the same way as the congregation, prayed. One felt the congregation united with him by audible expression, and with upraised hands. Corporate praying is very much a part of a Muslim's worship.

7.   The witness was bold and open. A good Muslim is not backward or apologetic in talking about his religion.

X.   CONCLUSION

By drawing attention to the socio-religio-cultural forms, we are not belittling the power of God, through the Holy Spirit, to change Muslim lives. Certainly there is no new birth apart from God and the redemption of Jesus Christ. But our ministries and attitudes must echo the words of James: "It is my judgment, therefore, that we should not make it difficult for the Gentiles who are turning to God. Instead we should write to them...it seemed good to the Holy Spirit and to us not to burden you with anything beyond the following requirements..." (Acts 15:19, 20, 28).

BIBLIOGRAPHY

Burdick, Eugene and William J. Federed
  1958   The Ugly American. New York: Norton Library.

SUMMARY OF PARTICIPANT'S RESPONSES

Many respondents felt this was one of the best papers, and that the author's emphasis on love and adaptation were excellent. "If we lack anything today," they said, "it is not money or even more missionaries. It is love."

One writer said that his reaction to the paper was emotional-- regretting that in his years of ministry...he was too "Western," too goal oriented, but gratitude for those times when (he) was able to put aside (his) "program" and sit down quietly for prayer with someone...sometimes a Muslim, who needed his help. "Here is a paper," he wrote, "that breathes the heart and soul of an evangelist for Muslims."

Along with the praise for the paper however, were many expressions of caution for Westerners desiring to implement the approach advocated by the author. They agreed, for example, that we should try to use the Muslims' cultural styles, but they were not so sure that we are the ones who can decide which should be used. "If you have no converts," they said, "then you are not able to make the decisions on what to keep and what to throw out..."

Relatedly, the description of the ministry of the Coptic priest, Rev. Brahim, was seen as very challenging, but it was doubted whether it was still possible to condition young missionaries, politically, socially, and spiritually to assume a similar role today. Further, there was some question about the accuracy of the description of this man's ministry, and what exactly makes him effective. Some readers asked, "if Rev. Brahim's ministry was so successful, where are his converts?" Another asserted: "The author claims that Rev. Brahim has baptized literally hundreds of Muslims. I know for a fact that the number did not exceed 25."

On the nature of Rev. Brahim's ministry, writers said that the author may have missed the real point of his success: "It is the spirit of [Rev. Brahim] that captivates. His methodology, the forms that he employs, are basically Coptic and Orthodox. But he is willing to spit into bottles for people to take away and give to sick people; he is ready to have his cloak pulled... by those seeking blessing. It is his spirit which comes across as saying, 'I am yours. I am at your disposal.'" It is clear, as other readers suggested, that we need to seriously consider and learn from Rev. Brahim's ministry, but much more needs to be known about him before we can assess the true value of his methods.

AUTHOR'S REJOINDER TO PARTICIPANT'S RESPONSES

In summarizing the responses to "Incarnational Witness to the
Muslim Heart," two basic facts are worthy of note. One is that,
in general, the 83 responses were overwhelmingly positive, with
58 of them being very positive, 17 being positive with some
reservation, 7 being negative and one non-committal. The
other fact that is note-worthy is that of the 9 non-western
responses included in the 83 above, 4 were negative, 3 were
positive and 2 were positive with some reservation.

One can immediately see that the percentage of those accepting
or rejecting in the latter group is almost a complete reversal
from the responses of those from the West. Whatever else we
may conclude from these differing responses, certainly there is
indication that enough of a divergence exists to demand that we
communicate in depth and humility with each other to find what
God is saying.

Recently, three men who have spent much of their lives in
reaching Muslims (one having been born in a Muslim country, and,
incidently, on the Lausanne Committee) stated, "The greatest
obstacle to a Muslim coming to Christ is not theology, but
fear." If this is true, then certainly the whole subject of
this paper takes on added importance, for the more we can reduce
the "culture shock" of Muslims coming to Christ, the less they
will fear to come.

The following model, taken from Scripture, may be useful to
illustrate the paper. Try introducing the Muslim on the right
spectrum and the Westerner on the left.

A MODEL FOR INCARNATIONAL CHURCH PLANTING

Paul, a cross-cultural incarnational witness to Gentile and
Jew, I Cor. 9:19-23:

```
+-----------------------------------------------------------------+
|     Gal. 2:3          |                     |    Acts 16:1-3     |
|  Cultural Bridge      | Bridge in Christ    | Cultural Bridge    |
|Gen.*-------Gen. Ch.*  Gen. Ch.---Jewish Ch. Jewish Ch.-------Jew |
+-----------------------\  /------------------\  /----------------+
|   Acts 15:1-29         \/  Eph. 2:11-22      \/   Acts 22:12, 13 |
|Gen.          Gen. Ch.  Jew Ch.        Jew Ch.             Jew|
|   Cultural           |    |        Barrier |    |               |
|                      |Cultural  //  Barrier                    |
|   Cultural           |        //          Barrier              |
+-----------------------------------------------------------------+
```

Acts 11:1-3; John 4:9, 27

*Gen.--Gentile; Ch.--Christian

The incarnational approach to Church planting (where Christ is allowed to be incarnate in and come through any given culture or subculture) is very important in keeping the bridge intact between the Christian and his people in order to facilitate a mass movement of that culture to Christ. The love of God, as displayed at Bethlehem and Calvary in identifying with men, is essential in constructing that bridge.

If in the above model, we move the Jewish Christian too far to the left, by partially or fully destroying his culture, then we erect a natural barrier to other Jews coming to Christ, for Christ in the Christian (the point where Christ becomes visible on earth) takes on a Gentile-like form which the Jews despise, thus making it difficult for them to come to Christ.

In my opinion, two movements in our day illustrate this principle--the Jesus revolution and the Jews for Jesus movement. Would a mass movement to Christ have occurred in the hippie subculture had there been insistence on their adopting the "straight" culture? Would there be the movement among Jews today if they had to lose their identity as Jews to become Gentiles in culture? Many failed to see much desirable in a rather weird hippiedom, yet there was something inherent in the "Jesus freak" that identified him with his subculture that was more than "just Christ." It was Christ expressing himself through a sanctified version of that subculture. That was the bridge over which thousands walked and ran. Judaism is rejected by God today as the vehicle of God's grace and salvation, yet there is something inherent in the Messianic Jew that relates to his religio-cultural group. Does not the Bible and recent church history teach us that to see a movement begin in a given culture, we must somehow "lock into" or "bridge into" that culture in an incarnational way. Is Islam further afield than hippiedom or rejected, legalistic Judaism so that we can't allow a similar bridge to be built between the Muslim in Christ and his religious culture?

THE MUSLIM CONVERT AND HIS CULTURE

Harvie M. Conn

How has the evangelical missionary looked at the relation
between conversion and culture? How has that perspective
affected the way he approaches Muslim evangelization? What
part does it play in the planting of Millat 'Issawi (churches
as Jesus fellowships) and the development of a Muslimun
'Issawiyun (submission to Jesus) movement? Are the barriers
to fruitful evangelism "primarily theological?" Or "primarily
socio-cultural?" What steps are needed by the cross-cultural
evangelist to erode those barriers in the strength of the
Holy Spirit?

I. A TRADITIONAL EVANGELICAL RESPONSE

Until recently, the emotional response to such terminology
could often be expected to be negative. To some, they connote
an unwillingness by the evangelist to disassociate the convert
from the religion of Islam. To another, they speak of tenuous
support for resistance to public confession and baptism, secret
belief. To still others they veil the syncretistic baptism of
Islamic ritual and belief, a euphemism for Christian casuistry
in the interests of numbers.

There is no doubt that, on the lips of some theorists, these
charges could be real. And there is no doubt either that,
depending on the practical outworking of such theories, the
dangers of syncretism and casuistry can become more than merely
dangers. At the same time, behind these fears may also lie the
remnants of an apologetic approach to Islam whose weaknesses
were being identified more than a half century ago and now, with

the contributions of cultural anthropology, are being
increasingly corrected.

Exemplified to some degree in the earlier formulations of
Samuel Zwemer (Vander Werff 1977:235), this traditional approach
reflects the legacy of the 19th century which pits Christianity
as a monolithic system over against Islamic as a purely
theological construction. We have no desire to downgrade the
past for what the present has only recently learned. History
is not only a ruthless reminder of what we have not achieved.
It is also a gracious call to thanksgiving for what was achieved
and to humility for what we still have to discover. Here too
Zwemer can serve as a model of change. To his criticism of
Islam as a system, he added increasingly a growing sensitivity
to the Muslim as a man and to the effects of "popular Islam" on
theological constructs. He remained aggressively aware of Islam
as an animated system but added to that perspective an understanding that such a system was neither as monolithic or
impregnable as the past had supposed. Recent studies in the
relations of systems building to ethnic views of culture and
society are reinforcing even more his later studies.

At the same time, the remnants of the old patterns remain
with too many. Its razor edges made less cutting through the
missionary's self-sacrifice and love, the methodology still saw
Islam as an ideological construct relatively untouched by the
ethnic worldviews with which religion is integrally bound.
Academic studies provided no tools to put theoretical wings on
the practical love of the missionary for the Muslim as a person,
and a culture-builder. Islam remained largely a theological
system, not an ethnic lifestyle living out a "faith-commitment"
(Conn 1978:41). Without this sensitivity to the relation between
religion and cultural worldview, the approach of Christianity to
Islam was often conceived of as the confrontation of one linear,
rational, universal system with another linear, rational,
universal system. This tendency was reinforced on the side of
Christianity by a long history of evangelical apologetics deeply
infiltrated from western cultural captivity to Aristotelean and
Cartesian cognitivism. Ever since Aquinas had seized on
Aristotle's rational categories in his Christian polemic against
Islam, Christian apologetics has, to greater or lesser degree,
made use of the same tools. Kept by the Christian naivete of
compassion and respect for the whole man from plummeting into
something worse, its allegiance to the truth as purely rational
has kept it from ascending into something better. So a Henry
Martyn could find himself caught between the two, losing through
the failure of rational controversy, "all hope of ever convincing
Mohammedans by argument," yet continuing to make use of debate/
dialogue and its presumptions of Christianity as a rational,
propositional system (Vander Werff 1977:34). Pfander's The

Balance of Truth remains in that same culturally bound dilemma, piety and rationalism struggling for control. With such presuppositions, evangelism becomes polemics rather than elenctics, the call to repentance and faith that repeatedly asks, "What have you done with God?" (Bavinck 1960:221-272).

Contemporary titles on evangelism to Muslims continue to show this same struggle, though not as blatantly as older materials. Reinforced by a long pattern of resistance on the part of the Muslim to the gospel, evangelism retreats further into a pattern of ideology comparisons aimed at breaking down "misunderstandings" and "misconceptions" (Elder n.d.:1). C. R. Marsh is deeply sensitive to the need for conveying the gospel "in such a way that he will be able to understand and grasp it" (Marsh 1975:7). But, in keeping with the conflict inherent in the older tradition, that concern for the gospel being "heard" is understood in rational categories, conveying "the message to his mind." Marsh tells us that "the whole man must be reached," but that is defined in terms of dealing with "theological problems," and prefaced by the sentence, "We must show him that our faith is logical" (Marsh 1975:10).

May we not recognize in this language the remnants of an older model of approach which presumed a monolithic concept of culture, culture as a more or less static macrocosm united in an impregnable way to its "primitive," "heathen" center. Too often the terms, "primitive" and "heathen," have been used in the colonialist, western sense of "non-civilized." And this "hidden curriculum" was combined with the pietistic roots of evangelicalism into a "Christ-against-non-western-culture" mould that made no effort to transform or possess Islamic culture for Christ. There was little "eye for what God has spared in his mercy" from the complete deterioration of sin. There was little awareness of the historical, sociological shifts in culture's histories. Through those shifts, what a theologian might call the "common grace" of God, culture's components, though basically an indivisible whole integrated by man's relationship to God, became more detached from that coherence, losing their original character.

Reflections of this mentality are multiplied in the collection of testimonies edited by Muriel Butcher from North Africa. Malika is said to have resisted the compromise of her young faith by calmly saying, "Christians don't keep the fast" (Butcher n.d.:14). Jamel's "spontaneous joy" was sapped by disobedience and compromise in keeping the fast and smoking (though refraining from both in the presence of the missionaries) (Butcher n.d.:41-42). Aziza's lack of a clear stand during Ramadhan is related to the near death of her daughter and her daughter's recovery to her eventual acknowledgment that "God was

punishing me for keeping the fast." "She could never again
follow Christ <u>and</u> Islam" (Butcher n.d.:68-69). Our purpose at
this point in quoting these examples is not to defend or attack
the legitimacy or non-legitimacy of Christian participation in
Ramadhan. It is to offer concrete examples of the missionary
concept of culture that has characterized the traditional
approach.

Increasingly, however, evidence is mounting to question the
simplism of these older efforts. Frederick and Margaret Stock,
analyzing a 97 percent Muslim Pakistan, comment, "Too often we
assume that theological differences are the primary barriers to
winning Muslims. This has been repeatedly disproved. Many are
theologically convinced of Christianity, but cannot hurdle the
social and cultural obstacles to faith" (Stock 1975:202).
Following Donald McGavran's emphasis on sociological barriers
as the primary obstacle to faith, the Stocks may be guilty of
falling into another kind of simplism here and overplaying
sociology at the expense of "theology." At the same time, we
must recognize they are speaking of Pakistan and not other
cultural settings. We take their statement as a corrective to
the tendency of past methodology to isolate religious commitments from their sociological and cultural dimensions. This
corrective is reinforced by Avery Willis, Jr., in his extensive
study of Javanese church growth in the last decade, a movement
comprising "the largest group of people ever to become
Christians out of a Moslem background" (Willis 1977:4). Willis
fears that growth will be impeded as the Church tends to view
"theology:" as the antithesis of culture and to call for
conversion in terms of a radical rejection of any Javanese
enculturation (Willis 1977:203-204). Peter McNee, writing of
Bangladesh, dreads "to think of...how many Muslims have been
turned away because of their inability to adjust to the Hindu
thought forms through which Christianity is expressed in
Bangladesh, or consider how many Muslims have reverted because
they were never trusted in a Hindu convert church" (McNee 1976:
122).

So, written testimonies of converts echo a Muslim
identification of Christianity not simply with theological kufur
(blasphemy) but with colonialism and western culture. Butcher's
collection of biographies from North Africa provide several
examples. Malika's refusal to fast is met with the angry
rejoinder of her brother, "You've been eating at the missionaries' home; they're turning you into a European." She is
accused of becoming a "blasphemer and a European dog" (Butcher
n.d.:14). Norria's family meets her new faith with warnings
against "the false religion of the Europeans." "Didn't she know
that Mohammed was her prophet and Jesus the prophet of the
Europeans?" (Butcher n.d.:21). Erik Nielsen, the former General

Secretary of the Danish Missionary Society, remarks, "How often has it not happened that I would talk with a person, for example, in Indonesia and ask him whether he was a Moslem. He would say, 'Yes.' And I would say, 'I am a Christian,' to which he would reply with a smile, 'Yes, that I can see.' He could see that by the color of my skin. To be a white man was to be a Christian" (Nielsen 1964:222).

In none of this are we seeking to reduce or belittle the theological barriers between Islam and Christianity. Nor are we arguing that the primary obstacles are simply sociological. We fear the simplism of the past that has reduced the conflict to primarily one of a purely "religious" sort and the simplism of the present that can reduce the conflict to primarily one of a purely sociological or cultural sort. Religion is never that pure and neither is sociology. Both interact constantly on one another in a cultural continuum. And in many situations, the sociological dimension of the continuum may be the more impor-tant as the "real" barrier to the gospel. The traditional evangelical approach, by its view of culture, inhibits us from seeing that continuum. How may this insight help us in correcting our understanding of the barriers?

II. BARRIERS TO MUSLIM CONVERSION

A. OUR UNDERSTANDING OF CONVERSION AS ONE-STEP DECISIONISM

Under the cultural impact of pietism, missionaries like India's Ziegenbalg have understood conversion as leading "a single soul belonging to a heathen people to God" (Christensen 1977:118). Though modified by a concern for man's social needs, (Verkuyl 1978:176-181) this narrow individualism was reinforced by puritan moralism and Protestant scholasticism. In the process, conversion was reduced to merely an act of repentance and faith distinct from other isolatable categories like sancti-fication, adoption, etc. The end result has been to downplay or lose altogether a sense of conversion as a comprehensive designation for the entire renewal of man (Calvin's view), conversion as a sign of the Kingdom come in Christ and into which we are daily engrafted. Conversion as the process of change of vesture (Eph. 4:24, Col. 3:9-10), conversion as metamorphosis over a period of time (Rom. 12:1-2), has become narrowed down to its necessary initiating deed of transferal, turning from idols and turning to God in Christ (I Thess. 1:9). In so doing, the Pauline perspective on conversion as an eschatological on-going event begun with Christ's power encounter with the sinner but not consummated until the coming of his Son from heaven (I Thess. 1:10), has become isolated from glorification and narrowed to conversion as initiation. In keeping with this same perspective, repentance has become known

by its fruits, though John clearly reminded his hearers that
their deeds were not per se their repentance. "Bring forth,
therefore, fruits worthy of repentance" (Luke 3:8) (Warfield
n.d.:94-95).

This strong focus on individualism and one-step decisionism
as a feature of conversion was a cultural bias theologized by
the pietist against a European background where there were huge
numbers of nominal Christians. It can easily be repeated in
the face of nominalism also present in Christian communities in
the Muslim world. McNee sees it as a grave hindrance to the
cultivation of "people movements" among the Muslims of
Bangladesh (McNee 1976:119-120). "Sound conversions" become
largely limited to one-step transitions of allegiance. That
step is essential as initiation into the process. But it must
not be isolated either from the process of growing in understanding of what commitment to Christ means or we face again
the onslaught of "nominal Christianity." Faith thus becomes
devaluated to the act of one moment, rather than the attitude
of a lifetime that has a beginning at a moment in time, but
which for some people may not be capable of "western" definition.
That apparently has happened in the Punjab where "Muslims are
urged to make a personal decision for Christ that inevitably
leads to ostracism and social dislocation, with all the
psychological upheaval this involves" (Stock 1975:201). Understanding conversion as a life-long process of allegiance
conformity to Christ, initiated by a confession of submission
to the resurrected Lord (Rom. 10:9), should help us in seeing
that it is not an absolute degree of attainment that proves a
Muslim is a child of Abraham and not Ishmael. It is rather
"discernable progress in the right direction" (Taber 1976:3).
Conversion must be genuine by all means. But its genuineness
will be tested by a lifetime of fruitbearing, not a quick step
to some altar rail more ideological than biblical. In that
sense, we must distinguish between what makes a Muslim a
Christian and what shows outwardly that he is a Christian.

This one-step mentality can also reinforce the custom in
many circles of delaying baptism until full instruction or
lengthy fruit-testing has been completed. The effect is to
reduce baptism from the sign and seal of our entrance into the
Kingdom of God and the beginning of life-long training as
Kingdom disciples (Shepherd 1976:71) and make it the last stage
of incorporation in our rite of passage from Islam to
Christianity. In too many "Jesus Muslim" communities, baptism
is not so much the biblical mark of our initial passage from
death to life in Christ, as it is the sociological mark of our
culturally conceived notions of what constitutes "adequate
understanding for sound conversion." Discipline, the God-given

tool for discipling and for correcting nominalism, is virtually administered before the convert is initiated into the Kingdom community. The end result can be the encouragement of "secret believers." For "as soon as a Muslim becomes a Christian, we have to put him through a test; we have to teach him, teach him, teach him in order to baptize him. And this very often discourages him and he goes away, or he falls away" (Marzeki 1974:84). Conversion is conceived of simply as passing a point rather than as a process. This is then misunderstood by the Muslim community (Stock 1975:225). Baptism "is seen, not as a sign of the convert's new life and of a new and positive attitude to the Lord and to the community, but rather as the last vile step on the road to apostasy" (Anderson 1976:299).

Much of this is reflected in one of the testimonies contained in Mark Hanna's volume, The True Path. When a convert approached a Christian requesting baptism, he met the reply, "How can I baptize you when I don't know you?" When the convert met the Christian elders, he was asked what errors he had seen in Islam. "I stated that it was not so much what is wrong in Islam as what is right in the Christian faith that brought me to my commitment to Christ" (Hanna 1975:4). After some clarification of the basis of his conviction, the convert was baptized. Wisely he was not turned away. But operative in the mind of the elders may have been more than the biblical demands of faith and repentance. In addition to these, may have been a concern that baptism required an intellectually formed articulation of what was wrong in one system rather than an affirmation of allegiance to Christ in the other.

B. OUR UNDERSTANDING OF CONVERSION AS AN INDIVIDUAL DECISION

Western cultural emphasis on the individual-centered nature of conversion is willing to concede the gathering of the fruits of conversion into the group solidarity of the Church. But, often like Jens Christensen, it warns against any similar expression of solidarity or group coherence in the turning of a whole ethne to Christ (Christensen 1977:128ff). "On the contrary, the covenant theme of the Old Testament and the household baptisms of the New Testament should lead us to desire, work for and expect both family and group conversions...Theologically, we recognize the biblical emphasis on the solidarity of each ethnos, i.e.: nation or people. Sociologically, we recognize that each society is composed of a variety of subgroups, subcultures or homogeneous units. It is evident that people receive the gospel most readily when it is presented to them in a manner which is appropriate and not alien to their culture and when they can respond to it with and among their own people" (Willowbank Report 1978:22). Muslim evangelization must continue to stress the necessity

for a personal relationship to Christ as an essential part of
conversion. But it must also be recognized that in the world's
cultures such personal relationships are entered into not always
by isolated "individual" decisions in abstraction from the group
but more frequently, in multi-personal, infra-group judgments.
"Personal" cannot be equated with "individual."

   This sense of community within the Islamic decision process
has long been recognized by Christians as a barrier to conversion. But, combined with an insensitivity to the diversities
of cultural ethnicity in its impact on Islam, it has augmented
the myth of Muslim impregnability to the gospel (Conn 1977:6).
In doing so, it has deadened awareness that Islam's cultural
continuum may extend far enough for an adherent to be an atheist
but still call himself a Muslim. Deep doubts may be veiled
"under a cloak of external conformity to traditional Islamic
practices and customs," the fast of Ramadhan observed "primarily
because of social pressure and the fear it induced" (Hanna 1975:
43). Islamic objections to the gospel in some cultures may be
as much cultural barriers as theological. So Don Corbin writes
of evangelistic effort among the Muslims of Senegal, "We have to
go through Islam and into black culture as well, into the tribal
setting that [sic] Islam exists in Senegal...Islam, for the
Sengalese, is black" (Corbin 1974:40). Martin Goldsmith bemoans
his failure to revisit a remote village of about 200 people in
the Muslim area of south Thailand. "It was a Muslim village, but
it had no _imam_ or religious establishment of any sort...It was,
in fact, an ideal situation for a possible group turning to
Christ" (Goldsmith 1976:319). Avery Willis notes that "The
majority of converts to Christianity," in Indonesia's recent
history, "have come from...syncretistic, Javanistic Islam rather
than the orthodox _santri_ variant. Of the 163 interviewees who
were Moslem converts to Christianity after 1965, 63 percent
specified that they were from the 'statistical Islam' or
animistic Javanese background..." (Willis 1977:48).

   Increasingly, the analysis of Muslim conversion patterns is
recognizing the communal nature of the decision process, and
recognizing also that such conversions have taken place within
the ethnic microcosms that constitute Islam. Too many hints
and too much research still undone prevent us from simply saying
that "there have never been mass movements of any significance
among Muslims in India or Pakistan" (Inniger 1963:124). In the
1830's, 560 persons were baptized in the Nadia district of
Bangladesh, drawn from a sect "half Hindu and half Moslem" (McNee
1976:106). Even the bleak picture of Muslim resistance drawn by
Stock is not totally unsupportive of possibilities yet to be
explored. Of the 43 adult baptisms registered by the United
Presbyterian Mission from 1855 to 1872 in the Punjab, 9 were

Muslims (Stock 1975:23). In the Sialkot area 53 converts were
baptized from 1954 to 1964. Why not more? "Significant church
growth from the Muslim community is unlikely until some means
can be devised of winning responsive segments of them in whole
family units" (Stock 1975:261). False assumptions of Islamic
society as a monolith, evangelization directed at individuals
apart from their family environment reinforce a methodology not
geared "to win the natural leaders of potentially responsive
segments of Muslim society" and, through them, whole clans and
sects, "conversion...without severe dislocation" (Stock 1975:
201-202).

Even in cultures which have been Islamicized for half a
millennium, a new emphasis on the communal character of the
gospel's good news, a careful and patient cultivation of
Christian communities in Muslim societies, can be a living
demonstration of redemption. And, in addition, it may supply
what some now call "the redemptive analogy" to the communal
nature of Islam. One respondent to this paper speaks of the
Tariqa in East African Islam as such an example. "There are
redemptive analogies in the Tariqa theological stance as well
as its model of community which seems remarkably anticipatory
of the gospel and Church. I believe that the Tariqa fissure
(in the Sunni Umma) helps to make Church understandable and even
acceptable, providing the church models are Tariqa sensitized."

C. OUR UNDERSTANDING OF CONVERSION AS PURELY 'SPIRITUAL'

The western bifurcation of the sacred from the secular,
combined with a pietistic hostility to the cultural side of the
missionary task, has not helped us in seeing the totalitarian,
radical demands of conversion as a sign of the Kingdom of God
come in Christ and the Lordship of Christ over the whole of
life. As a result, our gospel for Islam frequently does not
make the total claims for all of life that Islam itself makes.

The fruits of this are displayed in a Christian community
where Kingdom lifestyle is narrowed to the confines of an
ecclesiasticized subculture and there is little interest in
the larger questions of culture and society. Turning to Christ
is not always seen as also a turning to culture, where the
believer rediscovers his human origins and identity, and a
turning to the world in acceptance of the mission on which
Christ sends the believer in eschatological pilgrimage (Costas
1978:17-20). In this process, conversion does not remake; it
unmakes. The results of this are tragic for Muslim listeners.

The radical nature of conversion involves a recreation,
through union with the resurrected Christ, a resurrection from
spiritual death, the "putting off" of the old and the "putting

on" of the new. But too often for the Muslim, that rupture with
the spiritual "past" is interpreted as discontinuity with his
culture, treachery to his or her own cultural origins. So, with
the Kabyles, a Berber tribe of 1,000,000 in eastern Algeria.
Though they represent what is the "only tribe in the once-
Christian Maghreb to have in any way responded to the Christian
faith in the present century," the acceptance of Christianity
became identified not so much with allegiance to Christ, as
"often coupled with the acceptance of French culture and
civilization" (Beaver 1973:248). The universal dimensions of
the gospel are thus lost and Muslims continue to successfully
represent the Christian faith as a white man's religion
(Parshall 1975:75). A random sampling taken by Avery Willis in
Java of non-Christians generally sympathetic to Christianity
reveals that "93.4 percent said lack of acculturation by the
churches was a hindrance to their becoming Christians" (Willis
1977:195). What is needed is a view of conversion and the
believer's relation to the past "as a combination of rupture
and continuity" (Willowbank Report 1978:21).

For the Christian, the bifurcation of conversion change
from life creates cultural assumptions of what motivations are
"proper" for conversion. "Spiritual need" is isolated from
politics, social relationships, social unrest, and other
"secular" questions. The Christian Church becomes wary of any
conversions for motives other than "spiritual" ones. In so
doing, the whole area of human "felt needs" troubling the Muslim,
and often providing a more fruitful "point of contact" than
technically "religious" ones, is unused. We concentrate on
theological problem areas of the Trinity, the Sonship of Christ,
and neglect what to many may be larger doors for opening--
bitterness towards parents, guilt over immorality, frustrations
on the job, loneliness.

The same reluctance that prompted the research of Waskom
Pickett into the caste movements of India to Christ in the
1920's continues to inhibit the comtemporary Church from
utilizing other than "spiritual factors." How can we use the
discovery of Willis in Java that, from 500 interviewees, one-
half were motivated by "spiritual factors," but one-fourth came
because political factors and one-fourth from social factors
(Willis 1977:212, 221-226). The Pauline perspective that saw
all of life as God's did not make conversion a signal to efface
the forms of his culture, whether Jewish or Gentile (I Cor. 7:
18-19), or even to abandon the social distinctions of slavery
(I Cor. 7:21-23). The Pauline advice does not mean, "Remain a
worshipper of Zeus." Neither does it mean, "Abandon all your
culture since none of it can be used in the service of God."
Paul still says to the evangelist within Muslim cultures, "Use
those elements of your culture which adorn your calling in

Christ and which do not endanger it" (I Cor. 7:24, 31). In all
things that do not deny Christ, let each man abide with God.

All of this is simply to underscore the need for a fresh look
at the understandings, motivations and expectations Muslims in
their diverse cultures bring to the encounter with the Christian
and with Christ. What are they looking for and why? These
understandings and motivations differ widely from Muslim to
Muslim and from area to area. Yet they have also many common
elements that only informed research can identify.

An increased awareness of the diversity of motivations in
coming to Christ and of the comprehensive character of the
gospel of the Kingdom means also that the communicator need not
ever restrict himself to one formula in the presentation of
Christ as Savior and Lord. The call to conversion in culture
is a call to "present the message in such a way that people can
feel its relevance...and can then respond to it in
action" (Nida and Taber 1969:24). The wide-ranging nature of
the gospel (I Cor. 10:31) permits us easy access to any context
in which the culturally conditioned hearer re-encodes the
message within his own frame of reference. To the recently
delegitimized Ahmadi sect of Islam, long an antagonist of
Christianity but now rejected as a genuinely Muslim system, a
new door of opportunity for evangelism might be opening. What
effect will it be in their disenfranchisement to hear of Isa as
the Builder of a new community? To the small coterie of Muslims
in northern Nigeria, still loyal after persecution to their
leader, Ibrahim, and to his prophecies that God would one day
reveal the true faith to them concerning Isa, the Word of God,
the Breath from God, the message in 1913 from a missionary
concerning Jesus as Fulfiller turned them to Christ (Jarrett-
Kerr 1972:319-320). From West Africa comes news of the Banu Isa,
the Jesus People, "Large groups of Muslims who have been gathering at Bima Hill in the Gombe area of Bauchi State in Nigeria
to await the coming of 'Isa the Mahdi' and who have requested
the Evangelical Churches of West Africa to instruct them about
Isa" (von Sicard 1978:335-336). The appeal of a Christology
built around Jesus as the Mahdi who breaks crosses by
being broken on one, who kills swine by putting to death the
impurities they symbolize. Under this Mahdi there will be
eternal security and prosperity. Lions and camels, bears and
sheep will live in peace and a child will play with serpents
unhurt.

We are under no illusion in all of this that a new sensitivity to our own failings and to the cultural conditioning of
Muslim responses to Christ will obliterate the "stumbling block"
that the gospel will always be. Even when Christ came to "his

own," they received him not. His entrance into any culture always brings crisis. We are simply insisting that it must be Christ who is the "stumbling block." Part of our task as effective evangelists is to seek the removal of any other "stumbling blocks," whether cultural or social or ideological, so that the Muslim may fall on Christ alone. If, for the Muslim the word "conversion" has become a verbal symbol of cultural denial, we must look for a verbal equivalent similar to the Jews for Jesus movement who speak instead of being "completed in Christ." Hopefully someone will undertake the study of the motivations behind conversions from animism or other systems to Islam. Why are people switching to Islam? Our goal in all this study and self-reflection must be a willingness to be "all things to all men, that I may by all means save some" (I Cor. 9: 22). The changeless, comprehensive gospel must be made intelligible and relevant to Muslim contexts, to their felt needs (Conn 1978:75-76).

BIBLIOGRAPHY

Anderson, John D. C.
1976   "The Missionary Approach to Islam: Christian or
        'Cultic,'" Missiology 4:285-300.

Bavinck, J. H.
1960   An Introduction to the Science of Missions.
        Philadelphia: Presbyterian and Reformed Publishing
        Company.

Beaver, R. Pierce, editor
1973   The Gospel and Frontier Peoples. South Pasadena:
        William Carey Library.

Butcher, Muriel
n.d.   By Faith - Character Cameos from North Africa.
        Highgate: North Africa Mission.

Christensen, Jens
1977   The Practical Approach to Muslims. Upper Darby:
        North Africa Mission.

Conn, Harvie M.
1977   "Missionary Myths About Islam," Muslim World Pulse
        6(2):1-13.

1978   "The Cultural Implications for Conversion: Some
        Theological Dimensions from a Korean Perspective."
        Unpublished paper read at the Lausanne Consultation
        on the Gospel and Culture, January 6-13, 1978.
        Willowbank, Bermuda.

Corbin, Don
1974   "Demonstration of Resistance Problems," Media in
        Islamic Culture. C. Richard Shumaker, ed. Marseille:
        International Christian Broadcasters and Evangelical
        Literature Overseas, pp. 37-40.

Costas, Orlando
1978   "Conversion as a Complex Experience," Gospel in
        Context 1(3):14-24.

Elder, J.
n.d.   Biblical Approach to the Muslim. Houston: Leader-
        ship Instruction and Training International.

Goldsmith, Martin
    1976   "Community and Controversy: Key Causes of Muslim
           Resistance," Missiology 4:317-323.

Hanna, Mark
    1975   The True Path. Seven Muslims Make Their Greatest
           Discovery. Colorado Springs: International
           Doorways Publishers.

Inniger, Merle W.
    1963   "Mass Movements and Individual Conversion in
           Pakistan," Practical Anthropology 10:122-126.

Jarrett-Kerr, Martin
    1972   Patterns of Christian Acceptance. London: Oxford
           University Press.

Marsh, C. R.
    1975   Share Your Faith with a Muslim. Chicago: Moody
           Press.

Marzeki, Jonathan
    1974   "Amplifying the Problem," Media in Islamic Culture.
           C. Richard Shumaker, ed. Marseille: International
           Christian Broadcasters and Evangelical Literature
           Overseas, pp. 82-87.

McNee, Peter
    1976   Crucial Issues in Bangladesh. South Pasadena:
           William Carey Library.

Nida, Eugene and Charles Taber
    1969   The Theory and Practice of Translation. Leiden:
           E. J. Brill.

Nielsen, Erik W.
    1964   "Asian Nationalism," Practical Anthropology 11:211-
           226.

Parshall, Phil
    1975   The Fortress and the Fire. Bombay: Gospel
           Literature Service.

Shepherd, Norman
    1976   "The Covenant Context for Evangelism," The New
           Testament Student and Theology. John H. Skilton,
           ed. Nutley, N. J.: Presbyterian and Reformed
           Publishing Company.

von Sicard, S.
    1978   "Maranatha: Advent in the Muslim World," <u>Missiology</u>
              6:335–341.

Stock, Frederick and Margaret Stock
    1975   <u>People Movements in the Punjab</u>. South Pasadena:
              William Carey Library.

Taber, Charles
    1976   "When is a Christian?," <u>Milligan Missiogram</u>
              3(3):1–4.

Vander Werff, Lyle L.
    1977   <u>Christian Mission to Muslims: The Record</u>. South
              Pasadena: William Carey Library.

Verkuyl, J.
    1978   <u>Contemporary Missiology</u>. Grand Rapids: William B.
              Eerdmans Publishing Company.

Warfield, B. B.
    n.d.   "New Testament Terms Descriptive of the Great
              Change," reprint from <u>The Presbyterian Quarterly</u>,
              pp. 91–100.

Willis, Avery, Jr.
    1977   <u>Indonesian Revival. Why Two Million Came to Christ</u>.
              South Pasadena: William Carey Library.

<u>Willowbank Report – Gospel and Culture. Lausanne Occasional</u>
<u>Papers. No. 2.</u>
    1978   Wheaton: Lausanne Committee for World Evangelization.

SUMMARY OF PARTICIPANT'S RESPONSES

"I wish I could understand this. It sounds very important."

Several respondents leveled good natured barbs like this at Dr. Conn for his propensity to use difficult words and constructions in his excellent paper. Many agreed completely with him, and felt that if the conference did no more than deal with the three barriers he raised, it would have been worth the effort and cost. Many more agreed in general, but raised important specific questions about his approach or assumptions. A number of these comments clustered around the headings suggested below.

JESUS MUSLIMS?

The most frequent reactions had to do with the author's references to "Issa the Mahdi," (Jesus the Guided One"), "Masjid Issawi" (Jesus Mosques), and "Muslimun Issawiyun" (Jesus Muslims). Some were highly favorable to the idea. One, going further perhaps, than was being suggested by the author said, "Conn has shown masterfully that the barriers are not in Islam but in western Christianity and we can now move from apologetics to anthropology."

Others, however, objected. "It's improper," they said, "to compare Jews for Jesus with 'Jesus Muslims.'" There can no more be a "Jesus Muslim" than a Jesus Buddhist, a Jesus Hindu, or a Jesus athiest." Another argued that while Christians can accept all of the Jewish Scripture and the Jewish concept of God, we cannot accept all of the Quran or the Muslim concept of God. Two others were also critical, but approached from opposite directions:
--"We believe that much of Jewish culture was God-given...we do not believe that Muslim customs and cultures are in the same way God-given."
--"We don't need to dislocate them out of their cultures, but we do need to dislocate them out of their religion."

Perhaps most importantly, a Muslim convert asked if anyone had ever done research on this question of a "Jesus Muslim" movement. "Wouldn't it be wise," he asked, "to see if (the thousands of converted Muslims) want to be called "Issawiyun?"

ON THEOLOGICAL ISSUES NOT BEING THE PRIMARY BARRIERS

Dr. Conn's statement that it has been repeatedly disproven that theological differences are the primary barriers to winning Muslims, also met with disagreement. One respondent asked, "Where and how has it been disproved that theological differences were not primary?" Others did not like Conn's "belittling" the theological barriers between Islam and Christianity. "Theology is God within a culture," they said, "and therefore the most significant of the cultural barriers."

Others added:
--"Who is offended by the cross, they or we? Everything is offensive to the Muslim so we change it all. But what shall we do with the cross? We cannot translate it, we cannot change it. It will always remain an offense. There is a danger of our becoming men of anthropology, sociology, and culture but failing to be men of the Spirit."
--"The motifs of Islam and Christianity are opposite--the hijra and the cross. Thus the differences are more than terminological--they are profoundly theological and practical."
--"It's simplistic to say the theological barriers are not primary--they are monumental."

CONVERSION AS ONE-STEP DECISIONISM

The first of Dr. Conn's "Barriers to Muslim Conversion" had to do with some people's understanding of conversion as a single decision. By far the majority of the respondents agreed that conversion is more than a once-in-a-lifetime decision. They added that conversion is even more than a process saying that, "It's an event, a process, and a relationship," and also stressed that there must be a specific moment where there is a "power encounter."

The reaction against Dr. Conn on the conversion decision question was partly also a reaction to the statement by Dr. Taber, quoted by Dr. Conn, that conversion is "discernible progress in the right direction." "Who," one asked, "is to say what is the right direction?" "What is discernible progress?" "Does it ever reach a stage of breaking with the past?" And, "At what point can a man be considered a Christian, either by himself or those in the community?" "I'm afraid," one concluded, "that in following this logic, it will be very difficult to ever say that any man is or is not a believer in an Islamic culture."

Editor's Note: The author incorporated the essence of his rejoinder into a text revision.

DYNAMIC
EQUIVALENCE CHURCHES
IN MUSLIM SOCIETY

Charles H. Kraft

In this presentation I want to briefly raise five issues vitally
related to the concept of "Church" in the context of Christian
witness to Muslims. These considerations combine to produce
for us a new vision of what the people of God should be in
Muslim societies. The creation of groupings of God's people
who produce such an equivalently dynamic impact within their
societies is the goal of what I am calling "Dynamic Equivalence
Churches" (Kraft 1973). This is a "concept paper" and,
therefore, high on theory and low in illustrative material.

I. WHAT IS THE 'CHURCH' BIBLICALLY?

   The first issue concerns the nature of what we call the
"Church." To us this word is a <u>technical term</u> referring
primarily to particular buildings, organizations, times,
worship patterns and Christian people and their concomitants
as we know them from our experience with them in Euroamerican
cultures.

   In the Bible, especially in the New Testament but also in
the Old Testament, we are, however, dealing with largely <u>non-
technical</u> terms for groupings of people. The biblical terms
especially the Greek <u>ekklesia</u>, were in their culture much more
like the English words meeting, assembly or gathering than like
the English word church. Throughout the Greek Old Testament
neither <u>ekklesia</u> nor even <u>sunagoge</u> were intrinsically technical
terms. In fact, according to Schmidt in <u>Theological Dictionary
of the New Testament</u>, <u>ekklesia</u> "is a wholly secular term" in
the Septuagint, requiring the phrase "of the Lord" to make it

plain that it is "the people or congregation of God," rather
than some other gathering that is in view (Schmidt 1928-73:527).
The same non-technical usage, requiring contextual application
to God's people, characterizes the use of ekklesia in New
Testament times.

The significance of this fact for our topic lies in the
importance of recognizing the distinction between the valid
and necessary gathering of the people of God and the specific
culturally inculcated ways in which God's people gather and
organize themselves. We see, for example, radically different
customs employed by Old Testament and New Testament people of
God in their gatherings. But the same scriptural words are
applied to the various groupings.

I deduce from this that God is pleased to accept the
expressions of organization, worship, witness, behavior (as
long as it is moral) and doctrinal formulations that differ
considerably from what we as Euroamericans prefer. The peoples
of God described in Scripture were all committed in faith
allegiance to God and to each other. But they expressed these
commitments in terms of prevailing sociocultural patterns. Our
churches, in keeping with our culture's prevailing way of
organizing groups of people tend to be "associational." That
is, they are usually made up of people who voluntarily choose
to associate with each other, rather than of those born
involuntarily into extended kinship groupings. Among the
Hebrews, on the other hand, the ordinary basis for being a part
of a grouping of God's people was kinship. All other structuring of the life of the people of God was also channeled in
culturally appropriate ways, including the types and use of
ritual, prayer, communication, leadership patterns, music and
chant, postures, formulations of doctrine and the like.

God does not seem to have a single set of sacred forms
through which he requires that people express their relationship to him and to each other. There are, of course, deep
biblical meanings (such as a growing faith relationship with
God) without which there is no salvation or spiritual growth.
But the cultural forms through which these meanings are
expressed are to be as appropriate to today's cultures as were
those of biblical peoples to their cultures. Christians should
function in today's contexts. Only in this way can the needs
of God's people within his communities be met and the tasks of
witness to those who are not yet God's people be effectively
carried out.

II. VALIDITY OF THE WHOLE BIBLE TO PROVIDE MODELS

If a biblical view of "churchness" advocates the expression
of biblical meanings via the cultural forms of the receiving
people, we are not simply restricted to certain parts of the
New Testament for appropriate models. It has become fashionable
within much of western Christianity to give greater weight to
the Pauline epistles than to the rest of the Bible in seeking
scriptural guidance for faith and practice.

I believe that the primary reasons for this spring from our
ethnocentrism rather than from the requirements of biblical
Christianity. Without denying the importance of the Apostle
Paul in the early formulation and application of Christian
truth, I would like to suggest that we have often assumed that
the value of his contribution to us bespeaks the equal value of
his writings to those of every culture. My own experience in
Africa has, however, taught me that people of cultures more
similar to Hebrew culture see God and his message more clearly
via other portions of the Scriptures. Paul, the "Apostle to
the Gentiles," speaks well to Euroamerica, but other portions
of Scripture may speak the same message more effectively to
the members of other cultures.

I question the evolutionary understanding of the Bible that
sees God building a pyramid with Romans and Galatians at the
top, while overtly or covertly questioning the validity for
today of these portions of Scripture directed toward Hebrew
audiences. The Old Testament and the Hebrew-oriented portions
of the New Testament are not simply preliminary to those
portions couched in Greek thought patterns, they are equal to
them in inspiration and authority (even though not incorporating
the extent of revelational information available to the later
authors). They show, I believe, how God still seeks to work in
cultures more similar to Hebrew than to Greek culture.

Is it sub-Christian, still to define faith as faithfulness,
knowledge as experiential rather than intellectual and truth
as relation-centered rather than fact-centered as did the Hebrews
and as do many similar cultures today? Is it illegitimate still
to encounter evil spirits in the name of Christ, to expect God
to speak in dreams and visions, to communicate, educate, lead,
ritualize and otherwise structure Christianity in ways reminis-
cent of the Old Testament and Gospels where these are culturally
appropriate? The Bible shows such means to be adequate
expressions of divine-human interrelationships in Hebrew and
Hebrew-like cultures, whether or not they serve well in Euroamerican cultures. As we move through the Scriptures, of
course, the later revelations added to the earlier ones lead us

to greater understandings of God and his workings. While
recognizing this fact, we should not submit to the temptation
to regard as invalid any contemporary acts of God that are more
similar to those recorded in the Old Testament than to those
recorded in the New Testament epistles.

God's Word develops in detail God's approach to a Semitic
people. He starts where they are culturally and strongly
influences the course of their culture from that point on. He
accepts their cultural starting points with respect to everything except their basic allegiance. This allegiance must be
to him above all gods. But he requires at the start little if
any change in their customs and lifestyles, their family and
social structures, their leadership patterns, their concepts of
life, time, sin, morality, even their concepts of supernatural
beings, their kinds of ritual, music, communication patterns,
educational techniques and the like.

The point of all of this is to suggest that we go to the
Bible to discover how God wants us to reach Muslims and to
discover where God is already at work among them. For those
Muslims with Semitic cultures (and for most of those with non-
Semitic cultures as well) there are a great many parallels in
those parts of the Bible regularly ignored by Euroamericans.
When attempting to find approaches to peoples of cultures like
the biblical Semitic cultures we should look to the Semitic
portions of the Old Testament and New Testament rather than to
those portions aimed at Greco-Roman audiences, even though it
was in one of the latter that Paul most clearly articulated
God's principle in this regard: to approach Jews as a Jew and
Greeks as a Greek (I Cor. 9:19-22).

III. DISTINGUISH FAITH ALLEGIANCE
FROM RELIGIOUS STRUCTURES

A third point concerns the damaging effects of our continued
use of the word "religion." This word is terribly misleading
because it is used with two quite distinct meanings, even by
the same people in the same discussion. It is used most
generally to refer to a given cultural system made up of
cultural structures that are seldom evil in and of themselves.
These structures are, however, used to express the basic faith
allegiance of the people who employ them. If this allegiance
is to someone or something other than the Christian God, it
cannot be regarded neutrally by Christians.

A biblical example of the point I am making comes from the
story of Elijah and the prophets of Baal (I Ki. 18). Elijah
and the followers of Yahweh employed Semitic cultural structures

82

to express their allegiance to Yahweh. The followers of Baal,
on the other hand, employed very similar Semitic cultural
structures to express their allegiance to Baal. Both groups,
furthermore, probably believed in the existence of the others'
God(s). The point at issue was not, therefore, a difference in
religious structures, but a crucial difference in faith
commitment or allegiance.

The kinds of ritual, behavior patterns, places and times of
meeting, music (if any), prayer times and postures, even
doctrinal formulations are quite incidental to the allegiance
that is being expressed through them. That allegiance is,
however, a matter of eternal salvation. Unfortunately, though,
Christianity is often presented as a religious system in
competition with other religious systems rather than a faith
allegiance expressible through a variety of cultural systems.
As a religious system, any given expression of Christianity is,
like every other religion, the product of a given culture.
That product may be employed to express a truly saving faith
relationship to God through Christ. But it is specific to a
given culture, and any competition between religious structures
labeled Christian and those labeled Muslim is simply surface-
level cultural competition between one group's preferred
structures and those of another group. An encounter between
one deep faith allegiance and another is, however, a far
different matter.

As the anthropologist Homer Barnett (1953) has pointed out,
cultural innovation is the result of the recombination of
existing concepts to produce a new configuration (Diagram A).
We have ordinarily seen Christian allegiance in combination with
the religious forms of western cultures. This association is so
strong that both insiders and outsiders refer to these structures
as "Christian." Muslim allegiance has, likewise, been so
strongly associated with certain cultural structures that those
structures have been labeled "Muslim." I believe, however, that
it would be thoroughly biblical to work toward a recombination
of Christian allegiance with so-called Muslim religious
structures (Diagram C). In Kraft (1974c) I have outlined what
such a recombination might look like for many "Muslim" cultures.

Indeed, as I have stated elsewhere (Kraft 1974c), I believe
that this is what Muhammad himself was trying to do: to combine
an allegiance to the Judaeo-Christian God with Arabic cultural
structures. Abraham and Moses and Paul before him had performed
similar recombinations between that allegiance and the cultures
within which they worked. Most Christians would question whether
Muhammad succeeded in his efforts at recombination without
diverting the allegiance. Yet it may be that such a judgment on

the part of Euroamerican Christians is influenced more by our inability to imagine Christian allegiance in combination with any but western cultural religious forms, than by facts more relevant to the evaluation of faith allegiances.

The ambiguous use of the term religion has, I believe, muddied the waters at this point. Note in this regard how strange it sounds even to suggest the possibility of "Muslim Christians" or "Christian Muslims" to signify those who, while committing themselves to God through Christ simply remain culturally Muslim (as an American remains culturally American). We are already seeing Hebrew Christians and a large number of African expressions of Christianity in which this kind of recombination is manifested.

IV. DYNAMIC EQUIVALENCE CONGREGATIONS

The clearest model for such recombination lies in the area of interpreting or translating from one language to another. We all believe that it is possible to take meanings expressed originally in one language and to translate them adequately into another language. We know that there are always both losses and gains in such recombinations. The translation is never exactly the same as the original. But a good interpreter or translator recombines the meanings of the original utterances with the structures of the receptor language in such a way that the resulting combination 1) gets across the essential meanings expressed in the source language and 2) stimulates a response in the hearer of the translation equivalent to that which resulted from the original hearing (Diagram B).

Poor translations result from recombinations that exhibit so much of the source language structure that it interferes with the intended meanings. Typical inadequate recombinations such as the American Standard or Revised Standard Versions are phrased in a Greekized English that has no existence outside of the limited church context in which it is used. Such translations require that their users learn the strange forms and structures in order to extract the intended meanings from the partial recombination. A complete recombination, on the other hand, results in a product that effectively employs the structures of the receptor language to convey the original meanings with equivalent impact on the new hearers. A good translation does this so naturally that it does not sound like a translation.

In a very similar way the community of God's people should recombine the meanings expressed in the biblically approved illustrations of "people of Godness" with the cultural structures of today's cultures (Diagram D). These new combinations, then, while faithful to the original meanings, are so at home in the receptor culture that they do not require the receptors to learn a set of foreign structures in order to extract the message from them. Nor do they require interpreters from overseas to explain the meanings of imported structures. Overseas personnel are still needed to stimulate people to saving faith but not to teach them a foreign culture. For a dynamically equivalent community of the people of God does not look like it was constructed somewhere else and imported.

This is the kind of recombination that Paul was engaged in when he took God's message from a Hebrew cultural context to a Greek cultural context. Before him, of course, the translators of the Septuagint and the Hellenistic Jews had moved Hebrew religious concepts in this direction.

But in that case it was a matter of the same ethnic group learning to express its allegiance in a different language. Paul's situation is more like ours in that when he turned to the Gentiles he sought to move Christian meanings into a new sociocultural matrix operated by different (i.e. non-Hebrew) ethnic groups.

In comparing our problem with Paul's, we may isolate at least two helpful features. In the first place, we observe that Paul was moving the gospel message from a Semitic matrix into a proto-European matrix. In communicating effectively to Muslims, our problem is to reverse that direction by moving from a European matrix into cultures more similar to Semitic cultures. Secondly, Paul's task was simplified somewhat by the fact that large numbers of Hebrews had already made the linguistic and, to some extent, a cultural transition from Aramaic language and culture to Greek language and culture. Though Paul often went beyond these Hellenistic Jews in his use of Greek thought patterns and cultural structures, he was able to build on models such as the synagogue that had already been created by the recombinations of the Hellenists. In our efforts to stimulate dynamically equivalent Christian groups within Muslim societies, we have similarly helpful models both in the cultural structures now in use in these societies and in the Semitic cultural structures evident throughout the greater part of the Scriptures.

V. DEVELOPMENT OF NEW APPROACHES

In developing a new approach the first step is to determine the goals. I would suggest that the goal be the bringing into existence of groupings of God's people within so-called "Muslim" cultures 1) that are committed in faith allegiance to God in

accordance with biblical revelation and 2) that function within
their own sociocultural matrix in ways equivalent in their
dynamics to biblically recommended examples. A detailed ethno-
theological study of this goal and its implications would be an
important first step toward the development of genuinely new
approaches.

We need, however, to look realistically at certain major
barriers that will need to be overcome. There is the distinct
possibility that as Euroamericans with a tragic history of
relationships with Muslims, we may be disqualified from direct
witness in many areas. We will need to look much more seriously
than previously at the debilitating effect on Christian witness
of the widespread antipathy on the part of Muslims to those
historically associated with the Crusades, the establishment of
Israel and what Muslims regard as theological aberration. We
might, therefore, need to seek indirect means of approach.

A related barrier stems from the fact that overall Euroamerican missionary strategy has been so thoroughly intertwined
with the colonialist mentality and has, therefore, been
successful wherever people have been greatly impressed, even
intimidated, by Euroamerican cultural achievements. We have,
like the Judaizers, been most successful where people have been
willing to convert to at least parts of our culture (including
Euroamerican theological formulations as well as our technological, medical, and educational structures) along with
conversion to our faith. Muslims have, of course, largely
resisted such cultural intimidation, especially in theological
areas, leaving us without a missionary strategy. We have to
learn, therefore, how to win or earn the right to be heard on
the basis of the appeal of the biblical message to needs that
Muslims feel. Demanding a hearing on the basis of our cultural
achievements, though still successful in many parts of the world,
must be replaced as an approach to Muslims (or anyone else).

A third barrier that must be recognized and dealt with in
developing new approaches is the already existing Church in at
least certain Muslim lands. It seems to be true today, as it
was in the days of Jesus and Paul, that some of the greatest
barriers to doing the work of God are erected by those who
consider themselves orthodox. Like the Pharisees and the
Judaizers, many Christian groups today have developed an
exclusivism that combines with unfamiliar (to Muslims)
terminological and structural symbols of their piety to
alienate outsiders rather than to attract them. John the
Baptist, Jesus and Paul did not seek to win people to such
groups. The development of more effective (and biblical)

Christian witness to Muslims may demand that at least certain
of the existing Christian communities in Muslim lands be
bypassed.

In developing new approaches our primary concern must be
that both our ends and our means be truly Christian. Spirit-
guided common sense should, however, also lead us to consider
such questions as: Who within the Muslim world is likely to
be receptive? Who are those to whom the receptors are likely
to respond? What methods are likely to meet with a positive
response? The Spirit of God will, of course, be constantly at
work. But he apparently brings greater results via some
people and methods than via others. I have elsewhere (Kraft
1974a and 1974b) critiqued methods that approach Muslims on the
basis of a competition between their structural and conceptual
system and a western one with the aim of converting them to a
western cultural understanding and expression of Christian
allegiance. Most of us are against such methodology. But we
need to probe in greater detail the deep implications of our
ethnocentrism and consequent commitment to competitive
strategies.

Can Euroamericans overcome these barriers in dealing with
such a sensitive area as basic faith allegiance? Or are we
disqualified? If we are disqualified, are there those whom we
can assist to do the job? If we can function effectively, on
what basis? Can at least some Euroamericans develop the ability
to identify with Muslim peoples as Jesus and Paul did in order
to be able to appeal to them from within their cultural
matrices? Could one be a Muslim-Christian in the same way that
Jesus, Paul and many of their converts were Hebrew Christians
(Diagram C)?

Receptive populations of Muslims seem to be more often
reported today than previously. These populations should be
studied and the conditions on the basis of which they are
receptive analyzed. These understandings plus a whole-Bible
view of the approaches that can be used could lead to genuine
breakthroughs.

DIAGRAMS

A. Basic Model (after Barnett 1953:188).

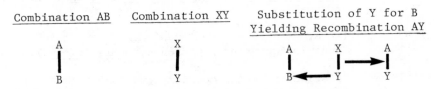

B. Model Applied to Translation – Goal: Equivalent Function of
Original Message (A) among Hearers Employing the New
Language (B).

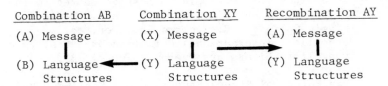

C. Model Applied to Religion – Goal: Equivalent Function of
Christian Allegiance in and through Near Eastern ("Muslim")
Cultural Structures.

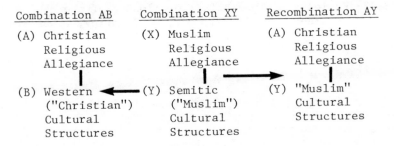

D. Model Applied to Church – Goals: Equivalent Function of
Community of God's People in New Cultural Structures.

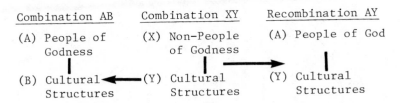

BIBLIOGRAPHY

Barnett, Homer G.
    1953   <u>Innovation: The Basis of Cultural Change</u>. New York:
            McGraw-Hill

Kraft, Charles H.
    1973   "Dynamic Equivalence Churches," <u>Missiology</u> 1:39-57

    1974a   "Distinctive Religious Barriers to Outside
            Penetration," <u>Media in Islamic Culture</u>. C. Richard
            Shumaker, ed. Marseille: International Christian
            Broadcasters and Evangelical Literature Overseas,
            pp. 65-76.

    1974b   "Guidelines for Developing a Message Geared to the
            Horizon of Receptivity, Parts 1 and 2," <u>Media in
            Islamic Culture</u>. C. Richard Shumaker, ed.
            Marseille: International Christian Broadcasters and
            Evangelical Literature Overseas, pp. 17-33.

    1974c   "Psychological Stress Factors Among Muslims," <u>Media
            in Islamic Culture</u>. C. Richard Shumaker, ed.
            Marseille: International Christian Broadcasters and
            Evangelical Literature Overseas, pp. 137-144.

Schmidt, K. L.
    1928-73 "Ekklesia," <u>Theological Dictionary of the New
            Testament</u>. G. Kittel, ed., G. Bromiley, translator.
            Grand Rapids: Eerdmans. Vol. III, pp. 501-536.

SUMMARY OF PARTICIPANT'S RESPONSES

People do not tend to be neutral toward Dr. Kraft's writings.
The responses to his paper for this conference are indicative
of this fact:
--"By far the best and the worst (paper) we've seen so far."
--"Irritating in the right places. It is long overdue."
--"I differ greatly with Dr. Kraft's ideas...but I like his
   innovative thinking."
--"An excellent, stimulating paper..."
--"The least satisfying paper."
--"Provocative but not very realistic."

A number of specific issues provoked a variety of responses
from our readers. In this summary it will be most useful to
simply quote various responses under each of the topics below.
Again, while probably most respondents were in agreement with Dr.
Kraft, we will zero in on those whose opinions tended to differ
from those of the author.

ON 'PROGRESSIVE' REVELATION

--"Three cheers for Dr. Kraft's insistence on using the whole
   Scripture."
--"Progressive revelation does not mean and has never meant what
   he describes it as meaning."
--"The Scriptures themselves refer to the progressive nature of
   God's revelation to men."
--"Despite the possibility of obtaining models from the Old
   Testament for the community of faith,...the body concept, the
   giving of gifts, the horizontal commitments of believers,
   simply cannot be fully understood...without proper theologi-
   cal background of the post-resurrection community."
--"Certainly the Old Testament is equal to the Pauline letters
   in inspiration and authority, but I don't develop a church...
   on the teachings of the Old Testament."

ON MUSLIM CHRISTIANS (AGAIN)

--"Arab Christian and Hebrew Christian are equivalent terms.
   Muslim Christian and Hindu Christian violate each term."
--"Dr. Kraft seems to delight in baiting us with loaded terms
   like 'Muslim Christians.'"
--"Should be 'Christian Muslim' rather than 'Muslim Christian.'"

ON THE DYNAMIC EQUIVALENCE CHURCH

--"Worthy goals, beautiful thoughts."
--"A valid and urgent concept...but it needs a biblical/
   theological wholeness and exactness someone else will have

to bring."
--"Did the early church live out the complete expression of
what God intended His people and His church to be?"

ON RELIGIOUS ALLEGIANCE

--"Kraft's statement that we have been hampered by our inability
to imagine Christian allegiance in combination with any
other but western cultural religious forms...disregards the
many efforts around the world that missions and Christians
have made to adapt to the culture in which they live."
--"It is not necessarily true that indigeneous religious
structures adequately express religious allegiance when that
allegiance is to the Christian God. The reason is clear:
The gods of previous allegiance were false."

ON FORMS AND MEANINGS

--"In [this] essay we have a slightly modified form of the
gnostic heresy. The faith is reduced to deep biblical
meanings (such as a growing faith relationship to God)
...rather than the mighty acts of God in history to save
which are God Himself acting uniquely to save. These become
illustrations of 'meanings' which (we are told), must be
conveyed in the new setting...why not talk (to Americans) of
George Washington crossing the Delaware River (rather than
Moses crossing the Red Sea)--a much more appropriately
enculturated illustration for modern Americans. (For the
meanings, we are told, are the heart of the matter.)"

AUTHOR'S REJOINDER TO PARTICIPANT'S RESPONSES

I want to thank the 118 people who responded. I am gratified
that the majority felt helped, sorry that a few misunderstood
and humbled by the seriousness with which most took my paper.
My response takes two forms: 1) several slight revisions of my
paper, and 2) the statements that follow concerning the major
issues raised.

The knottiest problem is the practice of separating a people's
faith allegiance from their religious structures. As one respondent said, part of being a Muslim is <u>not</u> to differentiate
between allegiance and structures. I have no easy answer but
will suggest 1) the need to clearly conceptualize what the
basic issues are (as I have tried to do), 2) the need for research to discover if, in fact, at least some Muslims can
conceptualize and act on this distinction, 3) that a continuing
allegiance to one's culture is not wrong as long as it is an
allegiance to culture as a <u>means</u>, but to God as the end, and
4) that making this distinction and getting the priorities
straight might be the single most crucial matter in the communication of the true Gospel to anyone, anywhere.

Note that God started his work with Abraham by focusing his
attention on God as the goal (end) for which Abraham would now
use his culture. This was a "power encounter" over whether
Abraham's supreme allegiance (the end for which he would use
his culture) would be something (e.g. gods, family, tradition,
wealth) contained within the cultural system or to the true
God who exists outside of it. And this is the same encounter
that we see throughout the history of Israel and Christianity
(and Islam?)--that between an allegiance to the system with but
nominal allegiance to the true God and a total sellout to God
himself. Note Jesus' statement contrasting allegiance to himself with that to family (Matt. 10:37) and Paul's contrast between
outward and inward circumcision (Rom. 2:28, 29) as two of many
Scriptural treatments of this point.

My suggestion to bypass existing churches elicited considerable comment. Most of the internationals and several field
missionaries were quite positive. The major concern (and I
share it) is that any bypassing include a loving attempt to
communicate the reasons to the members of the existing churches.
I question, however, contrary arguments based on 1) the desire
to preserve existing organizations and/or western concepts of
unity (i.e. uniformity), and 2) the willingness to sacrifice
the Christian evangelistic mandate to the fear of further
fragmentation of Christian groups.

Though dynamic equivalence theorists will need to discover within Scripture just what kind of impact God desires, I see nothing that causes me to question the power of the model. The model comes from communications, not from linguistics and is, therefore, able to deal with many more aspects of culture than simply language. More research and exemplification does, however, need to be done.

I deny that my concerns are more anthropological than theological. I am simply recombining Scriptural data with an anthropological perspective (AY below) in place of the combination of Scriptural data with the philosophico-historical perspective (AB) of traditional theology. This is simply a different contextualization of theology.

Combination AB (Traditional Theology)	Combination XY (Anthropology)	Recombination AY (Christian Ethnotheology)
(A) Scriptural Data	(X) Cultural Data	(A) Scriptural Data
(B) Philosophico-Historical Perspective	(Y) Anthropological Perspective	(Y) Anthropological Perspective

My view of "progressive revelation" does not question the increase of revelational information as we move through Scripture. What I contend is that all of Scripture is inspired and usable today--none of it should be ignored simply because it doesn't appeal to us or because there was a significant later revelation. How well a portion speaks to the receptor people should be the prime (though not the sole) consideration, since the saving message of Scripture pervades every part.

POWER ENCOUNTER IN CONVERSION FROM ISLAM

Arthur F. Glasser

Any discussion of conversion in connection with Muslim evangelism must begin with the biblical data. Recently, I participated in the mission consultation of a major denomination, convened to define its mission policies for the next decade. What particularly impressed me was the ambivalence of a majority of the delegates. Whereas they willingly affirmed the biblical mandate for mission and included the great commission (Matt. 28:18-20) in their basic policy statement, they deliberately rejected a proposal that mission in Islamic countries involved making Muslims disciples of Jesus and baptizing converts into the life and witness of his Church--the specific stipulations of the great commission. The contention was that "mission among Muslims" did not demand such arrogant imperialistic objectives.

So then, we begin with the language, illustrations and theology of conversion found in the New Testament. Only then will we be in a position to relate this to "power encounter" in conversion from Islam.

I. THE BIBLICAL LANGUAGE OF CONVERSION

The words "shub" (OT), "epistrepho" (NT), and their cognates, when used to describe a conversion that is Godward, embrace the idea of turning back or turning around--a change in direction that involves both mind and spirit. The normative Old Testament reference is the conversion to Yahweh of the commonwealth of Israel in the light of her covenant history. Such national "turning" (involving repentance) was often accompanied by the recommitment of the people to the ordinances of worship and to the ethical standards of the Sinaitic covenant (e.g. in

Hezekiah's day: II Chronicles 29 and 30). On occasion we come
upon the record of a city (e.g. Nineveh in Jonah 3:5-10) or a
king (e.g. Manasseh in II Chronicles 33:12, 13) going through a
turning around (turning back) conversion experience.

In the New Testament "epistrepho" is used to describe the
spiritual reorientation of a person turning from an unworthy
allegiance to the Lordship of Jesus Christ. Through preaching,
people are "awakened" by the Spirit and under his influence
"turn to God" from their idols (Acts 9:35; 11:21; I Thess. 1:9).
On occasion, reference is made to the Lord himself as instru-
mental in bringing about this change (e.g. Acts 3:26).
Strangely, the cognate "conversion" appears only once, but it
is used to summarize what Paul and his company reported as the
result of their missionary efforts. It was this news, "the
full story of the conversion of the Gentiles," that caused
"great rejoicing" (Acts 15:3 NEB).

So then, the biblical data is rather explicit. Conversion
involves the decisive, Godward reorientation of a person's
inner world that changes his basic relationship with God.

II. ILLUSTRATIONS OF CONVERSION IN THE ACTS

Luke has selected five converts of different backgrounds,
nationality, temperament, prior religious experience and sex:
the Ethiopian eunuch (ch. 8), the Pharisee Paul (ch. 9), the
Italian Cornelius (ch. 10), the merchant Lydia and the Roman
jailer (ch. 16). Although their histories are markedly
different, they are surprisingly representative. When we
examine them closely we find some striking similarities in the
sequence of events that brought about their conversion to God
through commitment to Jesus Christ. Although none were directly
challenged to "convert to God," their varied conversion
experiences endorsed the overall thrust of the evangelistic
preaching of the apostles - that God had reconciled the world
to himself through Jesus Christ and was calling men and women
to himself in love and grace. All men are under the obligation
as his creatures to turn to him in repentance, in faith and in
expectation of his triumph in history (Acts 14:15; 17:31). The
commonality of human sinfulness and rebellion against God is
presupposed and "the call to conversion is similarly universal
in scope" (Kummel 1963:18). The core of the apostolic "kerygma"
is the incarnation, death and resurrection of Jesus Christ.
Indeed, the good news is that God has "visited" his people
through these redemptive acts and even now is moving to the
nations to take from them a people for his name (Acts 15:14).
For this reason the Jerusalem Council was determined to "impose
no irksome restrictions on those of the Gentiles who were
turning (converting) to God" (15:19). When we realize

that Luke equates apostolic evangelism with proclaiming the
Kingdom of God (8:12; 19:8; 20:25; 28:23, 31), we cannot but
underscore the dimension of universality. The use of this
sublime phrase must mean that conversion to God is at the
center of his will for all Muslims.

In his brilliant essay on conversion in the New Testament,
Stephen Smalley has analyzed the conversion accounts of these
five individuals and notes the following distinctives
(summarized):

First, all went through a period of preparation - the
Ethiopian reading the Scriptures (8:28); Paul's training
in Judaism and the Law (22:3; 26:5) and in the doctrine
of those he was persecuting (9:2; 22:4; 26:9-11);
Cornelius was a God-fearer and a man of prayer (10:2);
Lydia was a worshipper of God and also in the habit of
praying (16:13f); and even the Philippian jailer may
have been given the opportunity of listening to Paul
and Silas preaching since the apostles were in Philippi
"some days" before they were imprisoned (16:12).

Second, the preaching about Jesus, or his presence.
Philip explains the good news of Jesus to the Ethiopian
(8:35); Jesus himself forms the content of Paul's vision
on the road to Damascus (9:5; 22:8; 26:15); Peter preaches
to Cornelius and the other Gentiles God's visitation in
Jesus of Nazareth (10:34-43; 11:14); Paul delivers some
kind of proclamation in the hearing of Lydia (16:13f);
and Paul and Silas deliver the logos ton Kurion to the jailer
and his household (16:31f).

Third, there is inquiry. The Ethiopian questions Philip
about the passage he is reading (8:34); Paul asks Jesus
for his identity (9:5; 22:8; 26:13) and, in one account,
for his commission (22:10); Cornelius asks the "angel"
for an explanation of his vision (10:4); and the jailer
asks the pertinent question of Paul and Silas, "Men,
what must I do to be saved?" (16:30).

Fourth, there is prominent evidence of the activity of
God. The Spirit is associated with the ministry of
Philip, who is the agent of the Ethiopian's conversion
(8:29, 39); Paul encounters the Lord directly (9:4ff),
and at the hands of Ananias, also prompted by God
(vs. 10ff) presumably receives the Spirit before
baptism (vs. 17ff); Cornelius sees an angel of God in
his vision (10:3, 30), and also receives the Spirit
before baptism, the evidence of which is speaking in
tongues (10:44ff; 11:15; 15:8); and the Lord "opens

the heart" of Lydia (16:14).

<u>Fifth</u>, the convert in each case undergoes baptism
(8:38; 9:18; 10:48; 16:15; 16:33). This one stage
belongs inseparably to them all with its implicit
confession of faith. Note that in no case does an
explicit confession of faith occur by itself, and
apart from baptism (Acts 8:37 is a "late" inter-
polation).

<u>Finally</u>, in each case there are evident results of the
conversion. The Ethiopian and the jailer rejoice
(8:39; 16:34); Paul preaches Christ (9:20, 22;
26:22f); Cornelius speaks with tongues, extolling
God (10:46); Lydia and the jailer display the
Christian virtue of hospitality (16:15, 34; cf I Pet.
4:9). Given the limitations of our evidence, certain
features are sufficiently common to all these accounts
for certain general deductions to be permitted. First,
the spiritual experience in question is more than
simply the work of a moment; second, it is frequently
occasioned by preaching; third, some kind of
intellectual activity, however elementary, is involved;
fourth, the conversion is undertaken by an individual
who is treated as a whole personality; fifth, the
believer is related more or less immediately to the
total life of the Church by the instrument of baptism,
often directly associated with the gift of the Spirit;
and finally, as the premise of all that may be said
about conversion in the New Testament, the work is
from first to last a response to the <u>opus Dei</u> (1964:
193-210).

III. THE THEOLOGY OF CONVERSION

Viewed externally, conversion involves "stopping, turning,
and pursuing a new course" (Routley). More is involved than
mere repentance over the past and resolution touching the
future. There is the deliberate disposition of heart and mind
to surrender to the will and power of God, encountered in Jesus
Christ, and to turn away from the things that are not of God.
This reorientation of the whole life and personality is the
<u>sine qua non</u> of entrance into the Kingdom of God. Perhaps it
was for this reason that the Apostle John completely replaced
the synoptic terminology of repentance with that of the new
birth (John 3:3). And the Apostle Paul struck a parallel with
the death and resurrection of Christ. The convert has been
"baptized into his death" and "raised to newness of life" in
the Spirit (Rom. 6:2-4; Col. 2:12). Actually, this conversion
paradigm of repentance and faith, of death and life, becomes

the subsequent pattern of the Christian life (I John 2:6). The
converted Luther was fond of saying: "I live by repentance and
the forgiveness of sins."

Another integrating concept is the centrality of baptism in
the total conversion experience. Bishop Stephen Neill has
pointed out that admission to the churches of the apostolic age
was "by faith and baptism" (his emphasis) and added: "The New
Testament knows nothing of membership in the Church by faith
alone, without this accompanying act of obedience and
confession" (1964:188). Baptism marks entrance into the divine
ecclesia - the people of God. It follows then that one should
not downplay any of the interrelated components of baptism:
the hearing and believing of the gospel (Acts 2:37ff),
repentance (Acts 2:38), faith (Col. 2:12), the gifts of both
the forgiveness of sins and of the Holy Spirit - in short, all
that has to do with the spiritual reorientation of the whole
life and personality. Luke's summary of Paul's ministry in
Corinth was: "Many of the Corinthians hearing Paul believed
and were baptized" (Acts 18:8), and this sequence embraces the
totality of the conversion experience. Indeed, the witness
of Scripture is clear: the apostles all believed in the
essentiality of a conversion that manifests itself in the
regenerating work of the Holy Spirit. Behind this essentiality,
of course, is the reality of God's holiness and the alienation
from him that man's sinfulness has occasioned. There is only
one eternal God who governs all things according to his eternal
purpose. That he, a "deciding and disposing" deity, should
graciously seek to restore fallen man to full fellowship with
himself implies that he has the right to impose the conditions
of man's restoration. The condition he has imposed through the
Church is repentance: "All men everywhere" are "commanded to
repent" (Acts 17:31).

IV. POWER ENCOUNTER

The central issue in God's confrontation of any man is his
authority and Christ's Lordship. This means "power encounter" -
for the divine power that confronts and woos is inevitably
resisted by the human spirit. Perhaps this is why Luke tells
us that those whom God overwhelms with his grace and who enter
his Kingdom do so "violently" (16:16), whether they are Jews or
Muslims, humanists or Marxists, Catholics or Protestants. When
the whole thrust of the gospel is that Jesus Christ is not to
be admired only, but "received" with a transfer of allegiance -
submitting to his rule - the trauma of conversion is inevitable,
for this involves being delivered from the kingdom of darkness
and transferred into God's Kingdom (Col. 1:13). Any true
conversion involves a resolution of the issue of power. Indeed,
the evangelistic commission given to the Apostle Paul contained

the specific task: "Open their (Gentile) eyes, that they may
turn from darkness to light and from the power of Satan to God"
(Acts 26:18). All men are involved to a greater or lesser
degree with the powers. Their coming to Christ involves a
transfer of power. As Alan Tippett has stated so well:

> "Man is the victim. He is bound. He is under an
> enslaving authority, trapped and imprisoned. The
> situation is such that it is quite beyond human power
> for man to save himself or escape. In this desperate
> plight a Saviour from outside must be introduced into
> the situation or man will perish. We are faced with
> the power (dunamis) of the enemy, we are entrapped in
> the works (erga) of the devil, we are victims of the
> craftiness or method (methodeias) of the devil, and
> we are under the authority (exousia) of Satan. Only
> through a greater power and authority can mankind
> hope for deliverance. ... Hence Vicedom does not
> spare the pagan religions or advocate mere dialogue
> with them. 'In the last analysis they are to be
> understood from the viewpoint of the other Kingdom
> set over against the mission of God. While they may
> contain much that is good, it is embedded in evil
> and covered over by evil'" (1969:89-91).

V. CONVERSION FROM ISLAM

At this point, and with the biblical data on conversion
clearly in mind, we commence our evaluation of the factors
involved in the "power encounter" between Jesus Christ and the
Muslim believer under the instrumentality of a Christian
witness. We shall assume that the encounter takes place in a
context of freedom and mutual respect (the Christian and the
Muslim), unmarred by any form of human coercion. Obviously,
at the outset we must recognize that no two Muslims are alike
in much the same way that no two professing Christians are
alike. In their religious thought and practice Muslims vary
from those who are totally indifferent or quite careless, their
worship rarely extending beyond the perfunctory, to those whose
ardor in worship approximates that of the mystic Rabi'a of
Basra (8th Century) who prayed:

> "O Lord, if I worship thee from fear of hell, burn me
> in hell, and if I worship thee in hope of paradise,
> exclude me thence, but if I worship thee for thine
> own sake, then withhold not from me thine eternal
> beauty" (quoted by Bavinck 1948:96).

In our day "situation oriented" missiologists can be so
impressed with the religious devotion of many Muslims that they

tend to set aside the stark realities of the biblical witness
we have just considered. Their dominant focus is on this
impressive devotion and they make it the starting point in
their theologizing on religious encounter. They stand in awe
of the Muslim caught up in the adoration of God's majesty,
power and essential greatness. They resonate with his felt
obligation to submit to God's inscrutable will ("Islam" means
surrender and submission). They envy the Muslim's jealousy for
the honor of God - the One who in his sovereignty acts not as
an arbitrary desert sheikh but as the supreme Lawgiver and
Ruler, the One absolutely above all, the God behind all
phenomena and whose will none can successfully resist. Surely,
these men argue, such intensity and devotion to God exceeds
their own. Does it not approximate the devotion of the Apostle
Paul who sang: "Of him and through him, and to him are all
things: to him be the glory forever" (Rom. 11:36). Why then
should we distinguish between Paul's Christian devotion and
their Muslim devotion?

Certainly, it would be both absurd and offensive to confront
the devout Muslim with the bald assertion that his religious
devotion is futile because of his deliberate exclusion of the
Name and Lordship of Jesus Christ. But it would be equally
wrong to commend him for his worship of God. After all, God
is the only one qualified to judge whether a man's worship is
"in Spirit and in truth" (John 4:23).

Actually, a frame of reference is needed for the evaluation
of human religiosity. No better starting point can be
suggested than Paul's analysis of the religious devotion of man,
recorded in Rom. 1:18-2:16. Briefly summarized, religious
devotion (the reality, not the intensity or quality) is a
universal phenomenon. More, one finds the intensely devout
within every religious system. One has only to recall the
religious devotion of Saul the Pharisee prior to his conversion
to recognize that a man's intense zeal for God may not come
within the circle of the divine approbation. There is
something very significant in the fact that heaven noticed his
praying only after he was converted on the road to Damascus
("Behold he prayeth!" Acts 9:11).

Paul says that men in their religious devotion "stifle the
truth" regarding the true nature of God (1:18). Even when
convinced there is only one God, like the Jew or the Muslim,
the religious man may respond by unconsciously repressing those
elements of God's reality that are uncongenial to man's
fallenness. God must be reduced either to the ineffectiveness
of impersonality or expanded to a deistic remoteness ("a High
God far away in unreachable regions," Bavinck 1966:120). What
lies "plain before his eyes" in the universe around him - that

is, God's everlasting power and Godhead – somehow becomes
blurred and eludes his full comprehension. Although touched
by God, and responsive in part to his seeking activity, man
ends up worshipping a distorted image and unwittingly rejects
those ingredients most essential to his attaining a right
relationship with him. Touching Muhammad in this connection
Bavinck wrote:

> "In the 'night of power' of which the ninety-seventh
> sura of the Qur'an speaks, the night when 'the angels
> descended' and the Qur'an descended from Allah's
> throne, God dealt with Mohammed and touched him. God
> wrestled with him in that night, and God's hand is
> still noticeable in the answer of the prophet, but it
> is also the result of human repression" (1966:125).

So then, in all religions, Islam included, man becomes
preoccupied with his own manufactured substitutions – the
outcome of his fallenness – as he seeks to come to terms with
the truth of God confronting him in "natural revelation." In
similar fashion Christians are obliged to confess that in much
of Christianity – the human response to the revealed gospel –
there is likewise evidence of man's fallenness and even traces
of the demonic. Indeed, misdirected religious devotion with
its unconscious suppression and subsequent substitution,
characterized Saul the Pharisee prior to his conversion. And
what of John Wesley's experience prior to his experience of the
"rest of faith" at Aldersgate?

Moreover, the Christian witness to the Muslim can only
confront his evident religiosity with the humble yet courageous
word: "This God who has been seeking you and to whom you have
been responding would now address you in a new way through the
witness I bring of Jesus Christ." The Christian has no
alternative but to make such a claim, for Christ is "the Light
that lighteth every man" but whom man in his darkness has not
been able to comprehend (John 1:9, 5). To confront the Muslim
with Jesus as he is concretely revealed in the Gospels and to
accompany that confrontation with the personal confession of
having experienced his saving grace – this sets the stage for
the "power encounter in conversion from Islam."

VI. EVANGELISTIC METHOD

It follows then that the Christian should deliberately
resist the temptation to allow his witness to Jesus to descend
to the stale polemics of the past. Can he really convince the
Muslim that Christians have not falsified the Scriptures, or
that they are not polytheists, or that Jesus is more than the
quranic "Son of Mary," or that the crucifixion and the

resurrection of Jesus actually took place? More, all attempts
to affirm the ethical and social superiority of Christianity
are doomed to frustration because of the ineradicable evidence
of the demonic throughout the long and often tortured history
of the Church. Although there is a place for providing honest
answers to the questions Muslims ask, this should not be
central to the encounter.

The Christian must rather stand alongside the Muslim and
affirm with him the commonality of his humanness. In the name
of Christ he must speak of sin, righteousness and judgment.
This is the apostolic pattern discernible in the conversion
experiences we have already referred to (particularly in Acts
8:32-35; 10:26, 36-43; 16:30, 31). To adhere to this pattern
is to enter the stream of evangelistic emphasis that the Holy
Spirit will truly bless, since it was along these lines that
our Lord promised his accompanying witness (John 16:8-11).

VII.   CONCLUSION

All which brings us to the heart of the matter. When the
person set free by Christ meets the devout Muslim on a man-to-
man basis, what surfaces is rarely the "ideal" Islam of dogma
and practice. Indeed, both Christian and Muslim in that
context recognize instinctively that little is to be gained
through a discussion of the "iman" and the "din." These are of
little experiential consequence to the average Muslim. Of
greater concern and preoccupation are his efforts to cope with
the various acute problems and hostile forces which crowd his
world and keep him from peace of mind and heart. There is the
magic he feels he must practice. And what of the demons he
must placate? Or the fetishes he must not fail to use? Will
his invoking of the saints help him surmount his fears? On
and on. His world is dominated by "the evil eye," by sickness
and death, by sorcery and curses. Not by quranic Islam but
by animistic Islam, and the hunger of the heart it constantly
discloses.

And it is this hunger that the Christian witness must
address, for Christ alone can satisfy this hunger. Are there
destructive powers abroad in the world? Jesus is more powerful.
Is there hope in sickness and in death? He is both Healer and
Resurrection. Is there any purpose or meaning to life? Jesus
has his perfect will for each one of his people. The greatest
sin is that men do not turn to him in repentance and faith
(John 16:9). Only when Muslims reach out to Jesus and find in
him the solution to their immediate needs do they become aware
of their greater needs - access to God, the forgiveness of sin,
justifying grace and eternal life. And when they begin to seek
him as Lord and Savior, their "theological problems" begin to

evaporate and they enter the Kingdom of God--but not without the inner trauma of a "power encounter."

BIBLIOGRAPHY

Bavinck, Johannes H.
    1948   The Impact of Christianity on the Non-Christian
            World. Grand Rapids: Wm. B. Eerdmans Publishing
            Company.

    1966   The Church Between Temple and Mosque. Grand Rapids:
            Wm. B. Eerdmans Publishing Company.

Kummel, W. G.
    1963   Man in the New Testament. London: SCM Press.

Neill, Stephen
    1964   The Interpretation of the New Testament 1861-1961.
            London: Oxford University Press.

Smalley, Stephen
    1964   "Conversion in the New Testament," The Churchman
            78:193-210.

Tippett, Alan R.
    1969   Verdict Theology in Missionary Theory. Lincoln,
            Illinois: Lincoln Christian College Press.

SUMMARY OF PARTICIPANT'S RESPONSES

Dr. Glasser's paper was seen as an excellent contribution on the biblical basis and starting point for discussion of Muslim evangelization. It was "a good essay, well argued, and exegetically honest." Many readers agreed wholeheartedly with the author, finding it refreshing to have him turn to the New Testament to examine the necessary parts of the conversion process. The six distinct aspects in the conversion of the selected New Testament figures which Dr. Glasser drew from Stephen Smalley were especially insightful. The fact, though, that Dr. Glasser was so "on target" in defining biblical Christianity as we know it, raised questions as to why it has been successful in many parts of the world but not in Islamic countries. "Are we to reconsider the biblical requirements?" "Does God have something new to say to his Church?"

Numerous important issues were raised in response to these questions. A number appreciated the centrality of baptism in Dr. Glasser's presentation and further argued that there is no precedent for omitting it as some might, since it was foreign even, for example, to the Ethiopian eunuch, but still administered. Others wanted to legitimize delaying baptism and allowing "secret converts" in some cases, while on the other hand, some questioned the practice of delaying baptism in order to instruct converts (an average of three years in one study), suggesting such a delay reflects a lack of faith in the work of the Holy Spirit.

Readers also questioned Dr. Glasser's wording of "conversion from Islam," and his apparent denigration of so-called "natural revelation." There was also some disappointment in his brief section on evangelistic method. One reader complained that the only alternative Dr. Glasser offered to "stale polemics" was to speak of sin, righteousness and judgment, which is, in effect, the reader said, re-entering the theological battlefield again.

Various readers wanted to know more of the "how to" of "power encounter," and some wondered if in fact the Christian/Muslim encounter can take place in a context of "freedom and mutual respect" as Dr. Glasser assumes.

Finally, one reader saw the "power encounter" Dr. Glasser speaks of as only applicable for those who have a "life-arresting" experience such as Paul had. Others, he said, grow into a faith or come to Christ in a very cognitive route perhaps not needing a "power encounter" as such, and it may be from these groups that significant numbers come to Christ out of Islam.

AUTHOR'S REJOINDER TO PARTICIPANT'S RESPONSES

(*Editor's Note:* The following material has been compiled by the editor from a copy of the author's rewritten text.)

The author received a wide spectrum of responses to this paper. Some of the most significant comments were from Muslim converts from Africa, the Middle East and Asia. In general, they concurred in the substance of the theology of conversion that was advocated.

Baptism, of course, became the focus of considerable thought and response. Dr. Glasser felt that even though baptism is indispensible, the mode and the time should be left to the new believers and the Holy Spirit, trusting him to guide and lead, "individually as he wills" (I Cor. 12:11), in each particular context. Along with this was the idea, forcefully expressed, that missionaries should not impose arbitrary patterns as solutions, but should be very sensitive to both the theological and existential factors. Perhaps a "functional substitute" should be devised. Whatever the case, it would seem unwise for any outsiders to press baptism on Muslim converts and that, instead, through the teaching of Scripture, the Spirit of God moving in their lives will result in new converts eventually and voluntarily requesting baptism as the seal of their faith with insight into the manner of its administration.

This particular emphasis was heightened by Dr. Glasser's citing of the fact that there are approximately 3500 different ethnic varieties of Muslims and that this may lead to a great divergency of form, type, time and other such concerns in the local application of the principle of baptism.

One point also raised for clarification was that as "encounter" occurs, it must occur within the context of Islam in order for it to be valid. There will be no genuine encounter between the Muslim and Jesus Christ if our witness to biblical truth is clothed in thought forms alien to his or her culture.

New light was cast on what this might mean when the author made distinctions in modern Islamic society between the educated intelligentsia who might be considered somewhat liberal or free-thinking, the orthodox or pious, and the common people who may be practicing a form known as folk Islam. Approaches must be designed that meet these different categories of people at their own level.

This was also articulated in the concern that we must resist the temptation to descend to the stale polemics of out-of-date

methodology of the past--interacting only at the level of biblical
Christianity versus the "ideal" Islam of dogma and practice--but
must integrate into our approach the understanding of cross-
cultural communication and the theological implications of cultural pluralism. Our objective must be: "But God through me
has good news for you concerning Jesus Christ," fully expressing
the commonality of our humanness and the complete failure of all
men to meet the righteous demands of a holy God.

CONTEXTUALIZATION: INDIGENIZATION AND/OR TRANSFORMATION

Charles R. Taber

Picture a Muslim university student in Cairo, and ask yourself: What is there about the <u>context</u> in which he grew up and lives, the context that played a large part in making him what he is, that affects what the gospel ought to say to him, how he will interpret it, whether he will accept it, and what he does about it? The search for the answer to that question is close to the heart of contextualization.

I.   CONTEXTUALIZATION

The word contextualization is fairly new, and there are some who think it is no more than a new fad term for the old concept indigenization; others insist that the new term represents a genuinely new concept. It is my position that contextualization includes much of what indigenization had, but a good bit more.

Indigenization, the older concept, though it was first labeled as a missionary principle a bit over a century ago, is of course as old in fact as the first effort to cross-cultural barriers with the gospel in the early Church. Analogous problems were addressed through the centuries by persons like Augustine of Canterbury, Matteo Ricci, and Roberto de Nobili, before being systematically described by Rufus Anderson, Henry Venn, John L. Nevius, and more recently by an entire generation of missionary anthropologists.

Along with the indigenizers, there have always been the nay-sayers. The one school of thought emphasized communication of the gospel, the other "purity" of the gospel, conceived in propositional terms. The first labored to transmit the gospel by emphasizing the points of contact and continuity between the gospel and existing culture, the second the points of conflict and discontinuity. The first tried to make conversion as painless as possible in terms of cultural and social rupture, the others emphasized a radical break. Experience showed, paradoxically, that it was not the indigenizers whose efforts resulted in the worst syncretisms, but their critics; this was because the critics tended to propagate quite naively their own cultural patterns as the Christian way, with the result that people badly misunderstood the foreign and irrelevant message.

Indigenization, in other words, was a step in the right direction, but it did not go far enough, especially if we are to take seriously the 20th century context. Contextualization extends and corrects indigenization in the following directions.

1. Indigenization tended to focus exclusively on the cultural dimension of human experience: the use of intelligible and relevant concepts and symbols, appropriate music, liturgy, and architecture, forms of organization and leadership, and so on. Contextualization recognizes the importance of this dimension but insists that the human context to which the gospel is addressed also includes social, political, and economic questions: wealth and poverty, power and powerlessness, privilege and oppression. People's responses are conditioned not only by their culture in the narrow sense, but also by how well they are fed, and whether they feel free or bound, fulfilled or frustrated, important or insignificant. Furthermore, and this is crucial, the very shape and voice of the gospel will also depend on these things: Jesus did not preach recovery of sight to the lame, but to the blind.

2. Indigenization tended to define culture in rather static, traditional terms. The various aspects of culture are "given," and they sit there while the gospel works around them. There was insufficient appreciation for the flexibility and changeableness of culture. But we live in a world of explosive change, in which a static concept of culture, oriented to a traditional world that no longer exists and tomorrow will be virtually forgotten, will not help us today. It is crucial to take into full consideration not only ancient cultural roots but also present flowers and future fruits. This calls for a missiological model which understands cultural transformation as a broad secular process against which to analyze the specific changes brought about by the gospel.

3. Indigenization tended to think of sociocultural systems as closed and self-contained; the type society was the small

tribal group, isolated by distance and jungle from outside
influences. But for better or for worse, such groups are
vanishing from the earth, as people bump into each other all
the time, both directly and via the increasingly pervasive
media. Today groups and societies relate to each other, trade
with each other, fight each other, and defeat and exploit each
other within a vast politico-economic system which operates on
a global scale. Our model must take into account this global
system and its differential impact on the various groups,
societies, and nations of the earth. It must lead us to
recognize that many of the political, social, economic, and
cultural pathologies which are present in many poor countries
are at least as much to be blamed on what richer, more
powerful countries are doing to them as on their own alleged
sloth and corruption. The fact that most missionaries, even
today, go from the rich countries to the poor ones means that
the gospel _must_ address itself to the global system; if it does
not, it will increasingly be perceived as irrelevant, suspect,
or evil, even--or rather, especially--by the groups which
constitute the underside of the world. In more concrete terms,
how a missionary is seen to relate to the foreign policy of his
country and to the activities of its corporations will strongly
affect the credibility of his message.

4. Indigenization was almost by definition something that
happened "out there" on the mission field; it had nothing to
say about how the gospel related to the missionary's society
and culture on its own home turf; it merely said that the
missionary's culture was not for export. In fact, indigenization tended to take a rather too uncritical and optimistic
view of _each_ given culture in its home setting, and to see evil
only in the imposition of an alien culture on groups in the
"mission field." And since mission was going on out there, and
the problems of cultural imperialism were real out there,
indigenization took on a de facto exotic flavor. But
contextualization insists on two additional insights: that the
demonic as well as the divine is manifest in all societies and
cultures, and that the same processes of cultural confrontation
and/or syncretism plague churches in the West as in any other
place, and must be faced with the same attitudes and means.

5. Indigenization, on the whole, tended to deal with
relatively superficial questions such as the "expression" of a
gospel which was conceived to be "the same" in all contexts.
Contextualization argues that there is indeed a sense in which
the gospel is "the same" all over the world; but that universal
dimension is much more remote from the surface level of verbal
and symbolic expression than was previously acknowledged.
Every language is inextricably part of _a_ culture, and is used
in an irreducibly particular context. These insights pave the

way for a much greater diversity of approaches to both
evangelization and theology than were previously admitted.

    6. Finally, though indigenization was intended to place
responsibility, authority, and initiative in the hands of
national Christians, it usually did so in only a part of the
total missionary enterprise: the work of the local church.
More complex operations, such as hospitals and major schools,
were without question designed, financed, and controlled from
the outside. Seldom outside the writings of a few mission
theorists was the more fundamental question asked, whether the
very concept behind these efforts was itself sound. As a
result, extremely western patterns were perpetuated and
Westerners remained in charge, leading to frustration and
resentment on the local scene.

    Contextualization, then, is an attempt to capitalize on the
achievements of indigenization, to correct its errors and
biases, and fill in its gaps. It is the effort to understand
and take seriously the specific context of each human group
and person on its own terms and in all its dimensions--cultural,
religious, social, political, economic--and to discern what the
gospel says to people in that context. This requires a
profound empirical analysis of the context in place of flip or
a priori judgments. It does not, for instance, ask how the
gospel relates to "the religions," but how it relates to _this_
religion as understood and practiced by _this_ group or _this_
person; it is not even content to ask how the gospel relates to
Islam in the abstract, but only in each of its multitude of
particular versions. What usable concepts and symbols does
this religion provide for the approach of the gospel, on the
analogy of Paul's use of the Athenian "unknown god?" What
genuine insights does it offer into the character, activity,
and will of God? What are its gaps, its errors, its
distortions? What particular obstacles does it place in the
way of a true understanding of the gospel? It is on the basis
of such an analysis that contextualization tries to discover in
the Scriptures what God is saying to _these_ people. In other
words, contextualization takes very seriously the example of
Jesus in the sensitive and careful way he offered each person
a gospel tailored to his or her own context. At this level,
the gospel is open to a great many approaches and expressions:
it tells the blind that Jesus makes people see, and the lame
that Jesus makes people walk; it offers freedom from the
degradation of poverty, and freedom from the bondage of wealth.
The unifying element in all these expressions is God's concern
to restore lost, alienated human beings to their true destiny
in his Kingdom, a concern expressed in the historical events
centering on Jesus of Nazareth.

II. THE MUSLIM CONTEXT

It may be helpful at this point to mention briefly some of the dimensions of the Muslim contexts which Christian mission must take seriously.

1. There is the historical dimension, which Muslims tend to take more seriously than Westerners, especially North Americans. The history of relations between Islam and Christianity goes back to the very beginning of Islam, and the various parts of the Muslim world have their own specific pre-Islamic histories.

Islam is in an important sense an explicit reaction of Muhammad to what he understood of both Judaism and Christianity as well as to traditional Arabic religion. What did he understand by Christianity, and what obstacles does this pose for communicating a more accurate understanding?

There has been between Islam and Christendom a history of virtually ceaseless armed conflict: the Muslim conquests of North Africa and Spain, the Crusades, the medieval and Renaissance wars in central and eastern Europe, the colonial expansion of "Christian" western powers into Muslim lands, as well as recent confrontations over Zionism, Lebanon, and oil. During this history, "Christians" have quite consistently behaved in extremely unchristian ways, and thus greatly discredited the gospel. Of course, each particular part of the Muslim world has its own experience of these contacts, so that Islam in Algeria had a quite different experience than in Afghanistan.

Western Christians, in their ethnocentrism and nationalism, have often despised Muslim culture, forgetting the enormous debt that western civilization owes to medieval Muslim scholars who preserved and transmitted the heritage of antiquity, as well as original eastern innovations in mathematics and the sciences.

There has been a lengthy and checkered history of explicit missionary efforts in Muslim lands, going back at least to Ramon Lull. For better or for worse, we have to live with what our predecessors did.

Islam itself is an aggressively missionary faith, and throughout history it has incorporated many different peoples. Out of interaction between the "original" Islam and the varied local contexts have come a wide range of versions of contemporary Islam.

The prolonged history of contact has given Muslims the feeling that they know pretty well what Christianity is, and the behavior of its advocates has not in general commended its message.

To return briefly to our Egyptian student, his historical context includes great pride in Egyptian antiquity, in the achievements of his ancestors when ours were barbarians in the forests of northern Europe. There is the specific tradition of the presence of a Christian church older than Islam, but become a minority enclave with a quite different culture and even language from those of dominant Islam. The accepted modus vivendi is that people are Muslim or Christian by birth and initial social integration, and that neither side, especially not the Christian, seeks to convert the other. So for our Egyptian student, Coptic Christians, and even more those who are converts of western missionaries, are a species of foreigners.

2. There is the religio-cultural context. We might be tempted to distinguish the two parts implied by the hyphen, but that would be to falsify a fundamental feature of Islam. I can only mention some aspects of this reality in the form of questions.

Does the status of Islam as a religion of "the Book" facilitate or complicate Christian witness? In what ways?

How can we capitalize on the very high view Islam has of the uniqueness and transcendence of God? How can we overcome their conviction that we are tritheists?

How can we capitalize on Islam's high regard for Jesus, and lead Muslims on to acknowledge the biblical claims about him? How can we overcome explicit denials in the Quran of key parts of the New Testament revelation? Is it possible to communicate the reality contained in the biblical metaphor "Son of God" without using the phrase, so as to bypass the deeply ingrained misunderstanding of it?

Can we overcome our tendency to denigrate Muslim ethics on the basis of the very imperfect performance of Muslims, and make use of the measure of coincidence we find between Muslim ethical ideals and Christian ideals so as to call Muslims to obedience to Jesus Christ?

Can we help enclave churches overcome their ghetto mentality? Can we work toward an understanding of conversion that will not require of the convert sociocultural treason and suicide?

What style of approach can most effectively replace the
confrontational monologue and the triumphalistic attitude that
Muslims have too often seen in Christians? Do we not need to
clear a lot of boulders and brush from the field before we can
expect to plow, to plant, to water, to cultivate, and then to
harvest? Might not a form of low-key, mutually respectful
dialogue work better than traditional methods?

   3. Finally, there is the present political and economic
scene. On the one hand, how will the newfound clout and pride
of OPEC affect mission? On the other hand, how can we relate in
a Christian way to the desperate poverty of Bangladesh and the
West African Muslim countries? How can we overcome the deep
suspicion and resentment of Christian aid which characterizes
many Muslims? How can we offer help in a non-patronizing,
non-threatening way, with no hidden agenda?

   How can we disassociate ourselves from the stance of western
governments on the Israeli and Palestinian questions? Even more
urgently, how can we escape the taint of a widespread
hermeneutic among conservative Christians that identifies modern
Israel with God's promises to Abraham and justifies all Israel's
excesses as fulfillments of prophecy? And how can we avoid
salving the bad conscience of the West for our treatment of the
Jews at the expense of the Palestinians?

   As for our Egyptian student, his politico-economic context
includes such considerations as the poverty and over-population
of his country, the chances for a job, his attitudes towards the
Sadat government, and so on.

III. CONTEXTUAL EVANGELIZATION

   Given the realities mentioned above, what are some of the
imperatives of a sound Christian approach to Muslims?

   The first prerequisite, I think, is a genuine expression of
repentance for the nature of our (western Christian) historic
and present relations with the Muslim world. Unless we take
this step, I see no point in going further. And it does not
help for us to argue that we are not personally responsible for
the monstrous crimes of the Crusaders nor for Zionist terrorism
against Palestinians. Muslims have an understanding of
solidarity and corporate responsibility that makes us partakers
of the deeds of our predecessors, associates, and fellow-
countrymen, unless we explicitly and concretely denounce them
and act differently. Contextualization requires that we start
on their terms, not ours. In other words, we will have to
commit quite deliberately a variety of "treasonous" acts in
relation to our own nations, societies, and social groups. We

will have to abandon triumphalism and develop sincere respect, appreciation, and sensitivity for Muslim persons, for their faith, and for their way of life. Mission characterized by any other attitude ipso facto mutilates and misrepresents the gospel.

We must also take seriously Muslims' own expressions of their felt needs: how do they perceive their lives, their aspirations, their frustrations? How do they experience their own particular version of the lostness and alienation of humanity? We must, in other words, start by listening rather than talking, and then talk first of all to these perceptions, and only then lead on by careful steps to a fuller understanding of the whole gospel. Why should anyone listen to us if we do not take them seriously?

Once these fundamental attitudinal revolutions have taken place in us, we can then explore, in dialogue with Muslims, what the gospel says to them and how best to express and symbolize it. We can examine with them how best to express Christian conversion, and at what point in the process it should be made openly. And we can work out with them the broader implications of their faith in Christ.

As converts together study and obey the Scriptures, and as their testimony begins to penetrate the broader context, it is indeed the ultimate aim of contextualization to promote the transformation of human beings and their societies, cultures, and structures, not in the image of a western church or society, but into a locally appropriate, locally revolutionary representation of the Kingdom of God in embryo, as a sign of the Kingdom yet to come.

The question we must answer is this: do we have the faith, the love, the humility, the patience that will make this style of mission possible?

SUMMARY OF PARTICIPANT'S RESPONSES

Responses to the first part of this paper were overwhelmingly positive. Our readers were very grateful for Dr. Taber's clear distinctions between indigenization and contextualization. A few thought the distinction may have been somewhat arbitrary, but most felt that it made the paper very practical and that Dr. Taber's critique of indigenization was extremely useful. One response characterized well the responses to this portion: "I have seen no better writing on this subject."

Sections II and III of Dr. Taber's paper, "The Muslim Context" and "Contextual Evangelization" caused a good deal more concern and in some cases, opposition. Some were grateful for Dr. Taber's insistence that western Christians repent for the traditional nature of Christian relations to Muslims, and some felt the specific proposals were excellent. It seemed though, that a number of Dr. Taber's ideas or wordings raised red flags for many of the readers.

For example, concerning the author's comments on the "Zionist terrorism against Palestinians," one writer said, Dr. Taber is beginning to climb the soap box of political controversy which I believe will be a very destructive element...Arabs pay alot of lip service to the Palestinian cause, but in the end will not sympathize with the destructive tendencies of the Palestinian leadership. If we get into the tailspin of joining sides with either Arab or Jew in mutual incrimination, we will never get down to the work of sharing the Gospel as a ministry of reconciliation."

ON THE NEED FOR WESTERN CHRISTIANS
TO EXPRESS GENUINE REPENTANCE

Readers said:
--"Guilt feelings may be exaggerated..."
--"We must not be trapped into a false sense of guilt. Islam is in no way guiltless."
--"I totally disagree. Some who are looking for a cause will use this argument but thinking people consider it another form of Western adolescent humility."

ON ABANDONING 'TRIUMPHALISM'

--"Dr. Taber owes it to his audience to define 'triumphalism.' Does Taber believe that 'every knee shall bow and every tongue confess,' or is that too 'triumphalism'?"

ON THE AUTHOR'S SUGGESTION THAT WE MUST "COMMIT QUITE
DELIBERATELY A VARIETY OF TREASONOUS ACTS

--"I can see no connection between 'treasonous acts' and
   abandoning 'triumphalism.'"
--"If the Gospel is transcultural, it can include our (culture)
   as well as his."
--"Evidently contextualization means something else to Dr. Taber
   than to me...In fact, Christianity must mean something else
   ...we are not about to sacrifice personal integrity and
   truth to follow this appeal. I can think of no more extreme
   position than what he advocates."

Speaking more generally, another reader said, "The
reflections of the author are...helpful, but have little to do
with Islam...The essay has a handwringing flavor to it that is
counterproductive in any Arab context. There must come a time
when we stop talking about the giants and go in and possess
the land."

Dr. Taber has obviously raised many issues that need further
clarification and discussion. That his paper was so "daring"
was seen by some as its greatest strength, by others as its
downfall. The paper was certainly, as one respondent put it,
"provocative--and basic."

AUTHOR'S REJOINDER TO PARTICIPANT'S RESPONSES

I am pleased that a number of readers found my paper useful, and not surprised that some found it questionable. Since it would be futile to try to reply to each comment, I will single out five issues that were raised by several.

1. I am grateful for the corrections of fact that several offered to my interpretations of one or more Muslim contexts. Since I have never lived in a Muslim country, I was primarily concerned to stimulate certain kinds of questions, not to offer an analysis of Islam.

2. Several faulted me for not spelling out a set of procedures for contextualization. But as I have said, I am not knowledgeable about Islam. Furthermore, it is of the essence of contextualization that approaches must be designed specifically in and for each context, not in general. I would far rather have a missionary who is thoroughly familiar with his context and sensitive to the leading of the Holy Spirit than one whose head is full of all-purpose techniques which are supposed to open all doors and to solve all problems.

3. A number felt that indigenization properly understood already covered all that I assigned to contextualization. That may have been so for a few; but the literature and the practice of many missionaries who thought they were practising indigenization shows that it was not so understood by the many. Too much of it was left implicit by the sensitive, and not picked up at all by the rest. It is better therefore to urge people to do something that is visibly different rather than to play semantic games with the old term.

4. Some questioned my description of a low-key approach and my use of the term "dialogue," perhaps because it is associated with a highly visible W.C.C. program. But those who insist on a traditional hard-sell approach should point out how well it works; it was my impression that it was because the old way was not working that this consultation was convened. I was suggesting that a more respectful, more gentle approach might be more effective. It would have the added merit of being more biblical, in my judgment.

5. The part of my paper that raised the most objections was that in which I discussed our corporate responsibility for the acts of our society and nation, and suggested that a missionary could be called upon to take "treasonous" positions with respect to the national policies and interests of his home country. Several were outraged that I seemed to hold them personally responsible for the Crusades; what I was rather saying was that,

given the realities of the <u>Muslim</u> perspective (which is what
contextualization is all about--taking seriously where the
receptors are), we <u>are</u> corporately responsible for those acts
of our nation or civilization <u>which</u> <u>we</u> <u>do</u> <u>not</u> <u>expressly</u> <u>disavow</u>
<u>and</u> <u>repent</u> <u>of</u>. The way of the Cross, which is surely the way
of Christ, would go along with this rather than insisting that
Muslims adopt our view of purely individual responsibility
(incidentally, a good biblical case could be made for some form
of corporate responsibility). As for "treason," I hoped that
my use of quotation marks would make it clear that I was speaking
hyperbolically; and unless we take the position that our home
countries are Christian in all they do, in all their policies,
and in their understandings of "national interest," which of us
would feel that it is never incumbent upon a missionary from the
USA (for instance) to publicly put a distance between himself
and evil US policies?

NEW THEOLOGICAL APPROACHES IN MUSLIM EVANGELISM

Bruce J. Nicholls

Today we are witnessing a renewal of Islamic dawah, the fulfillment of the command, "To call men into the path of Allah" (Quran
16:125). The Muslim world is becoming alarmed at the growth of
Christian mission or at least by the publicity that is being
given to it. Khurshid Ahmad, Director General of the Islamic
Foundation, Leicester, exploded at a recent Christian/Muslim
dialogue (Cambesy, June 1976), "If there is a single instance of
Muslim intolerance towards Christians, it puts me to shame--
I would always be prepared to confess it and I am ready to do
whatever I can to rectify that situation. But for God's sake
don't compare such isolated incidents of human weakness with the
enormous exploitation of the Muslims by the Christian world,
through education, medicine, aid, etc.--all of which have been
used as conscious and deliberate instruments of a missionary
policy" (Ahmad 1976:456). It is not surprising that the agreed
statement of the conference declared, "The Conference, being
painfully aware that Muslim attitudes to Christian missions
have been so adversely affected by the abuse of diakonia,
strongly urge Christian churches and religious organizations to
suspend their misused diakonia activities in the world of Islam."
This study paper is concerned with exploring new theological
approaches in response to this challenge.

I. ISLAM AS AL-DIN

Islam is more than a religious faith, it is a complete way of
life, al-din. It is a system which integrates all religious, social, economic, and political institutions on the foundation of
iman, the conviction and commitment to accept God as the Lord and

to submit completely to His Will as revealed in the law, the shariah. Islam is a community faith which represents a social movement to actualize in space and time the demands of the hidayah" (al-Faruqi 1976:401). Islam teaches that man does not need salvation in the Christian sense, but hidayah or divine guidance to know and to obey the will of God. Dawah is a call to all men to recover their true rationality, innocence and dignity as God's khalifah or viceregent on earth.

The Lebensmitte or creative center of Islam is tawhid, the witness that there is no god but God. Tawid means that God is the Creator or Ultimate Cause of all existence and action and it asserts that man is free and responsible to actualize the will of God. Thus in Islam religion and culture are one. As Ismail al-Faruqi said, "Islam stands clearly within the Mesopotamian religious tradition where religion is civilization and civilization is religion" (1976:399). Two recent conferences which attempted to restate this holistic view of life may be noted. At the International Islamic Conference, London, April 1976 on "Islam and the Challenge of our Age," Islam was presented as a total system of values, as the inspiration of the achievements in science and humanities and as the one sure source of belief and conduct. Again, the World Conference on Muslim Education, April 1977, at the King Abdul Asiz University at Jeddah, called for an end to the secularizing influence of western education and for a reclassification of all knowledge from an Islamic point of view.

A modern Muslim may be indifferent to his religious faith but he will want to remain a Muslim for cultural reasons. To change his religion would mean to cut himself off from his family and the whole of Islamic society. Thus the Christian response to dawah must be cultural as well as religious if our evangelism is to be effective and new churches planted.

II. THE KINGDOM OF GOD IN BIBLICAL THEOLOGY

Biblical theology has many complementary relational centers. In this paper I am suggesting that we explore the biblical concept of the Kingdom of God as the one that effectively meets both the religious and cultural needs of the Muslim and offers a comprehensive response to the Muslim understanding of al-din and dawah. However, the Islamic context does not determine our theological framework. We must begin where the New Testament begins in the ministry of the Lord Jesus Christ if we are going to faithfully contextualize the gospel.

Evangelicals have not always taken seriously enough the fact that the framework for our Lord's ministry was the proclamation of the Kingdom of God. He began his ministry with this message

(Mark 1:15). He conceived of the Kingdom as the universal reign of God in heaven and on earth, in both the spiritual and the created realms. Jesus was aware that he was the bearer of the Kingdom, in him the Kingdom was realized, yet he looked for its consummation at the end time. He saw his mission as the anointed one uniquely sent by the Father to the whole person, to the whole world and to the whole fabric of society. He did not confuse spiritual salvation from sin with social justice and responsible social action, but neither did he create a dichotomy between them as Ron Sider has well shown (1978:70-88).

The mind of Christ on this holistic view of mission is clearly seen in his confession of his mission as the fulfillment of the prophecy of Isaiah (Luke 4:17-19) and also in his reply to the disciples of the imprisoned John the Baptist (Matt. 11:2-6). He taught that his power to forgive sin and the miracles he performed were signs of his messianic Kingship. His lifestyle was the confirmation of his preaching. He traveled the cities and villages "teaching in their synagogues, and preaching the gospel of the Kingdom, and healing every disease and infirmity" (Matt. 9:35). The early Church caught the vision of the centrality of Jesus Christ and the Kingdom of God in its missionary outreach (Acts 8:12, 14:22, 20:25, 28:23, 31).

Jesus' concept of the Kingdom was cosmic. His Kingdom was not of this world yet he taught his disciples to pray to the Father. "Thy Kingdom come, thy will be done, on earth as it is in heaven" (Matt. 6:10). In the casting out of the demons, the Kingdom came upon his hearers (Luke 11:20). In the victory of the Cross the ruler of this world was cast out (John 12:31). Paul expounded the same triumph of Christ over cosmic principalities and powers when he spoke of the Father delivering us from the dominion of darkness and transferring us to the Kingdom of his beloved Son (Col. 1:13).

Jesus had a profound sense of the interaction of the historic moment and the eschatological hope which he expressed in the reality of the Kingdom now and the Kingdom to come. Those who repent and believe enter the Kingdom (Luke 17:21). Jesus rules Now by grace but Then he will rule as a glorious king coming with all the splendor of heaven. The disciples of Jesus wanted to hasten the coming of the Kingdom, but Jesus pointed to the Not Yet (Matt. 24); the gospel of the Kingdom must be preached throughout the whole world but at the same time false Christs and prophets will arise and lead many astray. As a result of this proclamation of the gospel of the Kingdom there emerges from the rock of Peter's confession the Church, which Hans Kung rightly describes as "the community of the new people of God called out and called together." The Church visibly manifests as households of faith yet spiritually one body is neither to be identified with the Kingdom nor independent of it. A messianic Kingdom demands a messianic community. Wherever Christ reigns within the visible Church, there the Kingdom of God has come on earth. The Church transcends culture and yet deeply penetrates it.

The dynamism of the gospel as "the design for living" is seen in the ethics of the Kingdom which Jesus expounded in the Sermon on the Mount. Kingdom ethics penetrate the inner motives of the private life. They center on marriage and the family but extend to every structure of human society. The ethics of the Kingdom are concerned with the quality of life as love to God and to one's neighbor overflowing the boundaries of law. This the biblical concèpt of the Kingdom is a dynamic and comprehensive reality which transcends the somewhat absolutist and static concept of al-din. It points to the sovereignty of God over all without blurring the distinction between God and Caesar as does Islam.

III. PROCLAIMING THE KINGDOM OF GOD IN RESPONSE TO ISLAMIC DAWAH

If the Lebensmitte of Islam is tawhid it is equally true that the creative center of the gospel is the triune personal God. "God is love" and "Jesus Christ is love incarnate" are concepts of personal God that transcend the mathematical oneness of God. If God is ultimately personal then he is eternally personal. Jesus did not become the Son, he was eternally so. The early Church fathers understood the Greek prosopon and the Latin persona as relational in contrast to modern man who has reduced person to an autonomous individual which the Muslim understands as tritheism. If God is love then he is eternally love and the mystery of this inner relationship is made visible in the incarnation. All analogies of nature are totally inadequate to explain the personhood of divine love. This mystery of the triune God and the Sonship of Jesus Christ can only be grasped from within the circle of faith, so the evangelist must enter into an indepth relationship with the Muslim, leading to faith, before this doctrine can be grasped. Evangelical Christians have generally accepted the methodology of Augustine and Anselm "credo ut intelligum." I believe so that I may understand.

If the Kingdom of God is a community of love, then the Church must transcend the community of brothers who submit to God. Alas, how far short we Christians fall. This means that the starting point of our theological understanding of evangelism will be the Church and not the individual. The Quran teaches that Allah is merciful but he has no need of love. The two or three references to Allah's love for men are generally interpreted in te'rms of God's greatness. Yet the very reality of suffering and the tensions in the Islamic world have awakened within many Muslims a cry for a merciful God who cares and forgives. The demonstration of the gospel incarnate in the Church is our only answer.

The Kingdom of God is also a Kingdom of justice because law
is an expression of the character of God as holy-love. Paul
argues that law as an expression of the will of God is morally
good (Romans 7) while the Psalmist confesses his love for the
law of God (Psalms 119:97). By contrast the natural religions
of fallen man make law their master and teach obedience as the
way of salvation. This is the abuse of biblical law for it
makes law autonomous. The abuse of law in Islam is parallel to
the abuse of Old Testament law in Judaism. Islam as <u>din al-
fitrah</u>, or natural religion, assumes that every man is fully
competent to recognize the truth of the law and to keep it.
There is little or no need of grace. Islam calls all men, Muslims and non-Muslims, to submit and obey.

From the beginning of his ministry Jesus made it clear that
the response to the proclamation of the Kingdom is to repent
and to believe. The largely Pauline understanding of salvation
as justification by grace through faith is a particularly relevant understanding of the gospel in the Muslim context (as it
is for the Hindu and for modern secular man, though this is not
always realized). In justification by faith the transcendence
of God and the helplessness of sinful man meet at the Cross,
yet biblical salvation in the Kingdom looks beyond the Cross to
the resurrection and the Second Coming of Christ when nature
itself will be liberated and a new earth and a new heaven established. If justification by faith is a Christ-centered model of
salvation then conversion is a Holy Spirit-centered experience
which points to another relational center of the triune God.
Salvation is always Kingdom-centered.

The Kingdom of God is good news to be proclaimed. The great
commission is the mandate of the Kingdom. It is the call to
preach the gospel, to baptize the new believers, to teach the
new community and to heal the sick and to demonstrate the power
of God over the demonic. The resurrected Christ spoke much of
the Kingdom as he prepared his followers for the Pentecost experience (Acts 1:3). Evangelism and church planting, the pro-
phetic rebuke of social injustice, the compassionate service to
the poor and oppressed find their unity in the gospel of the
Kingdom. Thus service through medicine, education, aid, etc.,
is not an instrument of proselytization but the evidence of the
transforming power of the gospel. Jesus never debated the pri-
ority of one of aspect of mission over another; he just lived
according to his own mandate.

124

IV. SOME IMPLICATIONS OF THE KINGDOM OF GOD
FOR MUSLIM EVANGELISM

1. <u>We must think biblically about the gospel</u>. Colin Chapman
suggests that an attempt to think biblically may turn out to be
a new discipline which challenges our prejudices and helps us to
think in a more Christian way about Islam (1978:66). It will
mean much more than collecting proof texts. The hermeneutical
task means using the best of the traditional grammatico-
historical method and critically reflecting on our own culturally
conditioned understanding of Scripture. In order to think biblically we must both distance ourselves from the text and then
identify ourselves with it in commitment and obedience. At the
same time we must both distance ourselves from our own culture
and then fuse our horizons with the Islamic culture so that we
will be able to contextualize the gospel in the missionary situation. It is equally important that we help the Muslim to develop the same reflective spirit concerning the Quran; only then
will he be open to hear and receive the Bible as the true and
final Word of God.

Thinking biblically also means thinking symbolically. Jesus
preached the Kingdom in parables which enabled him to win from
his hearers a very different response from that normally achieved
by rational argument. Martin Goldsmith has shown how the Is-
lamizing of the parable of the Publican and the Pharisee can be
effectively used to teach the concept of sin to Muslims (1976:
321ff).

Thinking biblically will also mean using dialogue not in the
dialectical and universalistic way it is often advocated today,
but as a genuine interpersonal listening and sharing experience
within the framework of evangelism.

2. <u>We need to think culturally about Islam</u>. It is understandable that Christians with long centuries of mistrust and
suffering at the hnads of Muslims should have a love-hate relationship to Islamic culture. This had led to the formation of
distinctive "Christian" cultures in Islamic lands which make it
very difficult for Muslim converts to relate to the new community
into which they have entered. As the religious hold of Islam on
many weakens, so the task of transforming Islamic culture becomes more urgent. In this process we must look for both the
bridges and the road blocks. F. S. Khair Ullah has draw attention to the linguistic hang-ups in communicating with Muslims
(1976:305ff). Vernacular Bible translations of an earlier era
tend to perpetuate the linguistic barriers. Fouad Accad has
suggested seven Muslim/Christian principles in bridging understanding between the Bible and the Quran. For each principle he

quotes relevant passages from the Towrah, the Zabur, the Injeel
and the Quran. Kenneth Cragg has often suggested a number of
elements in Islamic culture that are "convertible," especially
in the area of our common opposition to idolatry, forms of worship including prayer and fasting and in aesthetic forms of
calligraphy and art (see his paper at Gospel and Culture consultation, Bermuda, 1978).

At the same time full recognition must be given to the cultural factors in which the two faiths are sharply divided, such
as aspects of the Muslim view of women, the use of force in
fusing religious culture with nationhood and the threat of death
with apostasy. The fundamentally different ways of thinking
about salvation and culture in Christianity and Islam can only
be overcome as the Lordship of Jesus Christ is acknowledged.
The obvious differences between the teaching of the Quran and
the popular practice of Islam widen this gap in understanding
as every missionary to the Muslim knows. The Kingdom of God
becomes the objective reference point to evaluate, reject,
adapt and transform culture in the faithful proclamation of the
gospel and the building of the Church.

BIBLIOGRAPHY

Ahmad, Kurshid
   1976   "Towards a Modus Vivendi," International Review of
             Missions 260:456-457.

al-Faruqi, Ismail
   1976   "On the Nature of Islamic Dawah," International
             Review of Missions 260:391-409.

Chapman, Colin J.
   1978   "Thinking Biblically About Islam," Themelios, pp.
             66-78.

Goldsmith, Martin
   1976   "Community and Controversy, Key Causes of Muslim
             Resistance," Missiology 3:317-323.

Khair Ullah, F. S.
   1976   "Linguistic Hang-Ups in Communicating with Muslims,"
             Missiology 3:301-316.

Sider, Ronald J.
   1978   "Evangelism, Salvation and Social Justice,"
             Evangelical Review of Theology 1:70-88.

SUMMARY OF PARTICIPANT'S RESPONSES

Our respondents liked this paper and most were in general
agreement with Rev. Nicholls. His emphasis on the Kingdom of
God was especially seen as right on target:
--"Mr. Nicholls' paper describes what I consider to be the
   theological approach to Islam. The Kingdom of God was the
   major proclamation of Jesus, and it will be impossible for us
   to improve on this timeless message."
--"Bruce has caught very well, and also expressed very well,
   the fundamental differences between Islam and Christianity
   as systems of religious thought and practice...We need
   very much the emphasis [he] has given to the concept of
   the Kingdom of God as we approach the task of interpreting
   the 'evangel' to Muslims...A continuing study of the
   implications of the concept...can only lead us forward in
   the evangelism of Muslims."
--"I cannot agree more with the need to approach Islam with
   a theology of the Kingdom. This, as Nicholls points out,
   provides a scope broad enough to deal with the total way of
   life advocated by Islam."

There were a few areas, however, where readers felt further
sharpening or clarification was necessary. The question posed
by Rev. Nicholls on God's rule within the visible Church, for
example, raised the further question of what he meant by the
"Church." "We need to answer this," one wrote, "for Islam is
a very visible rule of Allah in the political state and the
priesthood. We deny that such a visible rule is equated with
the Kingdom of God, although this has at times been affirmed in
the church. But then what do we offer as the test for the
presence of the Kingdom of God on earth or in the church?"

Another reader found "very impractical" Rev. Nicholls'
suggestion that it is equally important that we help the Muslim
to develop a reflective spirit concerning the Quran. "That goal,"
he said, "is as unrealizable as the argument for its necessity is
wrong: 'Only then will the Muslim be open to hear and receive the
Bible as the true and final Word of God.' It is the Bible itself
that convinces people it is true, which knowledge ought to spur
us on to getting as many Bibles into the hands of Muslim peoples
as possible."

Finally, some felt the author's argument on the love of God
could have been strengthened, if it had been noted that the
basic distinction between divine love in the Quran and the
Bible is that the former is reciprocal (God loves those who
love him or believe and do good), while in the Bible he loved us
while we were yet sinners.

Editor's Note: No rejoinder was received from the author to
the responses summarized above.

AN "ENGEL SCALE"
FOR MUSLIM WORK?

David A. Fraser

The fundamental issue facing Muslim evangelization is how
Christian advocates can fairly and sensitively persuade Muslims
to give their faith allegiance to Jesus Christ as Supreme Lord.
I am assuming that 1) apart from a consciously held commitment
to Jesus as Lord, without prejudging its cultural form of
expression here, no one has any assurance of salvation received
or the promise of eternal life from God's revelation, 2) we
have a significant role to play as God's appointed means in the
process by which people come to commitment to Christ as stewards of the good news, and 3) an understanding of the actual
factors involved in this process can have significant impact
on our communication and commitment-fixing strategies. This
paper is concerned with the process of decision-making for
Christ and the various components that make up the matrix in
which stable commitments are made.

I. CONSEQUENTIAL DECISIONS

People make an enormous variety of decisions throughout
their lives. A decision that concerns major lifestyle
changes such as marriage, vocation, or religious allegiance
is in most societies made only by the family, clan or community after a relatively significant period of deliberation.
The decision to place one's faith allegiance in Jesus Christ
after having been raised in another faith is such a major
decision. It gives rise to a proliferation of additional sub-
decisions, commits a person to a public role about which many
people surrounding them have strong feelings and opinions,
and involves long term, important rewards and punishments.

To pose questions concerning the process by which either groups or individuals actually make such commitments is to expose a rather large, unknown area. What do we know about peoples, families or individuals moving from a situation of ignorance or misunderstanding of Jesus Christ to a life choice to follow him as Supreme Lord? Can we construct a model of the stages or steps people typically go through as they awaken to the power of God and respond to his gracious call? Is the decision process significantly different for people moving out of a background of animistic, popular Islam, than for "orthodox" quranically-oriented Muslims? How does what we know about "conversion" from psychology, anthropology, and sociology relate to what the Scriptures bring into focus about that event?

For its part, science has held a great deal of interest in both conversion and decision-making. Communications theory and marketing research hold promise of application because they are focused on helping business management and politicians and their imagemakers shape opinions and attitudes of the public. Unfortunately, most of the studies deal with modern, western cultural contexts and subjects. Most conversion studies deal with its psychological correlates and are concerned with the impact of conversion on personality integration.

For its part, the Church has left the area largely virgin because of a misdirected feeling that such research invades a sacred area. To be concerned with human motivations and factors that increase the likelihood of favorable response smacks of transforming proclamation into another Madison Avenue sales job. There is a real tension here and we must never become complacent or naive in the use and impact of an increasing array of tools, means or techniques to guarantee the results we seek. Yet, we also must not fall into the trap that pits the Holy Spirit against the means the Holy Spirit is able and pleased to use. John R. W. Stott's wise words in another context can help us find balance here:

"Some say rather piously that the Holy Spirit is himself the complete and satisfactory solution to the problem of communication, and indeed that when he is present and active, then communication ceases to be a problem. What on earth does such a statement mean? Do we now have liberty to be as obscure, confused and irrelevant as we like, and the Holy Spirit will make all things plain? To use the Holy Spirit to rationalize our laziness is nearer to blasphemy than piety. Of course without the Holy Spirit all our explanations are futile. But this is not to say that with the Holy Spirit they are also futile. For the Holy Spirit chooses to work through them." (Stott 1975:127).

We are only at the beginning of our understanding of the processes by which people come to faith in Christ. Such understandings will have exceedingly powerful effects on how we carry out evangelism. The simple notion of the decision mechanism of multi-individual, mutually interdependent commitments that occur in people movements has suggested major shifts in mission strategy.

II. WHAT WE NEED TO KNOW ABOUT DECISION-MAKING

A number of studies and models have been set forth to interpret and organize studies of recruitment and conversion to Christian and pseudo-Christian groups (Toch 1965, Lofland 1977, Tippett 1977, Gerlach and Hine 1970, Beckford 1975, Carrier 1965). Drawing generally on their models, and realizing that they have been developed from non-Muslim contexts, the following matters seem crucial in understanding the matrix within which people, both individuals and groups, come to active commitment and incorporation in a religious movement:

1. Predisposing factors
2. Commitment context
3. Susceptibility
4. Decision-making mechanisms
5. Decision-bolstering processes

A. PREDISPOSING FACTORS

Evidence suggests that people and groups are <u>reluctant</u> to make new consequential commitments or decisions. This is not simply a matter of psychological inertia but also the result of the organization and nature of the religious beliefs and worldviews of societies. The vast majority of beliefs are organized into "self-sustaining" hypothesis systems. Humans seem to prefer under most conditions to keep what they already believe intact and ignore massive evidence to the contrary. Confrontations and relationships, experience or information that might lead to a new religious position are generally avoided except by certain marginal or risk-taking people. Muslims, like most humans, have a natural wariness of religious claims outside their own traditions and that wariness is reinforced with strong social sanctions against those who change allegiance.

For conversion to take place there must be certain tensions, problem situations, predisposing factors that push people and groups out of their normal equilibrium. These might be adverse physical conditions such as poverty, ill health, natural disaster or war. Or they might be more subjectively experienced conditions such as racism, sensitivity to socially tolerated hypocrisies, or low social status. Without such predisposing conditions, large movements to Christ do not take place. Avery Willis' study, Indonesian Revival: Why Two Million Came to Christ (1977), illustrates the importance of understanding background factors in explaining why so many Muslims came to Christ in the years 1965-1971.

B. COMMITMENT CONTEXT

1. Choice points: To what extent are there culturally structured opportunities for Muslims to alter their religious worldview commitment? Islamic societies, though there is some significant variation, tend on the average toward freedom curtailment. Choices permitted in religious identity are largely restricted to recognized variations of Muslim belief and piety. The Western European notion of religious freedom which makes piety and belief a personal matter of individual or family choice is not generally part of Islamic cultural patterns.

2. Cultural sanctions: Decisions for Christ can be either encouraged or discouraged by the sanctions of the social group. Can we expect people to be attracted to a Church or religious commitment when the penalties for making such a commitment are high? One might think of a continuum of cultural sanctions:

Required to be Christian	Very Encouraging to Christian Commitment	Indifferent	Very Discouraging to Christian Commitment	Required not to be a Christian

At the most positive end, perhaps epitomized by the high Middle Ages of Catholicism, virtually everyone is required to be Christian. Of course this generates the problem of "nominal or statistical" Christians. At the other end, where cultural sanctions are discouraging to Christian commitment, one might locate most Muslim contexts.

One implication of such a negative context is that the
appeal for Christ tends to be embraced by marginals or social
deviants who have a relatively lower stake or social status
in the Muslim community. Where such is the case, Christianity
becomes stigmatized. It gains no strong roots in the majority
community and is perceived as a subversive. The "average"
Muslim is confirmed in thinking that Christianity should be
resisted as alien. The Muslim convert feels embarrassment,
self-degradation, loss of family support, and social ostracism.
He loses vital contact with his community, becomes dependent
on the foreign-supported Christian community for job and marriage partner, and often is gradually removed from the remaining Muslim community.

Another implication is that the strategist will look for
contexts where Muslims are in encouraging settings, where the
cohesion of the group and severity of sanctions have lessoned.
This might mean immigrants such as the Turks in West Germany
or societies undergoing massive socio-cultural change would be
seen as strategic groups to reach with the gospel.

3. Piety profile: Muslim piety comes in a vast array of
differing styles and temperaments. Perhaps this diversity can
be illustrated by Geertz (1968). He argues that Moroccan
Muslim piety is activist, populist, laced with fervor, and
centered on "marobouts" whose moral intensity and blessing is
dispensed to loyal followers. Indonesian Muslim piety is more
inward, mystical, aesthetic. It is a contemplative Islam with
heavy overlays of Hindu animism. A successful form of Christian movement in Morocco might have to incorporate a more
activist, charismatic-leader type of Christianity. On the
other hand, Indonesian Christian forms would stress a more
philosophical, mystical piety with the search for union with
God. But most of this is speculative. What needs to be known
is what religion is seen to be and do for the people and the
piety forms they engage in in order to participate in the
"ideal" religious life recommended by their religious system.
An individual or group's commitment to Christ will be in part
shaped by the type and style of religious piety which they are
leaving.

C. SUSCEPTIBILITY (SUGGESTIBILITY)

1. Impact of predisposing factors: For an objective
situation to be translated eventually into commitment it must
make a specific subjective impact on a group. It must be emotionally and keenly felt and the people must believe that something can be done about it. Often this concept is discussed
under the rubric of "responsiveness." What it refers to is

that there are people groups and individuals, like Cornelius (Acts 10-11), who are already embarked on a search for a solution for which Christian faith is an answer. When they encounter the evangelistic appeal, they are ready to believe. They have what William James calls a "will to believe."

Until and unless people are dissatisfied with the help and meaning provided by their present commitment, they generally are unmotivated to give consideration to another option. It is no accident that the large movements into the Christian Church have occurred under situations of significant socio-cultural change and largely from among parts of the population who felt themselves peculiarly disadvantaged. Effective strategies aimed at producing consequential decisions will look for parts of the Muslim populations (social classes, occupational strata, ethnic groups, etc.) where the levels of discontent are high.

2. The nature and agents of the appeal: Susceptibilities are often latent or unconscious. The individual or group may be unaware that they are experiencing such strong needs or feelings until they encounter an appeal that brings them to the surface in such a way that the offered alternative is seen as highly desirable. Normally appeals do not create the need into which the offered solution fits but rather brings it to sharper awareness and show how the new way is dynamically relevant to that discontent. A communication of Christian faith that is not keyed into a susceptibility will be experienced as irrelevant, odd, alien.

Similarly the agents of that appeal must "earn" the right to be heard. Studies of who was the agent that recommended Christian faith show clear patterns of socially channeled influence. In the early Church it appears that a man as head of a pater familias could carry his whole family into the faith whereas a decision of a wife might remain solitary. All peoples have prejudices as to whom they respect and to whom they will give a hearing. One can raise the question as to whether the agent of evangelization has adopted a role in the people group which provides the kind of contact and confrontation that will activate the latent susceptibilities for faith. Pakistani charismatic evangelists are a case in point. Acting as healers and exorcists in rural villages, they have been literally besieged by "Muslims" in need. Their role and appeal, combined with vivid preaching of the gospel, activates latent susceptibilities.

Christian faith has been expressed in a variety of ways. The Church needs to draw on that diversity and utilize it in

offering Jesus Christ as Lord to the various ethnic varieties
in the Muslim world. Some western missions and missionaries
might be exceedingly uncomfortable adopting a charismatic-
healer role such as the Pakistani evangelists, and yet without
that style and expression of Christian commitment, latent
susceptibilities will never be tapped. This involves more than
the form of the appeal and the encounter which Muslims have
with Christian faith. It touches the forms they must adopt in
order to be part of the "Christian" community. Part of the
success of Paul in the early Roman world was his willingness
to utilize forms already customary and satisfying to his converts to channel their new-found love of Christ. Borrowing the
"synagogue" structure and building "Christian synagogues" is
exemplary for Muslim evangelization. If the decision for Christ
meant joining a "Christian mosque" or a Christian "Sufi brotherhood" instead of an utterly foreign Christian "church,"
decisions might be more frequent and more meaningful than they
have been in the past.

D. DECISION-MAKING MECHANISMS

We need to know how such decisions are made. Who is
involved? Is it all the family? The clan elders? If the male
head of a family makes a commitment, is that likely to be a
decision that the rest of the family will follow? What happens
when a woman in a family makes a decision? How can that decision become an open door to other relatives? When we consider
settings where relatively large numbers of Muslims have converted, we need to ask: Can the approach followed and decision-
mechanisms be generalized to other settings? One thinks here
of Indonesia's significant conversion rate in 1965-1971, and
a rural setting in Pakistan where 180 in a village have converted. If Islam is to be evangelized, it will not be by the
one-by-one extraction method that seems to be the present norm.
The moving of families and communities as a whole or nearly
whole units will have to happen.

Also, the method for registering the commitment is important.
The issue of secret believers and baptism is involved here.
What public and informal signs accompany that lifestyle
commitment and what does that say to the form in which we ask
commitment to Christ be expressed?

E. DECISION-BOLSTERING PROCESSES

All studies indicate that the period immediately following
the decision is crucial for the stability of the commitment
and the quality of the changes that occur in the personality
and lifestyle of the convert. Whether it be "group support

for changed cognitive and behavioral patterns" (Gerlach and
Hine 1970:110) or "solidifying belief" (Griffin 1976:169-212)
or "affective bonds to adherents formed" and "intensive interaction accomplished" (Lofland 1977:51-60). A post-conversion
period of evaluation, reassessment, instruction and preparation
is critical in giving a convert internal and external strength
to face the typically encountered resistance and discourage-
ment experiences growing out of the commitment. "Follow-up"
in the terminology of mass evangelism is as crucial as the
turning point where a person registers a "decision."

III.DEVELOPING MODELS OF DECISION-MAKING FOR MUSLIM EVANGELIZATION

Once we have some idea of what we need to know in order to
make sense of the process by which people commit themselves to
Christ, we need to bring experience to bear and discover patterns that are particular to given socio-religious-cultural
situations. This can be done partly by the case-study method
(Hanna 1975, Miller 1969). They represent one path by which
Muslims have come to Christianity. But the Muslim world will
never be evangelized if that is the major or only path people
must traverse to come to faith. At this point we must simply
say that the available information has not been analyzed, so
far as I know, to discover patterns of decision-making in terms
of the five elements discussed above.

Jim Engel, director of the Graduate Program in Communications
at Wheaton College Graduate School, has suggested a model of
the spiritual decision process which purports to be universal.
It was developed out of his marketing research and consumer
behavior skills and is the most serious attempt to develop a
model that might be useful in evangelistic strategy (Diagram A).

While it appears rather complex at first glance, its concepts
are not difficult to understand. It suggests that everyone
falls somewhere along a continuum in terms of relationship to
Christ. At one extreme are those who have no direct knowledge
of the gospel but know only what they have discovered through
nature, conscience, and what truths are found in their traditional culture.

"Others understand more fully the fundamentals of the
gospel (especially the truths of monotheism, the sinful
nature of man and the uniqueness of Jesus) and fall somewhere between positions -7 and -3. The people at these
stages, however, have not as yet reached the point where
there is a strong felt need for change and motivation to
open the perceptual filter to a serious consideration of
a life commitment to Jesus Christ. This occurs only where

there is a grasp of the implications of the gospel
accompanied by personal problem recognition (stage -2).
When the person is at stage -2 the only options are to
reject the message or to repent and commit his life to
Christ by faith, becoming a new creature. Assuming a
valid life commitment is made, the Christian growth
process begins. The first stage (+1) is often one of
post decision evaluation accompanied by doubts and
anxiety about the decision's validity and permanence.
Doubts can be reduced through proper follow up which
stresses the basic truths of the gospel again and the
meaning of faith. Simultaneously, the new believer is
assimilated into the fellowship of the body of Jesus
Christ, usually through the formal means of baptism (+2).
This stage is emphasized because spiritual growth is
otherwise drastically impaired or even impossible.
Growth and maturity then commence and continue throughout his lifetime" (Engel 1975:5).

The benefits of thinking about the decision process in this
fashion are several. It suggests that the goal of communication of the gospel is to move people in their decision
process toward Christ. It also provides other points beyond
"decision" or "baptism" for evaluating the effectiveness of a
communication method. Armed with the knowledge of where people
are in this process, we can avoid engaging in persuasion before
we have proclaimed the message sufficiently and brought people
to a suitable condition of gospel awareness. It also suggests
that post-decision events are important in ensuring stable,
enduring commitment.

While the scale centers on the question of what people know
and comprehend about the gospel, Engel (1977:31) also insists
that three other dimensions must be understood in developing
a successful communications strategy: 1) attitudes: how the
intended group feels about the subjects under consideration,
2) lifestyles: what the important motivations and felt needs
are that will affect the way the communication about the gospel
will be seen as relevant to the individual or group, 3) decision-
making style: what the manner in which people arrive at decisions is with respect to the subjects under consideration.

Does such knowledge help a strategist to sharpen up the
approaches and methods being used so as to be more effective?
If the percentage of a group that falls at -6 or -3 or -2 is
known, does it enable the evangelist to be more focussed and
relevant in communication so that the people can be moved down
the scale toward an eventual commitment to Jesus Christ? In
general terms I think the answer is yes. But I wonder if it

doesn't need significant modification if it is to apply to Muslim evangelization.

A. IS THE MODEL DESCRIPTIVE OR PRESCRIPTIVE?

It seems to portray the process as strongly cognitive. There are "truths" that need to be known and believed for salvation to take place. Conversion is viewed from the communication viewpoint--what needs to be communicated so that an "awareness" can develop. Follow up is a matter of reemphasizing truths and developing understanding. Does this model assume that there is an irreducible minimum of knowledge that must be known for the conversion to be valid? What is that knowledge and how should it be expressed for the many different Muslim contexts?

I suspect that conversion is multi-dimensional and that people come into relationship with Christ in at least several major fashions not easily portrayed by this model. I would stress a very experience-oriented method, as opposed to the very cognitive, truth-oriented method. The largest pool of potential converts are Muslim peoples who follow one of the varieties of popular Islam. They are heavily animistic, concerned with evil spirits and jinns. They know little of formal Islam. Their operative religion is one of amulets and charms, the seeking of power to give them success against the vicissitudes of life. For them, the entry point into another religious faith will be through a confrontation with a spokesman that can provide mundane benefits such as divine healing or the casting out of evil spirits. The most promising conversion story I have heard recently, where Muslims were becoming Christian in larger numbers than through the more intellectualistic preaching approach, involves a divinic healing ministry by a Coptic priest in Egypt. The turning point for adherents of popular Islam is the proof of "baraka" and power which the evangelist demonstrates. Understanding of the fundamentals of the gospel is an event that comes <u>after</u> they have confronted Christ and decided he is indeed Supreme Lord. All they know at the point of conversion is that <u>Jesus is powerful</u> enough to deal with their problems.

B. DOES THIS MODEL IDENTIFY THE CRUCIAL STEPS A MUSLIM TAKES IN SPIRITUAL DECISION?

My impression is that the more significant problem is not one of ignorance but of misunderstandings of Christianity that "innoculate" Muslims against hearing or understanding what Christian advocates are attempting to communicate. Perhaps the best we can do is to take the hint from Engel's model and develop a new one that is specific to Muslim experience and suggests the stages through which they commonly go, one of which may include a clearing away of misunderstandings about Christianity.

IV. THE NEXT STEP

We need to know how Muslims actually do make decisions for Jesus Christ. Such knowledge, when systematized and generalized into a scale such as Engel's spiritual decision process, can give us important clues as to how to be better stewards of the gospel. If we can discover the path the Holy Spirit typically uses to bring Muslims to Christ, we can more self-consciously and prayerfully conform our strategies and efforts to his activity. We can address Muslims with the knowledge and experiences they need to have, given their stage in the decision process. I believe such a "scale" can be developed. But I put this forth in a tentative way. The question mark at the end of this paper's title is meant to invite response to this assertion.

DIAGRAM A

THE SPIRITUAL DECISION PROCESS

GOD'S ROLE	COMMUNICATOR'S ROLE		MAN'S RESPONSE
General Revelation		−8	Awareness of Supreme Being But No Effective Knowledge of Gospel
Conviction	Proclamation	−7	Initial Awareness of Gospel
		−6	Awareness of Fundamentals of Gospel
		−5	Grasp of Implications of Gospel
		−4	Positive Attitude Toward Gospel
		−3	Personal Problem Recognition
	Persuasion	−2	DECISION TO ACT
		−1	Repentance and Faith in Christ
REGENERATION			NEW CREATURE
Sanctification	Follow-up	+1	Post Decision Evaluation
	Cultivation	+2	Incorporation into Body
		+3	Conceptual and Behavioral Growth
		•	Communion With God
		•	Stewardship Reproduction Internally (gifts, etc.) Externally (witness, social action, etc.)
		•	
		•	
		•	

ETERNITY

James F. Engel, Copyright, 1975 by Zondervan Publishing House. Reprinted by permission.

BIBLIOGRAPHY

Beckford, James
  1975   The Trumpet of Prophecy: A Study of Jehovah's
          Witnesses. Oxford: Basil Blackwell.

Carrier, Herve
  1965   The Sociology of Religious Belonging. New York:
          Herder and Herder.

Engel, James, D. Kollat and R. Blackwell
  1973   Consumer Behavior. Revised edition. New York:
          Holt, Rhinehart and Winston.

Engel, James and Wilbert Norton
  1975   What's Gone Wrong with the Harvest? Grand Rapids:
          Zondervan.

Engel, James
  1975   "World Evangelization," Spectrum, Winter.

  1977   How Can I Get Them to Listen? Grand Rapids:
          Zondervan.

Festinger, Leon
  1956   When Prophecy Fails. New York: Harper.

Geertz, Clifford
  1968   Islam Observed. Chicago: University of Chicago
          Press.

Gerlach, Luther and Virginia Hine
  1970   People, Power, Change. Indianapolis: Bobbs-
          Merrill.

Gilsenan, Michael
  1973   Saint and Sufi in Modern Egypt. New York:
          Oxford University Press.

Griffin, Em
  1976   The Mind Changers. Wheaton: Tyndale.

Hanna, Mark
  1975   The True Path. Seven Muslims Make Their Greatest
          Discovery. Colorado Springs: International
          Doorways Publishers.

Hoffer, Eric
  1951   The True Believer. New York: New American Library.

Janis, Irving and Leon Mann
    1977   Decision Making. New York: Free Press.

Lofland, John
    1977   Doomsday Cult. Enlarged edition. New York:
              Irvington Publications.

Miller, William
    1969   Ten Muslims Who Met Christ. Grand Rapids:
              Eerdmans.

Stott, John R.W.
    1975   Christian Mission in the Modern World. Downers
              Grove: Intervarsity Press.

Tippett, Alan
    1977   "Conversion as a Dynamic Process in Christian
              Mission," Missiology 2:203-221.

Toch, Hans
    1965   Social Psychology of Social Movements.
              Indianapolis: Bobbs-Merrill.

Willis, Avery T.
    1977   Indonesian Revival. South Pasadena: William
              Carey Library.

SUMMARY OF PARTICIPANT'S RESPONSES

Several respondents pointed to the absence of a question mark in the title of this paper. There should have been a question mark, and the editor apologizes for this oversight.

The pro and con opinions from our readers on the usefulness of the Engel scale for Muslim work could be measured by their attitude towards western marketing techniques and whether or not the Holy Spirit could work this way. For some, there is, as one put it, "a built-in resistance to the application of business management techniques to the Christian missionary enterprise." The problem seen is that the Engel scale grows out of a culture with a western-type marketing system, whereas, there are vast areas of the world where a barter system prevails which are not susceptible to such a western approach. Further, there is a built in assumption in the Engel scale that there is a logical progression to decision-making. It was pointed out that the role of visions, power confrontation, and healing, plus the desire just to explore a new world are often mixed in with the whole process. In addition, there usually are long chains of decisions involved other than the one implied by the Engel scale.

In spite of these concerns, many readers were very open to exploration in this area, and some were even expecting to have the author develop an Islamically specific tool they could begin to use immediately. Important suggestions were made in which the relationship of the communicator to the potential Muslim convert were assumed to be the determining factor in conversion. Using that assumption, the following adaptation was suggested for the upper end of an Engel scale appropriate for Muslim work:

-10 Awareness of Supreme Being but no effective knowledge of gospel.
-9 Established positive rapport with Christian communicator.
-8 Restudy of Quran on Jesus and clarification of misconceptions.
-7 Initial awareness of gospel through life of Christian communicator.
-6 Awareness of fundamentals of gospel through the Scriptures.
-5 Grasp of implications of the gospel.

Further confirming the centrality of the role of the communicator, a Muslim convert outlined his conversion experience against the Engel scale, highlighting the communicator's role at each step.

143

Mr. Fraser was criticized for implying that theological
differences are largely manifestations of cultural differences.
This was felt to belittle our concern for truth. Similarly,
there was criticism of the "dichotomizing" inherent in Mr.
Fraser's suggestions of an experience-oriented model as opposed
to a cognitive approach. The point argued was that we cannot
minimize either truth or experience.

With respect to Mr. Fraser's discussion of peoples and group
movements, some concern was expressed about the evidence which
indicates that it is often the marginal individuals in society
who are most susceptible to conversion. Marginal people, often
being somewhat deviant in behavior, are not the leaders who
could influence a group to begin thinking about Christ. At the
same time, all agreed that the old "extractionism pattern" has
not been productive and we must strive for a "people at a time."

A final concern was that the use of this scale on the field
might involve a huge data gathering system with highly trained
personnel. This is especially true since the scale needs to be
developed for each individual group of Muslims rather than just
a general one.

AUTHOR'S REJOINDER TO PARTICIPANT'S RESPONSES

1. My own version of a scale does not appear because I believe
it ought to be derived from actual experience within a limited
cultural context. Analysis of actual conversions should lead
to some models or paradigms for such a scale. I agree with many
respondents who felt the real beginning point of confrontation
was the misunderstandings Muslims have of Christian faith and
Christians.

2. To those who feel there is no "typical pattern" and so
eliminate the possibility of such a scale, I can only say that
such scales are already being developed by researchers in other
conversion contexts. It is not easy, but it can be done. I
suspect most of us already have informal models of paths of
conversion decision-making in our minds as we go about our work.
With an explicit model we can at least understand what we are
doing and relate our communication patterns to how we think
people make decisions.

3. The role of any such scale must not be misunderstood.
This is not a matter of creating a new "spiritual alchemy" or an
"evangelist's stone" that will turn failure into golden success.
It is a tool which helps us think more adequately and carefully.
Even if we had perfect information on which to base a scale (and
we don't and never will) and could place people inerrently on the
scale (and we can't), we would still have as much need as ever to
be filled with the Holy Spirit, to be ignited with a burning
desire to see Muslims encounter Jesus Christ, and to be creatively
loving and sensitive to their culture. Scale or no scale, we will
still need days and nights of prayer and fasting. But our zeal
and concern must be given direction and maturity by understanding.
We need to understand ourselves, the people we are attempting to
evangelize, and the patterns of decision-making which they follow.
It is time to get off the pious phrases that protect us from
facing our failure to learn from the experiences and insights God
is giving us. Zeal without proper knowledge and understanding is
like trying to heat a cold house by igniting the roof.

4. Likewise, the use of communications theory or the
principles of good management is legitimate, sensible and
spiritual. There is little threat yet that we are "technologizing
evangelism." Were we Christian farmers we would not pretend we
needed to be as ignorant and backward as possible so God could
really do His job well in giving the increase. As translators of
the Word of God we do not argue that linguistics is a stumbling
block to the Holy Spirit. As sowers of the seed which is the
Word of God we deceive ourselves if we think the harvest will be
greater in the measure to which we refuse to learn new insights
about how to sow the seed, analyze the soil, water and fertilize

the growing crop, or harvest the crop. It is not a matter of "manipulating" people into the Kingdom but rather of cooperating with the nature of things, people and culture as we attempt to be good stewards of the gospel we sow.

5.   Some were uncomfortable that I seemed to advocate making Christian faith more "attractive." I plead guilty. I don't think people respond to Christ when he _appears_ foreign, nonsensical or irrelevant to existential needs, or _seems_ to be asking people to betray their kinsfolk and give up their culture. I don't believe Christ _is_ that way, but we have made him appear so by many of our strategies and communication patterns. Maybe someone can explain to me why there should be more offense than the cross when we present Christ, as though he ought also to be offensive.

6.   Some wanted an emphasis that the Word of God is powerful, creating its own discontent and not simply fitting into pre-existing need. When sensitively presented in culturally appropriate ways, I would agree. But we cannot make a "fetish" out of the Word of God and suppose that a formulation that fits our susceptibilities won't need radical reformulation and focus on specific felt needs different from our own. God can make even an ass speak His Word effectively (as Baalam discovered), but even the word that dumb beast spoke was keyed to a concrete context with a specific need in focus. I believe the pattern we see in Scripture and throughout the expansion of the Church is one of constant rediscovery of how the Good News relates to radically different susceptibilities, how it can be phrased in radically different cultural frameworks and logic, and how it can break out of the straight-jackets we keep placing on it in hopes it will become _our_ gospel instead of the terrifying and liberating thing it is.

RESISTANCE/RESPONSE ANALYSIS OF MUSLIM PEOPLES

Don M. McCurry

"Open your eyes and look at the fields! They are ripe for harvest" (John 4:35). Jesus led his disciples into Samaria, among a people with a well-defined religion and center of worship that stood in contrast to Judaism with its center in Jerusalem. It is highly likely that the average Jew would have prejudged these people as resistant to the "true religion." Jesus showed his disciples that, contrary to popular prejudice, Samaritans were receptive to the truth.

In Taiwan, the Hakka people, formerly considered resistant by other ethnic groups of Chinese Christians, were actually open to the gospel when it was presented in a culturally congenial form. "In many cases, resistance is no more than a symptom of neglect.... They reject the Christian religion, not because they dislike it, but because they do not want to be swallowed up by another culture" (Liao 1972:13, 14).

Throughout the long history of Christian/Muslim relations it seems that there have been two notable ways in which we have erred. First, we have failed to see them as distinct ethnic peoples, and second, we have looked at them with eyes that have been prejudiced with hundreds of years of our own cultural-religious ethnic bias.

I. WHICH MUSLIMS?

How do you look at 720,000,000 Muslims? Are they just one huge impenetrable bloc of resistant people? A former worker in Indonesia states, "The Muslim world is no more a monolithic whole than is the Christian world. There are growing differences between Muslims at every level of their life: socially, educationally, and religiously. What may be true of the Ahmaddiyya emigre to Nigeria from Pakistan will not be true of the traditional Berber of North Africa.... The Indonesian Muslim with his syncretistic mixture of Hindu and animistic thought will differ totally from the strict Wahhabi in Arabia" (Goldsmith 1976:317). In commenting on the ethnocentrisms of Muslims, Bernard Lewis quotes several anecdotes showing the feelings that exist between Arabs, Persians, and Turks. He further noted their comments on the skin color between Iraqis, Ethiopians, Copts, Berbers, Indians, and Sindhis (Lewis 1974:199-216). A well-known Muslim writer wrote, "The unity of the Islamic world, however, is now partially broken as never before, not only politically--which had occurred already during the Abbassid period--but even religiously and culturally, by the erosion caused by westernization.... The spread of modernism has had the effect not only of sowing the seed of confusion in the minds of those who are affected by it and therefore loosening the hold of Islam upon them, but also of separating different parts of the Islamic world from each other more than ever before" (Nasr 1975:83, 84).

To further illustrate the wide varieties of Muslims within a given country, H.H. Risley, quoted in Crucial Issues in Bangladesh, provides the following schema on Bengali Muslims:

A. Ashraf (better class):
      Sayyids, Sheikhs (including Qureshis, Abbasis,
      Siddiqqis, and Faruqis), Pathans, Mughuls, and Maliks.

B. Ajlaf (lower class):
      Johahas, Faqirs, Rangnez, Chiks, Kasais, Laheris,
      Dais, Gaddis, Mallahs, Naliqus, Naliyas, Nikaris,
      Abdals, Bediyas, Dhobis, Hajjams, and Nagarchis.

C. Arzal (degraded class):
      Bhanrs, Halalkors, Higras, Kasbis, Lalbegis, Mangtas,
      and Mehtars.

In addition, both Bengali and Bihari refugees are mentioned. The author goes on to make the following comment: "Not realizing the importance of class distinctions, evangelistic work among Muslims is ineffective" (McNee 1976:2-5). What is true of Muslims in Bangladesh is also true of Muslims in India, Pakistan, Afghanistan, Nigeria, Chad, Indonesia, or any other country. They divide into more than the 44 countries that call themselves Islamic; into more than the 153 countries that list Muslim populations. The staff at the Missions Advanced Research and Communications Center (MARC) have developed profiles on 253 ethnic groups of Muslims, and they have only scratched the surface. Ralph Winter, in an unpublished chart on unreached

Muslims, estimates 213 ethnic groups of Muslims in Africa, and
300 in Asia, and possibly 3500 subgroups (homogeneous units)
throughout the world!

Why is this important? McGavran maintains that, "Right
strategy will divide the world into cultural units--those where
Christian mission is correctly seed-sowing and those where it is
correctly harvesting.... Wrong strategy fails to note the
difference between receptive and resistant segments of society"
(McGavran 1972:106). In Indonesia, where the gospel did spread
through these cultural units, "...whole communities became
Christian together. It was reported that in one place 25
mosques became 25 churches" (McGavran 1970:191). Undoubtedly,
this wasn't the only factor, but it was an extremely important
one.

In a country where the missions have been baffled by either
the monolithic concept or fallen into the individual approach,
one observer writes: "The Christian approach to the evangelization of Muslims in Pakistan is based on several false assumptions, leading to unproductive strategy. First, we have failed
to realize that Muslim society is not monolithic. It is
divided into many segments: various sects of Muslims, a variety
of tribal groups, class strata, different cultural and linguistic backgrounds. We approach them all alike.... So far most
evangelism has been directed at individuals apart from their
family environment. They are urged to make a personal decision
for Christ, that inevitably leads to ostracism and social dislocation, with all the psychological upheaval this involves"
(Stock 1975:201, 202).

In response to the question: "Which Muslims?," we reply,
"Those culturally homogeneous units of Muslims which show evidence of receptiveness." This means that you begin to see
beneath the overlay of Islamic labels into the wide varieties of
sub-units within a country, and you seek to avoid the pitfalls
of extracting individuals. "It is evident that people receive
the gospel most readily when it is presented to them in a manner
which is appropriate and not alien to their culture, and when
they can respond to it with and among their own people" (Willowbank Report 1978:19). But before we look for these receptive
units, we need to make sure our ability to "see" is not marred
by blind spots in us--the communicators.

II. IS THE RESISTANCE TO THE GOSPEL OR TO THE COMMUNICATORS?

In Traditional Societies and Technological Change, George
Foster wrote: "Only today are we beginning to realize that
major barriers to change, and to efficient directed-change programs, lie in the structure and dynamics of innovating organiza-

tions and in the culture and psychology of the people who staff
them" (Foster 1973:177). In pointing out the deleterious effect
of the anti-Muslim bias built into western culture, Norman
Daniel commented: "Communication suffered most, of course, from
the intolerable imperial relation of conqueror to conquered,
which only imagination of an exceptional quality could mitigate.... Interference (in communication) began because Europeans
refused to see the rest of the world as, like Europe, entitled
to its own cultural expressions.... The tragedy of the Christian
Church has been the confusion between religious and cultural
certainties" (Daniel 1975:145). A well-known Egyptian political
commentator wrote: "Europe, however, does not conquer in order
to spread a faith, nor in order to spread a civilization. What
it wants is to colonize; to this end it has made the Christian
faith a tool and instrument. That is why the European missions
never succeeded, for they were never sincere and their propa-
ganda had ulterior motives. They did not meet with any success
at all in the Muslim countries" (Haykal 1976:588). And even in
the area of ethnomusicology, Westerners come off badly. "To
hundreds of millions of people in Asia and Africa, the hymn
tunes of Europe and North America cause culture shock (!)....
Non-Christians are attracted by Christian music using indigenous
tunes and patterns, but they are repelled by much of our western
hymnody" (Morse 1975:33, 35).

Confusion of religious and cultural certainties! No success!
Asians and Africans in cultural shock from western hymnody!
Before we can talk objectively about the resistance/receptivity
analysis of a Muslim people to the gospel, we must make sure
"apparent resistance" to the gospel is not merely resistance to
our cultural imperialism (including political and economic
exploitation). Perhaps we can learn a lesson from Dhu'l-Nun
Misri: "The ordinary man repents his sins; the elect repent of
their heedlessness" (Shah 1964:1). Assuming we can learn to
communicate the gospel effectively with a minimum of culturally
offensive "Westernisms," let us have a look at parts of the
Muslim world today.

III. SELECTIVE OPENNESS IN PARTS OF THE MUSLIM WORLD

A local chaplain in the Arabian Gulf area writes: "The Arab
world of Islam was never as open to the 'People of the Book' as
it is today. Hundreds of thousands of Christians are the welcome guest-workers in every corner of it" (Accad 1976:342).
Although he didn't say it this way, the author meant that in
addition to being open to employing Christian guest-workers of
many nationalities, certain groups of Muslims are actually
showing a new interest in the religious concepts and literature
of their Christian guests. A veteran from the subcontinent
reports: "Muslims are listening to the gospel message with

unprecedented openness and interest" (Wilder 1977:301-320). In
Iran, a leading pastor proclaimed: "Now is Iran's time for the
gospel. Where are your evangelists?" And he went on to explain
where receptive ethnic groups were located. In Beirut, certain
types of Muslims have shown unusual receptivity to the gospel
especially since the civil war. In Jordan another veteran
shared: "The last 40 years of sowing the seed of the gospel are
now coming to harvest." In Egypt, through healing and exor-
cisms, Muslims are "seeing" the power of Christ and believing.
In Jummu-Kashmir, certain kinds of Muslims are finding their new
lives in Christ. Principals of Bible correspondence schools and
radio broadcasters are amazed at the responses coming in.
Questions that we need to answer are: "Who are these receptive
people?" "How and why do a people become receptive?" "How
can we find out and make evaluations for wise planning?"

IV.   DISCOVERING THE RECEPTIVE

    What are the clues as to what helps a people become
receptive to the gospel? Engel and Norton have identified one:
"Openness to change comes about as people begin to reappraise
their self-image, usually as a result of some kind of new
experience. The Muslim college age student in Indonesia, for
example, was virtually impenetrable with the gospel until the
post-Sukarno era when his country emerged into dynamic economic
development and growth. New experiential vistas opened, education opportunity burgeoned, and previous religious values began
to be challenged" (Engel and Norton 1975:83). Hodgson says it
this way: "Modernity...produces disruption of cultural traditions, which means at best...the uprooting of individuals and
the atomizing of society." "We confront a radical unsettling of
moral allegiances, and the need to find adequate human vision to
give people a new sense of what life can mean to them" (Hodgson
1974:417, 418). In his classic work, Innovation: The Basis of
Cultural Change, Barnett, in the section on disaffection wrote:
"Whole communities, tribes, and nations of individuals--or a
majority of them--can experience anxiety and hopelessness as a
result of large-scale misfortune. Consequently, a new idea that
offers prospects of relief may have widespread appeal" (Barnett
1953:395). None of the above necessarily means an affected
people will automatically be receptive to the gospel, but
mission research seems to indicate there is adequate grounds for
thinking so. From his own wide-ranging research, Peter Wagner
writes: "Wherever people are undergoing rapid or radical social
and economic change, churches are likely to grow. People who
are uprooted from familiar social surroundings and located in
new ones find themselves searching for a new orientation to
their lives. They are disposed to listen to the gospel, and
many of them will recognize that Christ can become the integrating factor they need in their personal lives and in their

community" (Wagner 1971:112). He goes on to identify factors
that induce receptivity: urbanization, new industry, reloca-
tion, colonization, Westernization, political changes, revolutions, and oppression (Wagner 1971:112-114). Each of the above
can weaken the ties of the traditional values held by the
individual and by groups. Persons undergoing one kind of change
are often open to another and this may be to respond to the
gospel. Roy Shearer has attempted to develop a "Conversion-
Readiness Questionnaire." I include it here, not as a defini-
tive tool, but as a suggestive model for us to further develop
for our own purposes. "To be useful, the questionnaire should
be scored to read out and estimate: 1) the amount of dissatisfaction a person has with his/her culture, 2) the amount of
dissatisfaction he/she has with his/her present religion, 3) the
strength of bond with his/her family and clan, 4) the amount of
freedom the respondent has to change and 5) the part his/her
family or clan group plays in a decision to change" (Shearer
1973:163). A modification of this might shift the emphasis from
the focus on the individual to that of a homogeneous unit of
people who make what has been called "a multi-individual decision" to change. Special attention might be paid to 3) with the
note that it may be the weakness of the bond with family and
clan that allows a unit to choose Christ. All of the above
discussion has been conducted on a purely horizontal level, in
sociological terms. There is another dimension.

V. THE SOVEREIGNTY OF GOD IN PREPARING RECEPTIVE PEOPLE

Jesus said: "The wind blows where it likes, you can hear the
sound of it but you have no idea where it comes from or where it
goes. Nor can you tell how a man is born by the wind of the
Spirit" (John 3:8). At the very outset, we bow before the
sovereign God and admit that we cannot know ahead of time who
will respond to the gospel. But we do know that the living
Christ has commanded us to make disciples of all "ta ethne," all
the ethnic groups of the world. We know that in the case of the
Samaritans, Jesus led his disciples into the harvest. We know
that he led his servants by visions, by closing doors, by circumstances, and in general, tended to the planting and growth of
his Church. And he is still doing it. He did give guidelines
then that pertain to today. When he sent them out, he told them
to work with the receptive and leave the resistant. He taught
them to be alert to fertile soil for the sowing of the seed of
the Word of God. Peter Wagner has neatly abstracted good working principles from the passages alluded to above: "Man's
chief responsibility in evangelistic work is to discern the hand
of God in preparing soil or ripening harvest and to move in,
under the power of the Holy Spirit, to sow the seed and gather
the sheaves" (Wagner 1973:69). And, "The obvious principle for
missionary strategy is that, before sowing the seed of the

gospel, we will do well to test the soil" (Wagner 1971:42). I
would like to modify that to the effect that after testing the
soil by the sowing of the seed, move in force to the receptive
areas--the good soil. Lastly, this principle so seldom practiced: "Well-directed research preliminary to evangelistic
efforts takes time, but it will pay dividends in the long run"
(Wagner 1971:189).

VI. A KEEN SENSE OF TIMING IS NEEDED

Stephen Neill has called our attention to the fact that
during the reign of Akbar the Great in India, the Jesuits had an
unprecedented opportunity which continued through the reign of
his son Jehangir, during which time several prominent Muslim
converts were baptized. He noted that this openness lasted only
22 years! (Neill 1970:37, 38). Commenting on the African scene
today, William Needham observed: "Major changes in the world
political scene have taken place within the past decade....
These changes have affected the fields of missionary service.
Some areas have closed...(some) more open to the Protestant
missionary presence include.... These changes and others emphasize that missionary opportunities are not static. They change,
often abruptly, and openings for Christian witness must be
seized wherever possible" (Needham 1971:133, 134). Is it possible that right before our eyes God has been preparing a wide
variety of ethnic groups within the Muslim world for coming to
know him through Christ in our time? There are many, many signs
that point to a coming harvest.

VII. A CHECKLIST FOR A RESISTANCE/RECEPTIVITY
ANALYSIS OF A MUSLIM GROUP

The following is meant to be suggestive. It would take pages
to work out the details of each item. These are the ingredients
of a beginning checklist:

1. Learn all that is necessary about cross-cultural communication to so communicate the gospel that we don't offend by
mixing our cultural baggage with the message.

2. Learn to look beyond the nationalism and Islamic veneer
of a country and discern the large number of units, each with
its own distinctives that comprise that society. Diagrams A-C
are samples of one way to do this.

3. Build a resistance/receptivity scale whereby you may
place the various groups of peoples that you have been able to
identify and evaluate.

4. In the light of your resources, divise a plan for "soil-

testing" through the written or taught Word of God, personal
witnessing, radio, Bible correspondences, and any other way God
gives you.

5. Realize that timing is important and that good steward-
ship means moving into receptive areas now.

6. Keep your communication with God so open that you become
sensitive to his leading to those prepared people he wants you
to disciple.

154

DIAGRAM A

PAKISTAN: AN OVERVIEW

76,000,000 = Total
Population

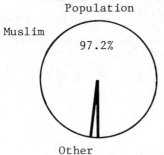

Muslim

97.2%

Other

DIAGRAM B

*MUSLIM POPULATION:
73,900,000*

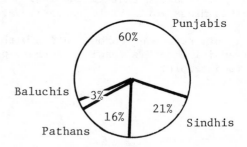

Punjabis

60%

Baluchis 3%

16% 21%

Pathans Sindhis

DIAGRAM C

PAKISTAN: A ROUGH APPROXIMATION OF SUBGROUPS

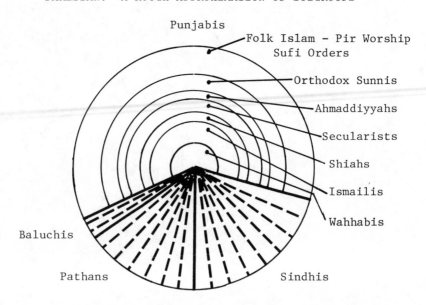

Punjabis

Folk Islam – Pir Worship
Sufi Orders

Orthodox Sunnis

Ahmaddiyyahs

Secularists

Shiahs

Ismailis

Wahhabis

Baluchis

Pathans   Sindhis

Among Punjabis, the concentric circles show major divisions.
Among Sindhis, Pathans, and Baluchis, striated lines show tribal
divisions.

Note: This model could be further subdivided into hundreds
of more homogeneous units.

BIBLIOGRAPHY

Accad, Fuad
    1976   "The Quran: A Bridge to Christian Faith,"
              Missiology 4:331-342.

Barnett, Homer G.
    1953   Innovation: The Basis of Cultural Change. New
              York: McGraw-Hill Book Company.

Daniel, Norman
    1975   The Cultural Barrier. Edinburgh: The University
              Press.

Engel, James F. and H. Wilbert Norton
    1975   What's Gone Wrong With The Harvest? Grand Rapids:
              Zondervan.

Foster, George M.
    1973   Traditional Societies and Technological Change.
              Second edition. San Francisco: Harper and Row.

Goldsmith, Martin
    1976   "Community and Controversy: Key Causes of Muslim
              Resistance," Missiology 4:317-323.

Haykal, Muhammad Husayn
    1976   The Life of Muhammad. Translated by Ismail Ragi A.
              Al Faruqi. Takoma Park: American Trust Publica-
              tions.

Hodgson, Marshall G.S.
    1974   The Venture of Islam: The Gunpowder Empires and
              Modern Times. Vol. III. Chicago: University of
              Chicago Press.

Lewis, Bernard
    1974   Islam: From the Prophet Muhammad to the Capture of
              Constantinople. Vol. II. San Francisco: Harper
              and Row.

Liao, David D.E.
    1972   The Unresponsive: Resistant or Neglected? Chicago:
              Moody Press.

McGavran, Donald A.
    1972   "Wrong Strategy - The Real Crisis in Mission,"
              Eye of the Storm. Waco: Word Books.

McNee, Peter

156

    1976   Crucial Issues In Bangladesh. South Pasadena:
              William Carey Library.

Morse, R. LaVerne
    1975   "Ethnomusicology: A New Frontier," Evangelical
              Missions Quarterly 1:32-37.

Nasr, Seyyed Hossein
    1975   Islam and The Plight of Modern Man. New York:
              Longman.

Needham, William L.
    1971   "Open Doors and Closed Borders," Evangelical
              Missions Quarterly 3:133-137.

Neill, Stephen
    1970   The Story of the Christian Church in India and
              Pakistan. Grand Rapids: Eerdmans.

Shah, Idries
    1964   The Sufis. New York: Doubleday and Company.

Shearer, Roy E.
    1973   "The Psychology of Receptivity and Church Growth,"
              God, Man and Church Growth. Alan R. Tippett, ed.
              Grand Rapids: Eerdmans.

Stock, Frederick and Margaret Stock
    1975   People Movements in the Punjab. South Pasadena:
              William Carey Library.

Wagner, D. Peter
    1971   Frontiers in Missionary Strategy. Chicago: Moody
              Press.

    1973   Look Out! The Pentecostals are Coming. Carol
              Stream: Creation House.

Wilder, John W.
    1977   "Some Reflections on Possibilities for People
              Movements Among Muslims," Missiology 5:301-320.

Willowbank Report
    1978   "The Willowbank Report. Report of a Consultation on
              Gospel and Culture." Mimeographed and distributed
              by the Lausanne Committee for World Evangelization.
              January 6-13, 1978, pp. 1-34.

SUMMARY OF PARTICIPANT'S RESPONSES

The responses to this paper fell into two broad categories:
1) Those who approved of the suggested procedures but wanted more input on how you do the various approaches outlined, calling then for someone else to do it, and 2) those who critiqued various oversights in the paper.

Among the former, the most frequent concern was with how you do soil-testing, and the problem of logistics in getting workers into all of the 3500 ethnic kinds of Muslims with its concomitant problems of recruitment and training for this kind of work.

One area of criticism was that the paper failed to deal with the theological aspect of Islam. Many felt that resistance to the gospel could be traced right to the quranic sources. Specifically, the things mentioned were the doctrine of God, being so totally other and distant, with no concept of his Fatherhood; the denial of the incarnation and the deity of Christ; the denial of the crucifixion and the possibility of substitutionary atonement; and the view of man being born without sin. These theological predispositions were thought to far outweigh any cultural barriers in explaining resistance to the gospel.

Another matter cited was an urging for us to be willing to preach, even knowing that people will resist, and not simply look for success possibilities. God in former days has raised up his Jeremiah's for the purpose of vindicating his justice in judgment. We must ourselves be prepared to be contemporary Jeremiahs.

A Muslim convert commented that Islamic society is more of a whole than we allow; it is also egalitarian and our concern with homogeneous unit and ethnicity are ideas that grow out of capitalistic societies. Relatedly, Marxist humanistic ideas, in certain Muslim situations, were said to open up Muslims to consider Christ and his teaching in a way that never happens under a totalitarian Islamic state. Cases were cited among the Somalis.

Confirmation for some of the sociological factors pre-disposing Muslims to be more open to the gospel came out of the situation in Lebanon. One writer cited the Arab-Israeli war, modern education, social change, urbanization, the civil war and the dislocation/relocation phenomena as factors that he felt contributed to a greater receptivity and number of conversions among Muslims.

A pair of comments on ethno-musicology came from a North
African Muslim convert and a Lebanese Christian worker. The
first pointed out that he has seen the "cultural shock" of
Westerners trying to use western music to communicate the
gospel. The latter noted that a current trend is now underway
in the Middle East in which Christian words are being put to
Arabic-type tunes from Egypt, Jordan, Syria and Lebanon and are
becoming popular ways of communicating the gospel.

Most poignant of all, was the frequent citing of the analysis
of the wide variety of ethnic groups in Pakistan as a good
beginning, but the lament that it was not accompanied by an
indepth resistance/receptivity analysis, and furthermore, what
we attempted to do for Pakistan should be done for all Muslim
countries.

Finally, a comment from a missionary, wise beyond his years,
to the effect that most missionaries know much that is useless,
don't know the things they should know, nor how to get a handle
on the right data. He appealed for better training of missionaries
in these matters.

AUTHOR'S REJOINDER TO PARTICIPANT'S RESPONSES

Knowing the human proclivity to take short cuts, it was not
surprising to read that many participants wanted their research
all done for them. Unfortunately, we are at that point in history when we have just awakened to the fact that we haven't done
our 'homework' with regard to Muslim peoples. At the current
writing, we have not researched any more than one-tenth of the
Muslim people groups we know about, and in very few cases have
we done anything like an adequate analysis on the receptivity
factor.

Before the conference convened, it was pointed out that this
was going to be a process rather than an event. By way of a
rejoinder, I would appeal to the participants to 'get into the
swim,' and help in the nine-tenths of the research that remains
to be done. This is going to take much cooperation between
missions and the already existing research institutes. One
way in which the author has sought to contribute personally
has been to help form the Samuel Zwemer Institute in Southern
California to do the very thing suggested by the respondents.

The same kind of argument pertains to the matter of 'soil-
testing.' The Protestant has not begun to mount the kind of
comprehensive seed-sowing/soil-testing operation that the
situation calls for. Nor have we determined the best way to

discover receptivity. In the author's opinion, we are just at
the threshold of new beginnings in our work with Muslims. Let
us join hands in moving forward in our unfinished task to
disciple Muslims.

The criticism concerning the light treatment of theological
issues is a valid one. The author did this deliberately for
the simple reason that early in the game, decisions had to be
made as to what kind of a conference we wanted to have. The
conclusion that prevailed was that we should save the highly
controversial theological issues that lead to rapid polariza-
tion, for smaller study groups after the conference. The
author also knew that many of the issues would surface in at
least two of the other papers. Having said all of this, I must
concur that the winning of Muslims is not going to be done by
'right techniques.' The theological barriers are real. Satan
is real. And human beings will not be forced. The latter part
of the paper tried to point out that our sovereign God is at
work and we must discover where he is ripening the harvests.

Again, the participants were right to point out that Islam is
far more of a whole than we allow. To say that they have a common creed, prayer practices, etc., does not mitigate the fact
that there are profound diversities and that there are varying
levels of receptivity which should serve to encourage us to
explore and respond to those who are receptive. We must not
allow generalities to blind us to the new possibilities for a
harvest that are evident when we examine people groups throughout the Muslim world.

ISLAMIC THEOLOGY: LIMITS AND BRIDGES

Kenneth A. Cragg

"The God of patience and hope..." is one of the great phrases
of the New Testament and these dimensions at the heart of our
worship must always dominate our thoughts and practice in
evangelism. "The wisdom which is from above," we read, "is
first pure, then peaceable, gentle..." and that sequence of
quality we must covet in integrity with truth and openness in
heart.

In study of what these may mean and require we concentrate
on the contents of theology rather than the practicalities of
evangelism. The latter belong elsewhere in this conference and
turn, of necessity, on our understanding of what is at stake
between the two faiths. Perhaps, therefore, it is right to
face at the outset the question of authority. The task of
reflection on the bridges and obstacles awaiting the Christian
in relating to Islam takes us at once to the Quran as the
central determinant of Muslim faith and life, and so to our
attitude to the Quran. But a plea must be made immediately
that we do not demand from ourselves a formal and prior verdict,
in the abstract, about the ultimate status of the Quran. To do
so would be to preclude the possibility of ever reaching one!
It is proper and intelligent to study and search the Quran
without staking such use on theoretical decisions about it,
either Islamic or other. We bring only a reverent respect for
the fact of Muslim submission to it, and we bring a patient
Christian desire to proceed as far as we loyally can within
what that submission means for Muslims, to whom the Quran is
the touchstone of what they should believe and why.

This is no merely pragmatic argument. Nor is it compromising

160

of Christian integrity. If Muslims are to understand new truth, or find fuller implications in admitted truth will it not be as the Quran can be recruited to their help? It happens (as these paragraphs hope to substantiate) that in fact the Muslim's Scripture has too often been undervalued by Christians for what we may perhaps call its "Christian potential." This is no doubt due to the long traditions of hostility and antagonism and mutual denigration. It is part of wisdom to transcend these and not to be deterred, in doing so, by the considerable problems and dissuasions we encounter from parts of the Quran itself or from our own misgivings about ventures of hope.

The potential of such hope is rich and there is precedent for it in the Christian reception of the Old Testament itself. No intelligent Christian will suppose, for example, that the gloom of Ecclesiastes, or the raw nationalism of such Psalms as 68 and 137, are compatible with the gospel. These, it will be said, are within a revelation anticipatory of the fullness of Christ, whereas the Quran, with its different sources of Christian disquiet, is subsequent to Christ. But when was truth essentially constituted by date? Place, as well as time, is an important factor if we are trying to understand the Quran's significance. Seventh century (A.D.) Arabia was more like the Samaria of Elijah than the Jerusalem of Jesus, the Alexandria of Philo, or the Ephesus of John.

Yet the final question for us is not how the Quran should be assessed in its own locale, but what clues it can yield for us now in the trust of the gospel in the world of Islam. "The wisdom which is from above," assuming we have its criteria rightly, would say that the clues are many and that they need to be put into currency with Christian "patience and hope."

We must begin, of course, with the inclusive Islamic, quranic sense of God, his being, unity, sovereignty, mercy and compassion. Islam is perhaps best defined in that phrase which Luther used to such good effect: "Let God be God." It has its own understanding of it. But the call to abandon and repudiate all idolatry, to acknowledge the sole authority of God in wisdom, power and mercy, to "have no other gods," either in creed or in trust, is the imperious demand of Islamic religion. "My little children, keep yourselves from idols" are perhaps the last words penned in the New Testament. They have a feel of their own and it is different from that la ilaha illa Allah of the minaret: "There is no god except God." Yet there is much in this single will to disallow the false and plural worships and to affirm the sole reality of God. That "much" there is here can be pondered, if we realize how pervasive is idolatry not least among the sophisticated. Any false absolute, a creed, a race, a party, a nation, a commerce, an ideology, to which we give an allegiance which is ultimate, is an idol and far more heinous than the stones and statues of the "primitives." How, of course, we can be freed from these idolatries is a large question on which the two faiths deeply differ (see below). But there is profound positive significance in the faithful insistence of Islam that only God is God and that only a right worship ousts the wrong ones.

But the question will be raised whether the God of Islam and the God of the gospel are the same. Here the answer cannot be either Yes or No; it must be both Yes and No. God as the subject of all language is necessarily the same, but what the predicate language makes about him differs widely. Since it is the purpose of predicates to define and describe the subject, the disparity in the predication enters into the sense of the subject. But that the disparity concerns the one subject is evident. For otherwise it would not be realized as disparity and there would certainly be no point in noting it. St. Paul brings to the people of the altar in Athens the news of the God of the gospel. But he says he is the God they "ignorantly worship." He does not ask them to deny the intention of their worship but to find it informed into the truth of God in Christ. What he denies is the predicate "unknown," (which may well be "indifferent" or "dubiously concerned with humans"). "Whom you in ignorance worship him declare I unto you." Christian evangelism is altogether concerned for men's understanding of the Christian criteria for God, all of which are wrapped up in the meaning, the mission, the wounds, the resurrection, of Jesus as the Christ. But it would be pointless to seek to bring those wondrous predicates of our faith if they did not in truth belong to Allah of Islam. What matters urgently is that they are not yet understood of him. It is that urgency which makes evangelism.

God, then, the subject of all theology is one. As to the predicates, as faith affirms and worship ascribes them, Muslims and Christians in part say Yes! to each others' predicates, and in part say No! Our bridges, roughly speaking, are the Yes aspects; our obstacles the No. These, in turn, ramify into issues about human nature, about sin, about history and the world.

Let us continue with the bridges. The Quran and the Bible have the common ground of belief in creation. "He only says: 'Be' and it is." God's is the creative fiat and the good earth, likewise, is seen as the habitat, the sphere, the "trust" of man. Man is "caliph" under God for the "ruling" of the natural order. As such he is guided by divine legislation. The divine intention for the world is understood in its amenability to man who is peasant, farmer, technician, artist, scientist, possessing and exploring and exploiting the world, under divine mandate and accountability. Man is creature under God, servant/master, vice-regent, deputy vis-a-vis nature, of the divine authority.

Here, not least for our contemporary issues of power and environment, of responsibility with resources and of social justice and compassion, are vast areas of common understanding for us to make good against all that militates against both human dignity and divine glory. For, as the Quran sees it (Surah 2:30f), Satan is the arch accuser. Having demurred at the status of entrustedness of the creature, and having rebelled against God on that score, it is Satan's aim in history so to tempt and disrupt and pervert the human handiwork and culture as to be able to demonstrate to God the folly he committed in so exalting the human role. For this, in Satan's view, was ludicrous divine risk.

These are profoundly stirring themes. If we are "to let God be God" we must "let man be man;" understand, that is, the crisis of our own vocation and how the divine purpose is staked in our response. Hence, of course, the urgency of the given law, the "guidance" (huda) as Islam calls it, the revelation which is to be the mentor of man in the crisis of his destiny in history. Hence, too, the sequence of prophets sent into the human scene in their sequence to exhort and teach the human response. Thus the quranic view of prophets in history is not unlike the perspectives of Jesus' parable of the vineyard, the husbandmen and the messengers. The particularity of Jewish vocation is absent. But the obligation of man in liability towards God for the trust of nature through time is deeply real in both the Islamic understanding of creation and in the centrality of prophethood to history.

There are, of course, obstacles here. But before we come to them there are other quranic features of this basic creaturehood which are our allies. Nature, in man's custody, is for the Quran a realm of "signs" (ayat). This term figures on almost every page of the Quran. The "signs" arrest attention and this is the ground of all science. Man notes, observes, classifies, and so harnesses phenomena. Islam here prides itself on encouragement of the human dominion through attentiveness of intelligence and the taking of careful pains. We stoop to conquer. Nature has not begotten technology by making statements; man has achieved it by asking nature questions to which "she" has replied.

But the attentiveness required by the ayat is much more than intellectual and scientific. It is, rather, religious and spiritual. The "signs" evoke gratitude in the attentive. The casual and the callous pass them by. A wife's fertility, or the earth's, is to the careless merely "ordinary." But to the worshipful it is endlessly awesome and wonderful. This sense of sacramentality (the word is not excessive) in the Quran has deep potential for our Christian ministry of Christ. For, if the natural order can be the sphere where what we call God's, namely mercy, goodness and care, is tangibly experienced, may not history, even personality, house the all inclusive "sign" the Incarnation is to us? Certainly the inner mystery of the Incarnation is not alien to the conviction that where God sets his signs is where we in turn can read them.

Further, "thanks be unto God," is the right temper of recognition. Is not Christian faith the most grateful of all creeds, having so much for which to praise, such dimensions, in the manger and the cross, of the divine self-giving? Gratitude is a conspicuous emphasis in the Quran. "Most of them never give thanks" is perhaps its most devastating comment on humanity. Can we perhaps enlarge the measure of the human gratefulness to take in the wonder, not only of nature and creaturehood, but redemption and grace? At least the clue is there. Significantly, the Quran sets as antonyms shukr (gratitude) and kufr (unbelief). Kufr is a broad term. It means whatever belies God. And we do this most culpably when we simply behave as if he were not there. The ultimate atheism, so to speak, is not the God we deny but the God we ignore. It is this negligence of God, this indifferentism, which is the ultimate quality of the kafir, the man who says No to God. Conversely the ultimate acknowledgement is not the lip of credence but the soul of devotion, "desiring the face of God" as the Quran puts it in another moving usage.

These reflections by no means exhaust what we had earlier in mind in stressing what we called the Christian "potential" of the Quran. Our task, surely, should be to recognize these assets with something like the insight of the apostle when he handled the Athenian altar or the author of the prologue to St. John the logos-wisdom of the Greek tradition. We have surely much more reason than the former and no less imaginative cause than the latter. The argument is not simply that it is irenic to do so. That might be merely tactical. It is, rather, that it is loyal, creative and right to do so, and to undertake the strenuous interpretative tasks as a positive and joyful duty. These tasks are both with the timorous or the doubtful of our own tradition whose loyalties must be respected and sifted, and also with the hesitant or resistant in Islam, sceptical perhaps of our sincerity or dubious about Christian intelligence with their communal book. Old reluctances die hard. But repeatedly the Quran stresses that it is meant to be understood. It is not, except perhaps for some esoteric pundits, an enigma

intended to conceal under the guise of telling. We can hardly
be reproached appropriately if we take it in its own seriousness
and, doing so, discover how far it takes us. On every count of
honesty and resourcefulness for Christ such seriousness is long
overdue.

Yet the more deeply we take such Christian stock of the Quran
the more surely we encounter the obstacles. It could not be
otherwise. Indeed a fuller awareness of what we have at issue
is one of the prime reasons for doing so. If we must be sure
we are under no illusions, we must also be sure that we are not
under the wrong ones, those, that is, of our own prejudice or
obtuseness. The more the "pure and peaceable wisdom" carries us
into and with the Quran, the more we must sense and feel the
barriers. Yet we shall have more "hope and patience" in
surmounting them.

They concern, of course, the understanding of man and of
Christ as Savior and Lord, two understandings which interdepend.
We have seen how Islam legislates for man under God. It further
believes that such legislation is feasible of obedience, given
certain prerequisites. These are the Islamic State over all,
the sanction of the political order to which from the time of
the Hijrah Islam was committed. There must also be the pattern
of habituation (five daily prayers, annual fast and pilgrimage,
periodic zakat) and the solidarity of the community or ummah of
Islam. Given these, and the reinforcing content of tradition,
man is held to be perfectible. Islam in general (though there
are significant exceptions) does not readily cry: "The good
that I would I do not and the evil that I would not that I do."
It has a confidence that law in revelation, mercy in community,
example in tradition, constraint in collective patterns, and the
aegis of Islamic rule, together suffice to attain that submission under God which is man's calling and duty.

Our Christian task is to offer our experience of the deeper
needs for grace and forgiveness and the new birth. Is there
not, we ask, a menace of pride, and so of disqualified good, in
law-abidingness? Is moral law not too often breached in the
observance either by the deadness of the latter or the
unworthiness of the spirit? The sin in which we stand before
God runs deeper than the culpability in which crime exists
before men. Then there is the negative dimension of law in that
it must needs condemn where it has been broken. In the
Christian view our need of grace is unmistakable and the very
sovereignty of God, to which Islam is so loyally committed,
affords it to us on conditions compatible with the holiness we
have offended.

In this part of our theology, there is urgent need, on the

negative side, to disabuse Muslim thinking of the sense the
phrase "original sin" is likely to hold for them. It is heard
to mean that somehow there is a reach of man's evil which is
beyond the range of God's creative goodness and that the
Christian gospel is darkly sinister in its view of the creation.
On the contrary, sin only matters because good matters. The
word "original" concerns the fact that man's self-centeredness
permeates the whole of personality and cannot be confined to the
evils of the body or to the external acts which infringe
revealed law. Indeed, the sins of the spirit, the pride of
piety, the warpedness of mind, are, in Jesus' view, more sinful
than the law-infractions of the "publican" and the sins of "the
flesh." We need patience and sincerity to interpret and affirm
the Christian meaning of man's condition before God.

But, central as that area of our witness is, the crucial
gospel has to do with the grace which, through Christ and him
crucified, suffices for our re-creation. Here the gospel of a
Savior's forgiveness has to face the focal puzzlement and
entrenched antipathy of Islam. But, even here, strenuous as the
tasks are, there are also assets of thought to be clarified.

Moving from the critical passage in Surah 4:158f, and from
other considerations deep in its theology, Islam believes that:
a) the Cross of Jesus did not happen, b) that is should not
happen and c) that it need not happen. There is the historical
denial of its actuality, the moral refusal of its possibility
and the doctrinal rejection of its necessity.

On the historical side is the familiar belief in the rapture
of Jesus to heaven and the substitution, by mistaken identity,
of another victim wrongly believed to have been Jesus. This, we
need to note, still leaves us with a Jesus men sought to kill
and with a Jesus who was ready to suffer. For the "rescue"
which "saves" him is only at the last moment and is, of course,
pointless unless there was mortal danger intended against him.
We can, therefore, still see in the will to crucify the
preacher/healer Jesus a measure of the sin of the world, which
is a large aspect of the gospel of the Cross.

But whether he truly suffered, whether God was in that
Christly suffering "reconciling the world to himself," these
questions of history can only be faced within the other two
Islamic disavowals of Christ crucified. Jesus, Muslims believe,
ought not to suffer in these terms. It implies an inability, or
a negligence, in God, a failure to vindicate his servant (all
the more if we say his Son!). God, on this view, "commends his
almighty power" in that Christ did not die. Moreover,
vicarious bearing of penalty for sin is not moral. "No soul,"
says the Quran, "bears any burden but its own" (Surah 6:164).

It is unjust to punish "x" for the sin's of "y." The gospel of substitution, they feel, is deeply immoral.

Yet have they, thus, understood what it says? The sense in which we can, and do, suffer for each other, is not in the having of guilt but in the taking of evil. In the story, the son's prodigal sin, the husks of the swine, the shame of the life, are all his, not the father's. But the father's is the unbroken love, the suffering heart, the restoring compassion. What is known to the boy as self-willed folly and sin, is known to the father as tragedy and grief. On the condition that the heart relationship holds (contrast the elder brother) the boy can, and does, "return to his father." This is sin-bearing and the Cross is its measure in the heart of God, because the Cross likewise, on the human side, is precisely the form of our Father-rejecting enmity and self-will. Truly seen there is nothing "immoral" about love's forgivingness, as we hear it from Jesus in his dying grace.

But is such redemptive suffering necessary to the divine omnipotence? God, says Islam, forgives, even as he creates. "He only says: 'Be' and it is." Forgiveness on God's part is effortless and majestic. To think of a Savior because of whom God is "enabled" to forgive us is to imply what otherwise must be divine inadequacy. Does God ever need "helping" to accomplish his will? How perceptive and careful we need to be in our language here, lest insensitive preaching play into the hands of misconception. How do we state the "necessity" of the Cross as the shape and fact of the divine adequacy in grace? For such in truth it is. Can our forgiveness be, as it were, a problem for God?

Evidently, if forgiveness is effortless, it is also unnecessary. For then there is no real offence, no veritable evil between man and God. Further, forgiveness is one of those things which cannot be had until it is wanted, nor given unless it is received. The forgiveness of such as ourselves is not a wave of the wand, or the lifting of a finger, but the restoring of a fellowship. The necessity of the Cross to an adequately divine forgiveness, adequate both to our human condition and God's divine grace, is the very pattern of that power in God in which Islam so tenaciously believes. For "Christ crucified is the power of God." The love of Jesus dying and risen is the shape of the divine competence. For here in the Cross is the "one perfect sacrament of that power by which, in the whole and in the end, all evil is redeemed." There we, too, are summoned to be redeemers, both of men's evils, but also of their high ideas. Our very obstacles, in that vocation, have to be our stepping stones.

There is much else which might be said. But papers have
limits. Whatever may be the "success" of our effort to
communicate, we may at least renew our hearts in the conviction
that a loyal Church will always be the means to the presence,
the saving relevance, in the world of these truths, and "with
God be the rest."

SUMMARY OF PARTICIPANT'S RESPONSES

Dr. Cragg's paper was appreciated both for its style and for the highly perceptive insights of this respected and eminently qualified Islamicist. For admirers of Dr. Cragg, this paper increased their admiration. One reader said that "he paints the theological issues on a broad canvas so that we are able to see the context of disagreement rather than merely the precise points."

The readers felt Dr. Cragg was realistic in affirming both the bridges and the obstacles, but that he had a positive readiness to highlight the bridges. Further, his arguments were seen as not merely tactical, but springing from a genuine appreciation for Islam and for Muslims, which as one reader noted, is the secret for the evangelism we hope to accomplish. "We should not be under any illusions as to the difficulty of the task," the reader warned, "but we must also be sure we are not under the wrong ones--those of our own prejudice or obtuseness."

A few respondents good naturedly critiqued the author's lofty style:
--"Dr. Cragg is so learned that at times he does not communicate with me."
--"With his usual mastery of the subject, Cragg uses no footnotes; with his usual modesty he uses no bibliography."

There were those too, who were not in full agreement with the author. One said:
--"Though Cragg was present at Willowbank, (The paper) remains profoundly pre-Willowbank. And that is a step back not only in time but in approach."

Some were against using the Quran in witness as advocated by Dr. Cragg. They felt that using passages from both the Bible and the Quran was, in effect, ascribing equal authority to each one. "Using Quranic 'bridges,'" one argues, "very well may sidetrack the discussion by bringing up the issue of inspiration." Another respondent disagreed with Dr. Cragg that openness to quranic truth is not compromising Christian integrity. "I believe," he said, "that in principle and sometimes in practice, it compromises...the doctrine of Sola Scriptura, that the scriptures alone are our authority."

Others pointed out that Dr. Cragg's expertise in quranic studies exceeds that of most Muslims, and argued that in the typical case scholars soon run into difficulty in the discrepancy between what Muslims believe about the Quran, and what it actually says. Other writers, affirming this caution

170

felt that Dr. Cragg's approach was limited to the 'elite' of
Islam, and that in areas where knowledge of the Quran is
minimal, "we accomplish little to begin with it."

Overall, the response to Dr. Cragg's paper was very positive,
and the critiques quite constructive.

Several of his ideas led to extensive development by the
enthused readers. One, for example, especially appreciated
the author's statement that "seventh century (A.D.) Arabia was
more like the Samaria of Elijah than the Jerusalem of Jesus...."
Expanding on this, the reader said, "we have for too long
assumed that all those who are chronologically A.D. are
accountable for the knowledge we have of God...We need to learn
to treat people more positively who live according to what they
know, even though not according to what we know."

AUTHOR'S REJOINDER TO PARTICIPANT'S RESPONSES

It was a matter of gratitude to find so many welcoming the
conviction that the Christian must be alert and open in his
attention to the Quran (as the matrix of Islamic thinking) and
competent in discerning how it bears upon his Christian commitment to "God in Christ, reconciling the world to Himself."
Some, it is true, had misgivings and hesitations. But one can
appreciate the instinctive sources of such reluctance and recognize the habits of mind that have to be overcome.

Certainly no "compromise" of biblical revelation (still less
any kind of "bargain" over some "give-and-take") was in mind.
Therefore, any cautions against such were unnecessary. But I
was pleading for an attitude to revelation which cares for its
content as the ground of its status, rather than the other way
around. Revelation is that which discloses truth, and so
possesses the reader (and the believer) of it. "Biblical" is
not an adjective like a label on a bottle which, therefore, an
alternative "bottle" may not carry. It is, rather, a consistent
reservoir of criteria as to God, man, nature, law, grace and sin,
by which we may be guided in critical appraisal of other sources.
Such sources the biblical may well corroborate as well as
repudiate, approve as well as reject. But, in either case, the
loyalty by which we are in trust with Christ (both within the
biblical and elsewhere) must needs be creative, intelligent and
enterprising--not timid, sluggish or weary. And we shall need,
in such loyalty, to receive as well as disown or we shall not do
either rightly. This, I believe, is very much the case with the
Quran.

For the rest, criticism seemed to fall into three main areas:

1. There was nothing about "folk Islam" and this (for many readers) was a far more important area of concern. Agreed. But then our task was "theological." We were aiming to deal with theology rather than "superstition." But it may be claimed that many of the "clues" run through both. The same kind of instinct to try and "see-from-the-inside" applies. Themes like <u>baraka</u> (the "blessing" availing for the "touch" in "sacred" things and places), the "evil eye," protective charms, etc., all present occasions for the lively interpreter of Christ, because they have to do with human fear and finitude, mortality and mystery. Certainly, let us not suppose a theological literacy where it does not exist. But let us not misread the <u>human</u> wistfulness where it yearns and seeks.

2. The paper presupposed a level of sophistication that, by and large, does not prevail today. Should we be educating Muslims, it was asked, in their own heritage and doctrine? What is wrong with ignoring the Quran? My reply would be that while there is a real distinction between "Muslim" and "Islamic," which it would be folly to ignore, the "popular" reaches back into the "ultimate." It is wise never to overestimate the use people make of their resources, but never to underestimate what they are. For reasons we have no space to explore, this is very necessary at the present juncture.

3. The paper was a failure in that it took no account of modern disciplines, sociology, linguistics and anthropology, and stayed in "abstract" theological realms just like Henry Martyn. One correspondent (whose careful analyses deserve, and will have elsewhere, a fuller answer) called it "profoundly pre-Willowbank." But is it not precisely the angle suggested by these other disciplines that requires us to question theological dogmatisms, to appreciate complexity and to alert our criteria more patiently. Yet, they do not require us to cease a theological <u>rapport</u>. For the very point of the gospel in context is that "the meaning <u>of</u>" and "the meaning <u>in</u>" should belong together. It takes a whole world to understand a whole faith.

POPULAR ISLAM: THE HUNGER OF THE HEART

Bill A. Musk

"In the name of Allah the Merciful, the Compassionate.
Truly Thou wilt preserve the one who carries this
writing of mine from the evil of all that might harm
him and Thou wilt appoint over him its angels and
servants and assistants who are entrusted with its
service and guard him by day and by night. Mohammed
is the Apostle of Allah and those with him are stronger
than the unbelievers. Among them are merciful ones
whom we see bowing and kneeling seeking kindness from
Allah and favour. Their marks are on their faces, the
effect of prostration, and that is their likeness in
the Pentateuch and the Gospel."

(Translation of a Talisman from a Muslim
book on the Names of God; Exhibit A)

"Buduh" is a common numerical talisman:

4	9	2
3	5	7
8	1	6

The numerical value of the first nine letters of the
arithmetically arranged Arabic alphabet are patterned so as to
add up to 15 in all straight-line combinations. The name "Buduh"

derives from the four corner letters (emphasized) "B (u) d u h."
The multiples of "5" have magic power against evil.

A lead or silver plate with small bells on the bottom, with
the following inscription, forms the most common Shiite amulet:

"Cry aloud to Ali; he is the possessor of wonders. From
him you will find help from trouble. He takes away very
quickly all grief and anxiety, by the mission of Muhammad
and his own sanctity."

(Translation of a Talisman from a
Muslim book on the Names of God)

Pinned to children, poked into crevices above door lintels,
strapped to the arm beneath outer garments, swinging from rear-
view mirrors in taxis and trucks, such amulets and talismans
betray to the initiated a second Islam: the Islam of popular
religious practice.

I. POPULAR ISLAM

Islam looks the same the world over. The "Five Pillars" are
famous, and any missionary to Muslims can expound on the "iman"
and "din" of Islamic, religious life.

But, beneath the surface, throughout the Muslim world, there
is at least one major divorce. In popular Islam, the meanings
attached to the forms of religious expression are radically
different from those understood by Bishop Cragg's muezzin
(Cragg 1964) or professor Anderson's students (Anderson 1970).
It is a division between "high" or "ideal" Islam, and "low" or
"popular" Islam.

The realities of the ordinary Muslim's everyday life are
rarely perceived by the unsuspecting, western missionary to
Islam:

"The student of Islam will never understand the common
people unless he knows the reasons for their curious
beliefs and practices...all of which still blind and
oppress mind and heart with constant fear of the unseen.
Witchcraft, sorcery, spells, and charms are the background of the native Muslim psychology to an extent
that is realised only by those who have penetrated most
deeply into the life of the people" (Zwemer 1939:Intro.).

Thirty-five years more recently, Rev. Detmar Scheunemann of
the Indonesian Bible Institute has asserted:

"Working for many years in a Muslim country, I have

come to the conclusion that the power of Islam does not lie in its dogma and practices, nor in the anti-thesis of the Trinity, against the Lordship of Christ and his redeeming death, but in the occult practices of its leaders, thus holding sway over their people" (Douglas 1975:885).

A. FORM, FUNCTION AND MEANING IN 'HIGH' AND 'LOW' ISLAM

A brief look at the foundational statements of faith and practice in Islam, as they are primarily understood by ordinary Muslims, will demonstrate the divorce before us.

Creed: The Muslim creed ("iman") includes a statement of belief in the only God, his angels, his books, his apostles, the Last Day (of judgment) and predestination. In popular Islam, the belief in the only God revolves largely around a magical use of the names of God (Exhibit A). Certain formulas compel God to do what is requested, and it is especially the use of the names of God that produce these results. There are many books on the magical use of the names of God, and the associated magic of numbers. The doctrine of angels includes, in popular Islam, demonology and jinn-worship. Involved in this doctrine is the concept of the familiar spirit, or Qarina--that is, the double of the individual, of opposite sex and a progeny of Satan, born at the same time as the individual:

> "The popular idea is that quarana [sic] come into the world from A'alam al Barzakhiya (Hades) at the time that a child is conceived. Therefore during the act of coition Muslims must pronounce the word 'bismallah.' This will prevent the child from being overcome by its devil and turned into an infidel..." (Zwemer 1939:Chap. 5).

The doctrine of God's books is turned into bibliomancy and bibliolatry in popular Islam. The Quran has the power of a fetish:

> "Certain chapters are of special value against evil spirits... The cure for headache is said to be the 13th verse of the chapter called 'Al-Ana'am' or the Cattle, which reads: 'His is whatsoever dwells in the night or in the day: He both hears and knows'..." (Zwemer 1917:2).

In popular Islam, the doctrine of God's apostles revolves largely around their dealings with the spirit-world. Both Solomon and Muhammad stand out in the popular mind because of their reputed intercourse with demons and jinn. Muhammad's hair has become famous as a fetish, and has power to heal.

The doctrine of the last day relates in the popular mind to
death and spirit-life. There is a belief in some saints as
mediators between God and the faithful--Fatima and Jesus
especially hold this position. The spirits of mortals remain
near their graves; hence the habit of visiting graveyards on
Thursday nights, and leaving food on the graves. The doctrine
of predestination (Qadr) has its effect on the popular mind
also. The 15th Shaban (the eighth month of the Muslim
calendar, also known as "the Prophet's month") is a holy night
in which God determines the fate of mortals during the coming
year.

Practices: The practices ("din") of Islam are also
interpreted differently in popular Islam. The five major
requirements are the confession of faith, the prayer ritual, the
legal alms-giving, the month-long fast, and the pilgrimage to
Mecca. The words of the confession are believed to be
supernaturally efficacious in driving away evil; they appear in
the wording on many amulets. Wensinck demonstrates the
significance of the belief in demons in the ordinary Muslim's
concept of the prayer-ritual. Demonic pollution is removed by
physical washing (Zwemer 1917:3). Part of the idea of alms-
giving in popular Islam, is the precaution being taken in
preventing the evil eye (of jealousy) from consuming one.
Similarly, with the month of Ramadan and the hajj, the various
accompanying rituals and performances in the popular mind have
to do with compelling God to protect, with driving out evil
spirits or sickness, etc.

Diagram A clarifies the issues referred to here, listing the
form, showing its intended function, and describing its meaning
in both "high" and "low" Islam.

Beyond this adaptation into the fears and hopes of everyday
life of the official religious "iman" and "din," popular Islam
has added a whole life-way of animistic beliefs and practices.
The use of the rosary for divining and healing, the use of
amulets and talismans (Exhibit B, the "Hand of Fatima"), the use
of hair-cuttings and nail-trimmings, the belief and practice of
saint-worship, the use of charms, knots, magic, sorcery, the
exorcism of demons, the practice of tree and stone worship,
cursing and blessing--these and many other animistic practices
belie the gap between the theological religion and the actual
religion. Comments Zwemer: "It is idle to talk of pure monotheism when dealing with popular Islam" (Zwemer 1920:Chap. 2.).

B. AUTHORITY IN POPULAR ISLAM

The sources for guidance of behavior in popular Islam are
found in the traditions, and in a theosophical interpretation of

the Quran. Power over peoples' lives is held, usually, by the local religious practitioners, the mullahs.

Out of the 1465 collections of traditions, only six are classical. Perhaps the best known of these are the ones collated by Bokhari and Muslim.

Zwemer comments on the contents of the traditions amassed by Bokhari:

"(They) touch every article of the Muslim faith and practice, deal with every detail of home-life, trade, politics, war, jurisprudence" (Zwemer 1916:Chap. 1).

Behavior patterns, learned in childhood in real life situations, rather than at a theological school, and reinforced by the pulls and presses of Muslim family, village and societal-cultural life, are rationalized from the traditions: "The illiteracy of Muslim lands means that people know, not Qur'anic Islam, but popular Islam" (Zwemer 1920:Preface).

A comment on the divorce between theological, Quran-based Islam, and popular, traditions-based Islam, is given indirectly by Goldsack as he speaks on the subject from a different perspective:

"We are convinced that it is pure ignorance of the contents of such standard collections as those of Bokhari and Muslim...which allows many intelligent Muslims to subscribe to the general Muslim belief (emphasis mine) that the Traditions are inspired, and, therefore, to be accepted as a divine rule of faith and practice" (Goldsack 1919:Chap. 6).

Scheunemann's comments on the power-holders in Muslim areas of Indonesia have already been cited. In modern Beirut, amulet-makers and fortune-tellers make good livings from their crafts (Exhibit C). From headaches to demon-possession, from love-potion to astral travel, the ordinary Muslim often depends for his very life, and certainly for his healing and help against his enemies, on a local religious practitioner. These men and women have real power!

II. THE HUNGER OF THE HEART

A Muslim in a village in northern Sudan receives a vision of Christ, and sets out to find a Christian to explain to him its meaning. An official in high Islamic circles in Egypt turns to Christ as his little child is miraculously healed. Or an Afghan student, lying sick in bed in America, recalls:

"I could not get out of my bed, or stand or walk.
The Christian woman sat beside my bed and prayed for
me constantly as she took care of me... As the Christian
lady prayed, I sensed something beyond her own sincerity
and earnestness. I knew she believed in Jesus, but I
also came to know something else that night. There was
another power, another presence, another person who was
alive and drawing near to me. The conviction was
inescapable. Jesus heard and answered prayer..." (Hanna
1975:63).

Our view of popular or "low" Islam brings before our eyes,
ordinary Muslims. Their beliefs and practices, and especially
their relationship to Islamic religious authority, belie huge
felt-needs. Popular Islam betrays a hunger of the heart.

A. FELT-NEEDS

Diagram B expresses what seem to be some of the major
felt-needs of ordinary Muslims. It describes ways in which
those needs are at the moment being met within their animistic,
Islamic life-way. Some of those solutions may be more
acceptable, from a Christian point of view, than others. Also
suggested is a goal at which to aim in our reaching out to
these people on behalf of Christ: How can they understand
Jesus Christ to meet those felt-needs?

B. HUNGER MET?

Accepting the radical difference between ideal and popular
Islam, there arises a philosophical and methodological problem
for the advocate of religious renewal in the actual situation.

Is he to seek to lead ordinary Muslims to a new, Islamic
faith-allegiance to God, within the cultural and religious
milieu of Islam? (Kraft 1977:603, 604) Here the recommendations
of Cragg, Anderson and others are essential, but are they
relevant for ordinary Muslims? Often, the ordinary Muslim
doesn't understand the "high" interpretations of the forms he
employs; one would have to educate him in his own religion
first.

Or is the advocate of religious renewal to seek a power
encounter which will promote a faith-allegiance directly to
Christ? The ordinary Muslim understands the power of the Quran
to heal, or the use of the rosary to divine and guide. He
needs to discover that Christ can heal, can give power, can
defeat demons, can speak supernaturally to man to guide him,
etc.

178

Of course, the choice of approach is not that simplistic, and the two methodologies are bound to overlap. Especially, it should be noted with the second approach, there will need to be developed creative, functional substitutes for the practices which previously formed part and parcel of the Muslim's life.

III. CONCLUSION

It is the proposition of this paper that, with popular Islam, a process emanating from power encounter be sought. Christ, in his dealings with the ordinary people around him, tended to free them from the "ideal" religion of the professionals. Why educate ordinary Muslims in their own faith so that Christ can meet them there tomorrow when he can meet them more fundamentally at the point of their felt-needs today?

The following appeal comes from Bangladesh:

"A skilled writer of Bengali, who has a passion for the salvation of his people must be sent around Bangladesh to collect together from the people involved, the accounts of the events – the casting out of evil spirits, healings and visions of Jesus... Tracts are needed which show how Jesus helps the ordinary Christian villager to live his daily life with less fear, more joy, and greater confidence. Tracts must show that God is real, in a way which has meaning for ordinary people" (McNee 1976:159).

Let a Turkish brother conclude, in his own words:

"...First I met her with her husband. They both were very distress in their souls, as if they didn't want to meet me. But God gave opportunity to tell to they more and more about the eternal salvation in Jesus. The man got saved first but he would still have many nights without sleeping and constantly flows of unceasing thoughts in his mind, so much that when you watch on his face as if he does not know the Lord, and death was on his face, both the same with his wife. Finally, one day I inquired about their previous life. First they didn't want to tell anything but they admit that they dealt much with evil powers. They told to me much about the sounds they were hearing while they were going to bed in the night and about the coffee cup how the demon split it into two pieces before their eyes, and many other things... Then soon I asked they if they still are afraid of the demons to disturb them. The wife said well once we are told to keep several pieces of things to protect us from this evil powers. I asked her to

bring them right there. She was very afraid, after I
insist she brought two pieces of silver, an eye (blue)
and some other things... Then I explain to her that
how the demons works through such things and asked her
to reject the authority of the demons through that
things over them and claim the victory on the Cross,
the Name and the Blood of Jesus to be free from all
bondages. She did, then she burst with tears confes-
sing her sins to Jesus, and asking Him to save her.
Much joy came to both of them and seemingly are going
well in the Lord..."
                    (Personal letter to author, Jan. 10, 1974)

A hungry heart satisfied?!

EXHIBIT A

A TALISMAN FROM A MUSLIM BOOK ON THE NAMES OF ALLAH

This talisman comes from "Shems-ul-Ma'arif" by Muhyee-ed-Din-al-Buni. The book treats the names of God and their use in amulets, healing, recovering lost property, etc.

The source reference is "The Muslim Doctrine of God" by Zwemer.

The translation of the talisman is given in the text of this paper.

EXHIBIT B

THE HAND OF FATIMA

An eye is cast into the palm of the hand. Such figures are commonly hung on, or painted onto, taxis and cars, etc., in the Muslim Middle East.

EXHIBIT C

AMULET-MAKER AND FORTUNE-TELLER
IN MODERN BEIRUT

Fatmeh is a professional amulet-maker and fortune-teller.
A friend of mine who wished to remain unidentified paid
her a visit last week with a big problem on her mind.

"It's not that I really believe in fortune-tellers," she
said, "but it was just a curiosity. I could hardly
believe my eyes when I got there, because there was such
a long queue of people waiting to see her it reached way
down into the street."

"When my turn finally came, I felt terrified, and my knees
were really wobbling. It didn't help either when the
first question she asked in a deep loud voice was: 'Do
you believe in me?'"

"She had never seen me before," she continued, "but
after a bit of thought she was able to pronounce my name
correctly and clearly - it seemed unbelievable."

She told how Fatmeh then began to tell her a lot about
her past - a lot of which was true. "She then spoke of
the future, and told me I was unhappy because someone had
written an evil spell against me. She gave me a piece of
paper to burn following that, which was supposed to break
the spell, and warned me that if I ever repeated what she
had said to anyone, my eyes would become swollen and red."

"The most incredible thing happened after I left though,
which scared the wits out of me," she added. "I started
yawning uncontrollably for half an hour, in a most
abnormal way - I barely had time to breathe in between
yawns!!"

"That's the sort of thing that sets you thinking about
fortune-tellers," was her last remark. "How can you ever
be sure that they haven't got powers we do not have."

Taken from article in <u>Daily Star</u>, January 4, 1974: "The
Evil Eye," by Nicole Haddad.

DIAGRAM A

INTENDED FUNCTION, FORM AND MEANING IN 'HIGH' AND 'LOW' ISLAM

INTENDED FUNCTION	FORM	MEANING IN 'HIGH' ISLAM	MEANING IN 'LOW' ISLAM
Expression of Submission to God	**1. CREED**		
	Only God	monotheistic confession of faith	magical use of names for God
	His Angels	servants of God at his pleasure	demonology and jinn-worship
	His Books	encoding of God's self-revelation	bibliomancy and bibliolatry
	His Apostles	vehicles of God's self-revelation	fetishes; worship of saints
	Last Day	ethical focus of man's life	spirit-life after death
	Predestination	ultimately, all in God's hands	used as sanction by religious practitioners
Expression of Belonging to Community of Faithful	**2. PILLARS**		
	Confession	proves one is a true Muslim	words are used to drive away evil
	Prayer Ritual	bodily purity for worshiping God	demonic pollution removed by washing
	Legal Alms	responsibility to fellow-Muslim	precaution against the evil eye
	Fasting	sign of commitment to Islam	rituals for dealing with evil, sickness
	Pilgrimage	visit the epicenter for the faith	rituals deal with evil, sickness, etc.

DIAGRAM B

POPULAR ISLAM:
FELT-NEEDS, ANIMISTIC AND POSSIBLE CHRISTIAN ANSWERS

FELT-NEEDS IN POPULAR ISLAM	ANIMISTIC ANSWERS TO FELT-NEEDS Not Acceptable...More Acceptable			CHRISTIAN ANSWER TO FELT-NEEDS
fear of the unknown	idolatry stone worship	fetishes talismans charms	superstition	security in Christ as Guide, Keeper
fear of evil	sorcery witch-craft	amulets knots	exorcism (?)	exorcism, protection in Christ
fear of the future	angel worship	divina-tion spells (?)	fatalism fanaticism	trust in Christ as Lord of the future
shame of not being in the group	magic curse or bless	hair/nail trimmings		acceptance in fellowship of believers
powerlessness of individual against evil	saint worship		baraka saint/angel petitioning	authority and power of the Holy Spirit
meaningless-ness of life		familiar spirit (?)		purpose in life as God's child
sickness	tree/ saint worship	healing magic (?)		divine healing

BIBLIOGRAPHY

Anderson, John D.C.
  1976   Christianity and Comparative Religion. Downers
          Grove: Inter Varsity Press.

Campbell-Thompson, R.
  n.d.   Semitic Magic.

Cragg, Kenneth
  1964   The Call of the Minaret. New York: Oxford
          University Press.

Douglas, J.D. ed.
  1975   Let the Earth Hear His Voice. Minneapolis: World
          Wide Publications.

Goldsack, William
  1919   The Traditions in Islam.

Goldziher, I.
  n.d.   "On Veneration of the Dead in Paganism and Islam,"
          Vol. I; "On the Veneration of Saints in Islam,"
          "On the Development of the Hadith," Vol. II,
          Muslim Studies.

Hamady, Sania
  1960   Temperament and Character of the Arabs. New York:
          Twayne Publishers.

Hanna, Mark
  1975   The True Path. International Doorways Publications.

Hughes, T.P.
  1885   Dictionary of Islam. Reprinted 1935; Revised 1964.
          cf "Arabic Alphabet," "Da'wah," etc.

Kraft, Charles H.
  1977   Theologizing in Culture. Pre-publication draft.
          Pasadena: Fuller Theological Seminary.

MacDonald, D.B.
  1909   The Religious Attitude and Life in Islam. AMS Press

  1911   Aspects of Islam. Books for Libraries.

McNee, Peter
  1976   Crucial Issues in Bangladesh. Pasadena: William
          Carey Library.

Moslem World
          "The War in Egypt," Vol. III, pp. 275-284.

Rahman, Fazlur
    1966   Islam. London: Weidenfeld and Nicholson.

Servier, Andre
    1923   Islam and the Psychology of the Muslim.

Wallis-Budge, Sir E.A.
          Amulets and Superstitions.

Westermarck
          Pagan Survivals in Mohammedan Civilization.

Zwemer, Samuel M.
    1916   The Disintegration of Islam.

    1917   Islam and Animism. London: Victoria Institute
            Transactions.

    1920   Childhood in the Muslim World.

    1920   The Influence of Animism on Islam: An Account of
            Popular Superstitions. London: Central Board of
            Missions and S.P.C.K.

    1939   Studies in Popular Islam.

SUMMARY OF PARTICIPANT'S RESPONSES

Respondents were enthusiastic about this paper which was seen as the most practical of the early topics. In perhaps half of the responses, were illustrations of Mr. Musk's point that there is, in fact, another form of Islam which is more common than orthodox Islam, and tremendously powerful in the lives of ordinary Muslims.

There was some concern that Mr. Musk relied too heavily on dated sources, especially Samuel Zwemer. The readers agreed that Dr. Zwemer may have "understood a lot more than we give him credit for," but some argued that "what was extremely prevalent in Zwemer's day is probably now on the wane due to Westernization." Several respondents pointed out that there are a number of more recent sources which could have added to the picture of contemporary popular Islam.

Referring specifically to the content, one respondent pointed out that there is another level of Islam more properly labeled "popular" Islam, and that is the agnostic or careless level. "These people do not understand the high Islam, do not practice the animistic Islam of which Musk writes, and abhor those who do." The respondent said that this group is perhaps more numerous than the adherents of either "high" or "low" Islam.

Several other readers noted the similarities between Islam and a "popular Christianity." Their calling on the names of God to deliver Muslims may be closely related to our calling on God only when we are in a time of need. "We say to the Muslim woman whose child is dying, to have faith in Jesus or to 'wait upon God,' instead of relying on amulets and the like, but we ourselves do more--such as taking the child to the hospital--in effect being as manipulative as they with their amulets." We must keep in mind, they said, that the Muslims' idea of Christianity is not the ideal evangelical Christianity that we profess, but what he sees in the life of ordinary Christians (mostly nominal) that he comes across.

The fact of popular Islam, and the importance of such related issues as the above led many respondents to question our traditional strategies. For example, one respondent wrote:
--"I would agree that popular Islam is...the most hopeful focus for evangelization and that the basic approach will have to be one that is experimental and power encounter oriented. But I expect too that it will be difficult to wean a people who have gained an appetite for amulets and fetishes and charms to a Christian Protestantism that does not permit that kind of form. I wonder if a people has such an appetite if they will not turn to Christian amulets and charms as a

functional substitute rather...bare unprotected...
protestantism..."

Another said that Christians in Muslim lands must show that
they believe in miracles as a major and integral part of their
daily lives, and argued that no missionary should be sent to the
Middle East who does not believe in the miracles that can be
performed through the power of the Holy Spirit. Many readers
concurred with Mr. Musk that "power encounter"--practical
applications of the power of Christ over sickness, evil spirits,
and superstition--is the best approach to adherents of "popular
Islam."

Some readers felt that this paper demonstrates that our
approach, especially to "low" Islam has been and continues to
be too rationalistic. We depend far too much on literature,
and explaining the message intellectually. We need to consider
whether a more charismatic approach and ministry may not be
needed, an approach which depends in a greater measure on the
Spirit's work in the individual, prayer for healing for
deliverance from demon possession and other specific needs.

AUTHOR'S REJOINDER TO PARTICIPANT'S RESPONSES

1. The 96 responses to this paper expressed confirmation,
surprise, criticism and have thankfully contributed towards a
more wholesome bibliography.

2. The exposé of a popular Islam, revealing in its adherents
a hunger of heart, provoked wide affirmation. "This was most
obvious to me in Oman," it described the "common person in
Pakistan," is "so clear in Morocco," appears even to be "not
divorced from sophisticated urban Muslims," embraces the reality
of "the Islam of West Africa" and "recently Islamised societies
in Eastern Africa." The "Muslim Melayu," the "Sudanese of
Indonesia," "Indian Muslims from Hindu background," and
"Palestinian Muslims"--all participate in some form of popular
Islam. No longer dare we speak of Islam merely as an "ideal"
theological system.

3. A dangerous temptation of the paper, however, is to
encourage the conception of a new monolith--that of "popular"
Islam. Huge variety at local level is demonstrated in the
matter of authority. In Lebanon, "mullahs and sheikhs lead the
Muslims in this kind of life," but in Pakistan the mullahs
remain custodians of orthodox Islam while 'pirs' "hold authority
over peoples' lives." In Turkey, "the village sorcerer has as
much authority as the village imam," while "the religious medi-

188

cine man is very important to Bangladesh Muslims."

4. Nor is the paper's description of popular Islam all-embracing. Some proposed the "agnostic or careless level, who are Muslims because they need to belong" -- neither theological nor animistic. Others mentioned the "person of the street" who is "pious and faithful in his/her practice of the elements of 'din.'" Sufism was also suggested as a popular expression of a quest for, and experience of, God. In reality, we are talking about a continuum -- from highly orthodox to deeply animistic. Perhaps "the average Muslim will hold together his strong belief in the Unity of God and in the finality of the Prophet of Islam along with his more superstitious beliefs...." But with the continuum recognized, we can fairly begin to talk about real, living Muslims, instead of academic, theological systems.

5. Other felt-needs were suggested, including community, honor, inward spiritual vitality, education, good family relations and social structures, etc.

6. In strategizing a relevant evangelistic approach to Muslims, can we now appeal to the experience as well as to the mind of the Muslim? It is not only theological truths which we must bridge to the Muslim (in as sweet a spirit as Cragg can motivate in us), but also Spirit-given power to release him from one kingdom to another. Christ must be seen, least of all as an alternative form of magic (several were concerned with Christianity's own "popular" forms), but as Lord and Saviour, or the whole man.

7. Concurrently, let us beware of merely justifying a triumphalist approach, simply because we are calling for "power encounter." Muslims need "to be met within the context of Islam." The spiritual revolution must occur "within the receptors' sociocultural context." Can we carry the living Christ with all his power to heal, exorcise and save into the real world of ordinary Muslims, and trust him to meet heart-hunger without implicit condemnation of their national and cultural heritages? Can Christ trust us that much?

A SELECTED BIBLIOGRAPHY FOR CHRISTIAN MUSLIM WORKERS

Warren W. Webster

This brief annotated listing of helpful books for Christian
workers has been compiled from hundreds of volumes in English
dealing with Islam and the Muslim world. The intent was to provide a basic list of 50-60 titles which is suggestive rather
than comprehensive. It is recommended that interested Christian
students of Islam and those beginning work with Muslims attempt
to get well acquainted with at least one volume in each section
of this outline while awareness gradually extends to some of the
other titles.

Some valuable materials unfortunately are now out of print,
but they generally can be located for research and study in one
of the libraries majoring on missions or Islamic studies. Many
hard to obtain volumes, especially some published in other countries, can be obtained through the Fellowship of Faith for
Muslims (205 Yonge Street, Toronto, Ontario, Canada M5B 1N2).

It is perhaps understandable why no attempt could be made in
this brief bibliography to include important works available in
Arabic, French, or other major languages of the Muslim world,
but the serious student should begin to acquire those materials
for the areas in which he is interested. Also in the interest
of brevity we could not include references to the many excellent
articles on the Christian mission to Islam appearing in such
periodicals as the Evangelical Missions Quarterly, the Muslim
World Pulse, Missiology, the International Review of Missions,
and The Muslim World. Magazines and journals, however, contain
some of the best current reports and ideas and should be
regularly consulted.

Hopefully, the bibliography and annotations which follow will
provide a helpful introduction to some available materials which
may contribute, directly and indirectly, to more effective communication of the Good News in Jesus Christ to Muslims.

I.   INTRODUCTION TO ISLAM

Fellowship of Faith for Muslims
  n.d.   "Focus on Islam" booklets. Toronto. *A series of
            inexpensive, informative booklets which may be use-
            ful in introducing laymen to the nature and chal-
            lenge of Islam. Titles include: "The Muslim
            Challenge to the Christian Church," "Islam: What
            is it?," "The Five Pillars of Islam," "The Ahmadiyya
            Movement," "The Life of Muslim Women," "From Islam
            to Christ--How a Sufi Found His Lord," and "The
            Qur'an Says. . ."*

Watt, W. Montgomery
  1968   What is Islam? London: Longmans, Green & Co., Ltd.
            *A generally helpful introduction by the Professor
            of Arabic and Islamic Studies at the University of
            Edinburgh.*

Wilson, J. Christy
  1959   Introducing Islam. New York: Friendship Press.
            *A brief, popular introduction with fine illustra-
            tions and a helpful glossary.*

II.   LIFE OF MUHAMMAD

Andrae, Tor
  1956   Mohammed, The Man and His Faith. Translated from
            the German. London: George Allen and Unwin Ltd.
            *A serious, but very readable, study based on vast
            knowledge and immense research which avoids
            extremes in interpreting the life of Muhammad.*

Watt, W. Montgomery
  1953   Muhammad-at Mecca. London: Oxford University Press.

  1956   Muhammad-at Medina. London: Oxford University
            Press.

  1961   Muhammad-Prophet and Statesman. London: Oxford
            University Press. *A series of detailed, classical
            studies by an outstanding scholar.*

III. THE QURAN (KORAN) AND THE TRADITIONS (HADITH)

Arberry, Arthur J.
   1964   *The Koran Interpreted*. New York: Macmillan. *A
            scholarly attempt to convey to the English reader
            something of the spirit and tone of the Quran in
            Arabic. It is said to be "the most poetic of the
            English translations"--and one of the best.*

Bell, Richard
   1953   *Introduction to the Qur'an*. Edinburgh University
            Press. *A technical and critical study of the origin
            and compilation of the Quran.*

Cragg, Kenneth
   1971   *The Event of the Qur'an--Islam in its Scripture*.
            London: George Allen and Unwin Ltd. *A modern Chris-
            tian attempt to sympathetically, yet critically,
            assess the meaning and significance of the Quran as
            an "event"--not simply a document--fusing Muhammad's
            personal charisma, poetic eloquence, Arab conscious-
            ness and vibrant theism into the Scripture of Islam.*

Guillaume, Alfred
   1924   *The Traditions of Islam*. Oxford University Press.
            *A somewhat dated, yet classic, introduction to the
            study of Hadith literature (traditions concerning
            Muhammad and his companions) which is regarded by
            many Muslims as having an importance and authority
            nearly equal to that of the Quran itself as a source
            of Muslim belief and practice.*

Jeffrey, Arthur
   1952   *The Qur'an as Scripture*. New York: Russell Moore
            Co. *A Christian scholar's assessment of how
            Muhammed came by his notion of Scripture and how he
            developed his own mission in terms of the pattern
            of prophetic succession he had learned from "The
            People of the Book." The last section of this small
            book is devoted to one of the best brief discussions
            available on the textual history of the Quran.*

Pickthall, Mohammed Marmaduke
   1977   *The Meaning of the Glorious Koran*. New York: Dover
            Publications. *An explanatory translation by an
            Englishman who became a convert to Islam.*

Watt, W. Montgomery
   1967   *Companion to the Qur'an*. London: George Allen and
            Unwin Ltd. *Notes on the quranic text giving helpful*

*background information and explaining illusions
which western readers might not understand. Based
on Arberry's translation but can be used with any
translation. Contains a useful index of proper
names in the Quran.*

IV. HISTORICAL DEVELOPMENT OF ISLAM

Boer, Harry
1969   A Brief History of Islam - A Christian
Interpretation. Ibadan, Nigeria: Daystar Press.
*A concise history of Islam written especially for
Christian readers by the principal of a theological
college in Africa. Special attention is given to
Muslim penetration and expansion in West Africa.*

Brockelman, Carl
1973   History of the Islamic Peoples. New York:
Capricorn Books. *A revised edition of a classic
one-volume history in English of all the Islamic
states and peoples. Reviews events country by
country. Complete with bibliography, index, maps,
etc.*

Gibb, H. A. R.
1973   Mohammedanism--An Historical Study. Oxford
University Press. *Another scholarly classic which
has been updated and reprinted with the addition of
a chapter on Islam in the modern world.*

Hitti, Philip K.
1970   History of the Arabs. New York: St. Martin. *A
comprehensive standard textbook on Muhammad's people
from pre-Islamic times to the present.*

Verhoeven, F. R. J.
1962   Islam, its Origin and Spread in Words, Maps and
Pictures. Amsterdam: Djambatan. *A well illustrated graphic aid to the understanding of Islamic
history.*

V. MUSLIM SOCIETY AND CIVILIZATION

Gaudefroy-Demombynes, Maurice
1968   Muslim Institutions. London: George Allen and
Unwin Ltd. *Translated from the French and reprinted,
a pocket encyclopedia dealing with most every aspect
of Islamic life, custom and law.*

Grunebaum, G. E. von
1951   Muhammadan Festivals. New York: Henry Schuman.
         *The story of the main Muhammadan festivals from
         their origins to the present day.*

Levy, Reuben
1957   The Social Structure of Islam. Cambridge University
         Press. *A sociological study of the effects which
         the religious system of Islam has on Muslim communi-
         ties, noting the common features of their social
         structure with respect to social classes, the status
         of women and children, morality, law, etc.*

Savory, R. M., editor
1976   Introduction to Islamic Civilization. Cambridge
         University Press. *A profusely illustrated study of
         Islamic art, literature, science, etc. with special
         reference to the modern Muslim world.*

Schacht, J. and Bosworth, editors
1974   The Legacy of Islam. Second edition. Oxford
         University Press. *An up-to-date edition of a
         standard reference volume which shows the signifi-
         cant influence of Islam on history, art, architec-
         ture, literature, law, science, etc.*

Westermarck, Edward
1933   Pagan Survivals in Mohammedan Civilization. London:
         Macmillan. *A valuable study by a capable anthro-
         pologist which provides the basis for understanding
         many common practices and superstitions which
         characterize popular Islam all the way from North
         Africa to Indonesia.*

Zwemer, Samuel M.
1920   The Influence of Animism on Islam, An Account of
         Popular Superstitions. New York: Macmillan. *One
         of Zwemer's early books, similar to Westermarck's
         study, which supplies keys to understanding the
         beliefs of ordinary Muslims regarding jinns, the
         evil eye, amulets, charms and exorcism.*

VI.   ISLAM IN THE MODERN AGE

Cragg, Kenneth
1965   Counsels in Contemporary Islam (Islamic Surveys
         Series, No. 3). Edinburgh University Press. *A
         survey of the main currents of Islamic reaction to
         the modern world in the Arab East, Turkey, Pakistan
         and India.*

McNeil, W. H. and M R. Waldman, editors
   1973   The Islamic World. Oxford University Press. *A comprehensive
           and penetrating study complete with documentation.*

Morgan, Kenneth W., editor
   1958   Islam--The Straight Path, Islam Interpreted by Muslims.
           New York: The Ronald Press. *A vivid and authentic description
           and interpretation of Islam for western readers by eleven com-
           petent Muslim scholars who represent each of the major Islamic
           areas from Egypt, Turkey and Iran to Pakistan, Indonesia and China.*

Smith, Wilfred Cantwell
   1957   Islam in Modern History. Princeton University Press. *A basic-
           ally sympathetic, yet keenly critical, view beneath the surface
           of events, providing perceptive insight into the tension between
           faith and history in the Muslim world.*

           (Note: No attempt has been made here to list any of the hundreds
           of contemporary books dealing with modern Islam in specific coun-
           tries or geographic areas such as North Africa, Turkey, the Middle
           East, Iran, the U.S.S.R., the Indo-Pakistan sub-continent, Malaysia,
           Indonesia, the Philippines, etc. Christian workers interested in
           specific areas of the Muslim world can readily develop a special
           interest reading list of their own through consulting libraries
           and purchasing local publications while living and working in
           those areas.)

         VII. INFLUENCE OF CHRISTIANITY ON ISLAM

Bell, Richard
   1968   The Origin of Islam in its Christian Environment. London: Frank
           Cass and Co., Ltd. *A reprint of earlier lectures showing how Islam
           was shaped from the beginning by both contact with, and misunder-
           standing of, the Christian faith.*

Jomier, Jacques
   1964   The Bible and the Koran. New York: Desclee Co. *A brief comparison
           between the Bible and the Quran written by a member of the Dominican
           Order and translated from the French.*

Nazir-Ali, Michael
   1983   Islam: A Christian Perspective. Exeter, England: The Paternoster
           Press. *A highly readable discussion of the principal influences
           in the rise, shaping and development of Islam. Attention is also
           given to Islam's current resurgence and the strengths and weaknesses
           of Western missionary activity, all presented thoughtfully by an
           able non-Western scholar.*

Parrinder, Geoffrey
   1965   Jesus in the Qur'an. London: Faber and Faber.

*A book intended for both Christians and Muslims. The author
systematically collects quranic teachings about Jesus and his
associates and discusses them in the light of parallels in the
Bible.*

Smith, Henry Preserved
   1897   The Bible and Islam. London: James Nisbet and Co. *An old
volume included here for its historic interest as an earlier
study of the influence of the Old and New Testaments on the
religion of Muhammad.*

Sweetman, J. Windrow
...1967   Islam and Christian Theology, A Study of the Interpretation of
Theological Ideas in the Two Religions (4 volumes). London:
Lutterworth Press. *A valuable, but copiously detailed, set of
reference books comprehensively treating the interaction of
Christian and Muslim thought from the beginning of Islam through
the Crusades and the Middle Ages.*

VIII.   THE CHRISTIAN MISSION TO MUSLIMS

A. HISTORY OF MISSIONS TO MUSLIMS

Addison, James T.
   1942   The Christain Approach to the Moslem, A Historical Study. New York:
Columbia University Press. *A survey of Christian contacts with Muslims during the first twelve centuries of Islam, followed by a more
detailed analysis, by geographical areas, of missionary efforts in the
last 150 years.*

Parshall, Phil
   1980   New Paths in Muslim Evangelization. Grand Rapids: Baker Book House.
*A discussion of the concept of contextualization, its usefulness and
limits in the world of missions. Application of contextualization
is made to the Muslim setting with illustrations from Indian sub-
continent.*

Parshall, Phil
   1983   Bridges to Islam: A Christian Perspective on Folk Islam. Grand
Rapids: Baker Book House. *An analysis of Muslim heartfelt meeds
as evidenced in folk Islam and especially Sufism. The importance
of missions addressing such heartfelt needs is stressed along with
suggestions of a strategy for doing so.*

Vander Werff, Lyle L.
   1977   Christian Mission to Muslims--The Record, Anglican and Reformed
Approaches in India and the Near East, 1800-1938. Pasadena: William
Carey Library. *A recent doctoral study analyzing lessons learned in
the mission to Muslims from the time of Henry Martyn to Samuel Zwemer.*

B. CHRISTIAN UNDERSTANDING OF ISLAM

Bethmann, Eric W.
   1953   Bridge to Islam, A Study of the Religious Forces of Islam and Christianity in the Near East. London: George Allen and Unwin Ltd. *An attempt
to build a bridge of understanding and communication between the two
religions. Valuable especially for the concluding chapter, "The Bridge
and Its Builders."*

Cragg, Kenneth
1964   The Call of the Minaret. London: Oxford University
Press. *The first, and perhaps best, of Dr. Cragg's
many books. A penetrating and stimulating interpretation of Islam, based on the phrases of the call
to prayer as given five times a day by the muezzin.
He first analyzes what the call to prayer means to
the Muslim, historically and doctrinally. Then he
finds in it for the Christian a call to understanding, to service, to retrieval, to interpretation and
to patience.*

C. CHRISTIAN MESSAGE AND METHODS
IN COMMUNICATING THE GOSPEL TO MUSLIMS

Brown, David
----   "Christianity and Islam" series. London: S.P.C.K.
*A series of books written by a former missionary,
with Muslim readers in mind, attempting to explain
to them God's revelation of himself through the
Messiah and the Scriptures. The fifth and final
volume is by another author. 1) "Jesus and God in
the Christian Scriptures," 1967, 2) "The Christian
Scriptures," 1968, 3) "The Cross of the Messiah,"
1969, 4) "The Divine Trinity," 1969, 5) "The Church
and the Churches," by Gordon Huelin, 1970.*

Budd, Jack
1976   How to Witness to Muslims. London: Red Sea Mission.
*Practical lectures by an experienced missionary in
East Africa and the Middle East. Suitable for group
study.*

Christensen, Jens
1977   The Practical Approach to Muslims. North Africa
Mission. *A timely reprint of a stimulating study
course first published serially in Pakistan by a
Lutheran bishop who spent a lifetime working among
Muslim Pathans on the northwest frontier. Bishop
Christensen was an original thinker who held that
the basic problem in the mission to Islam is theological and he calls for an honest rethinking of
our approach to Islam which is both radical and
practical.*

Christian Witness Among Muslims, A Handbook written especially
for Christians of Africa (south of Sahara).
1971   Accra, Ghana: Africa Christian Press. *As the
sub-title implies this manual is intended to help
the ordinary Christian know how to behave towards*

*his Muslim neighbors and then tells how to witness
about Christ among them. (This book has also been
published in India with some adaptations and an
additional chapter on the integrity of the Bible
for use in helping Christians witness to Muslims
there.)*

Crossley, John
   1960   <u>Explaining the Gospel to Muslims</u>. London:
            Lutterworth Press. *A brief, simple manual written
            by a missionary lecturer in Nigeria to explain the
            Christian faith to Muslims and to assist Christians
            in answering basic questions which Muslims commonly
            ask.*

Elder, John
   n.d.   <u>The Biblical Approach to the Muslim</u>. Houston: LIT
            International. *Written by a long-time missionary
            to Iran as a course for Christian workers in a
            textbook format intended for study by correspon-
            dence.*

Harris, George K.
   1957   <u>How to Lead Moslems to Christ</u>. 3rd printing.
            Philadelphia: China Inland Mission. *A concise
            manual originally written with the Muslims of China
            particularly in view but adaptable for use in any
            part of the world.*

Jones, L. Bevan
   1952   <u>Christianity Explained to Muslims, A Manual for
            Christian Workers</u>. Revised edition. Calcutta:
            YMCA Publishing House. *A painstaking summary of
            Muslim difficulties and an attempt to provide help
            in answering their arguments with regard to Chris-
            tianity. Intended for Christian workers rather
            than for direct circulation among Muslims. Somewhat
            oriented toward Indian Islam.*

Marsh, Charles R.
   1975   <u>Share Your Faith With a Muslim</u>. Chicago: Moody
            Press. *Written against a background of 45 years of
            experience among Muslims in Africa, this book sets
            forth many valid principles and helpful suggestions
            for Christian witness to Muslims--or to anyone.*

Miller, William M.
   1976   <u>A Christian's Response to Islam</u>. Nutley, New Jersey:
            Presbyterian and Reformed Publishing Co. *The author*

*writes out of more than 50 years of personal
evangelistic experience among Muslims in Iran and
in North America. His concern for the salvation
of Muslims permeates the book. The final chapter
sets forth 16 reasons why there must be a continuing
mission to Muslims.*

Parshall, Phil
1975   The Fortress and the Fire, Jesus Christ and the
Challenge of Islam. Bombay: Gospel Literature
Service. *Written from a biblical perspective
reinforced by many years of Christian work in
Bangladesh the author deals with the chief religious and sociological obstacles that traditionally
have prevented widespread acceptance of the Christian faith among Muslims and offers some radical,
but workable, solutions.*

Pfander, C. G.
1974   The Balance of Truth (Mizanu'l Haqq). Beirut. *A
recent reprint of a classic reply to Muslim objections. Originally written in Persian, it reflects
an older apologetic approach but is still of interest and value.*

Reaching Muslims Today, A Short Handbook.
1976   North Africa Mission. *A very practical and useful
compilation. It first surveys the Muslim challenge,
contrasting Christianity and Islam, and then outlines
the Christian reply to fundamental differences and
objections Muslims raise. The Handbook concludes
with a useful "how to" section outlining specific
things to do, and not to do, in presenting the gospel to Muslims.*

Shumaker, C. Richard, editor
1974   Media in Islamic Culture. Wheaton, Ill.:
Evangelical Literature Overseas. *Report of an
international conference of media experts in
Christian literature and broadcasting held in
France to focus on the cultural problems involved
in active communication of the Christian message to
the Muslim mind. Contains valuable resource materials not available elsewhere.*

Spencer, H.
1956   Islam and the Gospel of God. Delhi: S.P.C.K. *A
comparison of the central doctrines of Christianity
and Islam, prepared as a useful tool for Christian
workers, translators and writers among Muslims.*

Recently reprinted because of renewed demand.

Wilson, J. Christy
  1950   The Christian Message to Islam. New York: Revell.
          *A manual of methods of approach to Islam by one who
          spent 20 creative years in missionary service in
          Iran and the Middle East. Written not for Muslims,
          but for Christian workers concerned with presenting
          the gospel of Christ in a Muslim context.*

Your Muslim Guest, A Practical Guide in Friendship and Witness
for Christians Who Meet Muslims in North America.
  1976   Toronto: Fellowship of Faith for Muslims. *The
          purpose of this 15 page booklet is clear from the
          sub-title. It is especially helpful for people
          meeting and entertaining Muslim guests for the first
          time.*

          (Note: Limitations of space have not permitted
          including any of the fine biographies and
          autobiographies of Christian workers among Muslims
          from which many valuable lessons can be learned.
          Students of the subject are encouraged to read
          about missionaries of an earlier day like Raymond
          Lull of North Africa, Henry Martyn of India, Temple
          Gairdner of Cairo, Samuel Zwemer and Paul Harrison
          of Arabia, and George Harris of China as well as
          consult more recent biographies that are available.)

      D.   CHRISTIAN LITERATURE WRITTEN FOR MUSLIMS

Clark, Dennis E.
  1977   The Life and Teaching of Jesus the Messiah (Sirat-
          ul-Masih, Isa, Ibn Maryam). Elgin: Dove
          Publications. *A carefully prepared life of Christ
          based on the text of the Gospels, written with
          Muslim readers in mind, by one with long experience
          in living and working among them. In addition to
          English it is available in Arabic and several other
          languages of the Muslim world.*

Finlay, M. H.
  1968   Face the Facts, Questions and Answers Concerning
          the Christian Faith. Bombay: Gospel Literature
          Service. *Originally written in Singapore this com-
          pact little manual is just what the sub-title
          implies. It specifically replies to common Muslim
          questions about the Bible, the person of Christ and
          the Trinity.*

1973 The God Who Speaks to Man. Oak Park, Ill.: Emmaus
Bible School. *A 12-lesson Bible correspondence
course written especially for educated Muslims.*

Hanna, Mark
 1975 The True Path, Seven Muslims Make Their Greatest
Discovery. Colorado Springs: International Doorways Publications. *Testimonies by representative
Muslims who have discovered Christ in a personal
way. The book concludes with an extensive glossary
of Christian terms and appendices presenting additional information about the Bible.*

Miller, William M.
 1972 Beliefs and Practices of Christians, (A Letter to
a Friend). Lahore: Masihi Isha'at Khana. *An
excellent brief guide to Christian beliefs, well
written for Muslims in terms and categories which
they understand.*

 1969 Ten Muslims Meet Christ. Grand Rapids: Eerdmans.
*Classic stories of the grace of God in operation
in a hostile environment.*

Rhoton, Dale and Elaine Rhoton
 1972 Can We Know? Fort Washington, Pa.: Christian
Literature Crusade. *An examination of the basis
for religious knowledge and Christian commitment.
Without any reference to Islam or the authors'
years of experience in the Muslim world the book is
clearly written with the hope that Muslims--as well
as others--will make the discovery of life in Christ.*

   (Note: It is apparent that there are more useful
manuals about how to witness to Muslims than there
are good books written especially for explaining
the Christian faith to Muslims in ways they can
readily identify with and respond to. In addition
to the few titles listed above there are, however,
quite a number of tracts, leaflets, small booklets
and correspondence courses published for Muslims
in a number of languages. For further information
about literature for distribution to Muslims contact
the Fellowship of Faith for Muslims in Toronto,
Canada.)

IX.   REFERENCE MATERIALS

Encyclopedia of Islam.
     1954...   Second edition. Leiden: E. J. Brill. *The first
               edition of this standard reference work was published
               in four volumes, 1911-1938. Three volumes of the
               almost entirely new second edition were published
               by 1975. An expensive set for institutional use and
               scholarly purposes.*

Gibb, H. A. R. and J. H. Kramers, editors
     1953   Shorter Encyclopedia of Islam. Cornell University
               Press. *Includes all the articles contained in the
               first edition and supplement of the Encyclopedia of
               Islam which relate particularly to the religion and
               law of Islam.*

Pearson, J. D., editor
     1972   Index Islamicus (Guide to Periodical Literature,
               1906-1970). Cambridge: W. Heffner and Sons, Ltd.
               *A useful tool for serious students of Islam,
               periodically updated through the publication of
               supplements.*

Roolvink, R.
     1957   Historical Atlas of the Muslim Peoples. Cambridge:
               Harvard University Press. *Excellent colored maps
               depicting the extent of Islamic presence and in-
               fluence during various periods of history.*

Weekes, Richard V., editor
     1978   Muslim Peoples: A World Ethnographic Survey.
               Westport, Conn.: Greenwood Press. *An alphabetically
               arranged compilation of current ethnographic infor-
               mation describing most major groupings of Islamic
               peoples. Concise studies plus bibliographical data.*

SUMMARY OF PARTICIPANT'S RESPONSES

This paper went out late in the process and very few readers had
time to comment on it. Those who did respond recognized that Dr.
Webster could only cite representative selections from each
category and was not able to be exhaustive. Yet most suggested
other books which they felt Dr. Webster should have included.
These suggestions will not be listed here except to note the
need felt for inclusion of books by Muslim or Muslim convert
writers. Among these cited were:

Abdul
    Study in Islam Series I, II and III.

Hussein, Kamel
    City of Wrong.

Nasr, Seyyed Hussein
    Ideals and Realities in Islam.

Rahbar, David
    God of Justice.

Rahman, Fazlur
    Islam.

Editor's Note: The intended scope of this paper obviated the
necessity of a rejoinder by the author.

THE VALUE AND METHODOLOGY OF PLANNING STRATEGIES

Edward R. Dayton

I.   INTRODUCTION

There are an estimated 720 million Muslims in the world.   They are found in settings as different as the countries in which they live.   Some of these groups are relatively large and homogeneous, for example, the 60 million rural Javanese.   Others are quite small.   In a very real sense each group is unique.   Each group exists within certain national boundaries, a given cultural milieu, the flow of a given history and a particular set of immediate circumstances.

It follows that there is no one evangelistic method that will be useful to all of these many groups, neither is there one evangelistic strategy for reaching them.   We should not be surprised by this.   Our evangelical theology rests on the belief that God sees every individual as unique.   God has a particular concern and a particular "plan" for each person's life.   When unique individuals are placed together in groups, by definition the group is unique also.

This is not to say that we cannot learn a great deal from observing the effectiveness of various means and methods.   It does say that we need to do our homework before we begin.   There are no standard answers to Muslim evangelization.   However, there is a set of questions that may be very useful as we think about planning strategies for a particular group.   There is also an order to the way the questions should be asked.

II. A CIRCULAR MODEL

This paper will discuss one approach to planning strategies which is based upon a circular or iterative model.

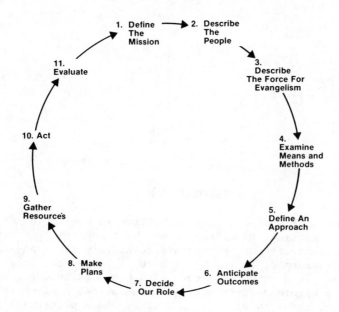

We begin by <u>defining our mission</u>. What is it that God wants us to do? What people does he specifically want <u>us</u> to reach? We can't reach every Muslim. What specific group of Muslims are we hoping to reach?

The next step is to <u>describe the people</u> as best we can. We need to see them within the context of their need before we move on to general planning.

Next we need to <u>describe the force for evangelism</u> that might be available to reach this people. By "force for evangelism" we mean potentially the entire Church. There are Christians all over the world who, because of their concern, can bring to bear their prayers, their resources and themselves to reach a particular people.

Next we come to examine <u>means and methods</u>. We realize for every people there will be a new combination of old means and methods that need to be reforged with new insights to tailor a program for each particular people. It's quite like the task of designing a key to unlock a door, in this case the door of the hearts of a special people. We need to see that each lock is different, and although there will be similarities, we need to assume that God has a unique way of reaching what to him is a very special people.

This then will lead us to define an approach, or develop an initial strategy. At this point in the process we can make a first statement about how we intend to reach this people.

God intends that we have results. Therefore we need to anticipate outcomes. We need to try to imagine what God is going to do in the lives of this people as we carry out this approach.

Too often we automatically assume that because we have a concern for a particular people that we are the ones who should be directly involved in reaching them. This is not always the case. Some of us are gifted in one direction, some have other gifts. We need to decide our role, either as an individual or an agency, before moving ahead.

Assuming that we have decided to move ahead, we need to make plans. In faith we need to anticipate what God would have us to do. Any statement about the future is a statement of faith. The larger our faith the greater our plans.

Plans will require that we gather resources. There will be a need for people, for funds, for facilities, for many different things. These need to be prepared.

Then we can act to carry out our plans, to set in motion that which we believe God would have us to do.

But as we act we need to evaluate. Things seldom go as we anticipate them. Plans will go awry. Situations will change. The Holy Spirit will lead in new paths. We need not to slavishly follow plans, but rather stay tuned with him. When we have carried out all our plans, modifying them as we go, we need to begin the cycle again, and define the mission.

So we view the task of planning strategies as a repetitive process, one which is useful for thinking about reaching any Muslim group. It is not tied down to any particular means or method. It does not make any assumptions about the people that we are trying to reach. Rather, it attempts to keep us in tune with what the Holy Spirit might be saying to us by leading us through a thoughtful process.

The questions that follow are intended to lead us through this approach. They follow the model on the previous page.

III. DEFINING THE MISSION

It may be the man and wife who are living next door to us. It may be a particular group of people within the city or neighborhood in which we live. It may be a group of Muslims who are living in a distant land. But it should be <u>a specific group</u> of people. Too often our strategies go awry because we have tried to cover too many people with one approach.

To what people has God called you?

IV. DESCRIBE THE PEOPLE

By a people group we mean "a significantly large sociological grouping of individuals who perceive themselves to have a common affinity for one another" (this is the definition of the Strategy Working Group ([SWG]) of the Lausanne Committee for World Evangelization ([LCWE]). See <u>To Reach the Unreached</u> by the author, MARC).

This affinity may be the result of shared language, religion, ethnicity, residence, occupation, class or caste, situation, or a combination of these and many other things.

The important thing is to put "boundaries" around a particular people, for it is just as important to define what group we are <u>not</u> trying to reach when we design a strategy. Most of us are used to thinking about a "people group" as being synonymous with an ethnic or a tribal group. However, there are many other ways of defining them. Here are some questions that need to be answered. (MARC and SWG have developed a detailed unreached people questionnaire that is available from MARC.)

1. What is the name of the people--how they call themselves?

2. Where does this people group live?

3. What is the population of this group and the population of any larger group of which they are a part?

4. What language(s) do they speak?

5. What makes them identifiable as a special group of people (language, location, class, religion, etc.)?

6. How many can and do read?

7. What is their religion(s) or philosophy of life?

8. How do you think these people see <u>themselves</u>? What do

you think _they_ would say are their important spiritual, physical
and emotional needs?

9.   What needs seem already to be adequately met? What
needs do they not have?

10.   How do _you_ see this people group? What would you say
their important spiritual, physical and emotional needs are?

11.   How do you know the answers to these questions are so?
Where did you get your information about these people?

12.   Who else might have accurate information about this
people? How might you go about discovering what they know?

13.   What are other key questions, peculiar to this people,
that are important for understanding them?

V.   WHAT THIS PEOPLE KNOWS ABOUT THE GOSPEL

The previous questions have dealt with the people group
within their milieu. Now we need to view them from a Christian
perspective. Where are they in terms of their relationship to
Christ? One of the most valuable ways of describing them for
evangelistic purposes is the use of the decision process scale
developed by Dr. James Engel and discussed in David Fraser's
paper "An Engel Scale for Muslim Work?" (Published as a working
paper for the North American Conference on Muslim Evangelization, 1978).

The questions that result from the Engel Scale are:

1.   What percent of the group have no awareness of Christ?

2.   What percent have an awareness of the existence of Christ
but have moved no further?

3.   What percentage have some knowledge of Jesus Christ but
really do not understand who Christ is?

4.   What percent have an understanding of who Christ is or
enough of the fundamentals of the gospel to be able to apprehend
him?

5.   What percent have grasped the personal implications of
what they know?

6.   What percent have recognition of a personal need in their
own life, a need that could be met by Christ?

7. *What percent are at the point of being challenged or making a decision to receive Christ?*

It is important to see that while it is not too difficult to answer questions 1, 2 and 3, questions 4, 5, 6 and 7 are intimately entwined and will vary from group to group. In most cases they can only be inferred by answers from the other questions. However, we are looking for estimates rather than precise data, for the intent of these questions is to help us select the right means and methods. (See below.)

Assuming then that there are those who have made a decision to receive him, we need to ask the following questions:

8. *What percent of those who have received Christ are in the process of evaluating their decision and have not yet joined a local fellowship?*

9. *What percentage are now incorporated into a fellowship of Christians?*

10. *What percentage have become active propagators of the gospel?*

Because so often there are those who have become incorporated into some Christian fellowship but show none of the marks of a Christian, we ask the question:

11. *What percentage appear to be Christians in name only?*

VI. GENERAL RECEPTIVITY OF THIS GROUP

The Engel Scale helps to locate where people are in relationship to coming to faith in Jesus Christ and becoming his disciples, but it does not tell us anything about their <u>movement</u> toward or away from Christ. Some people will be very stable as a group. Others may be in the process of rapid change. This leads to the following questions:

1. *How open is this group to religious change of any kind?*

2. *Why do you believe this is so? What specific evidences can you give?*

3. *What is your estimation of their attitude toward the gospel?*

4. *Why do you believe this is so? What specific evidence can you give?*

5. Does it appear this people are becoming less open or more open or not changing noticeably?

VII.   CULTURAL PRACTICES AND RECEPTIVITY TO THE GOSPEL

Culture--the present culture--will always have a bearing on a group's openness or closedness to the gospel (The Theology and Education Group of LCWE has developed a basic study in their Occasional Paper #2, The Willowbank Report--Gospel and Culture, 1978). The following questions help us think this through so that when we get to means and methods we will have a better understanding of what approaches to take:

1.   What cultural values, beliefs, practices of the people might be significant in their understanding of the gospel and a favorable feeling toward it?

2.   What cultural values, beliefs, practices of the people might produce a negative feeling toward the gospel?

3.   Are there some common cultural practices that seem to be clearly prohibited by Scripture? If so, what are they?

4.   Are there some common, important cultural values or practices which could be reinterpreted and incorporated with the Christian lifestyle? If so, what are they?

5.   Do the people find genuine satisfaction from their traditional religious or magical practices in the face of disease, sickness or death? What seems to make them content or discontent with their current religious involvement?

VIII.   THE RESULTING CHURCH

There is one last set of questions that will be helpful in our understanding of the people. These questions lead us to think about what kind of a church should result if the gospel truly impregnates this particular people group:

1.   If the members of this group become Christians, what kind of biblical, worshiping fellowship would be most likely to attract other members of the same group?

2.   What would be the means of worship?

3.   What would be the means of demonstrating concern for others?

4.   What would be the means of witness to others?

5. *What would be their relationship to other existing Christian groups?*

IX. DESCRIBE THE FORCE FOR EVANGELISM

There are many ways of discovering what other Christian groups are at work among the particular people group that we have chosen to reach. It is important to remember that the Church is described as a <u>body</u>. We need to work together:

1. *What churches, agencies or other groups of Christians are already working with these people?*

2. *What are they doing?*

3. *How effective, in your opinion, have they been?*

4. *Which groups or agencies appear to understand the basic need of this people?*

5. *If there are already established churches, which, if any, have shown significant growth (50%) in the last five years? Why?*

6. *Are the established churches accepted as culturally part of the group? Why? Why not?*

7. *What role in the culture should the evangelist or evangelizing group adopt to be effective?*

8. *Who appear to be the really key individual Christians or Christian groups to reach this people?*

9. *Where can we get more accurate information about the possible force for evangelism?*

Questions 8 and 9 are important. We need to listen to what the Spirit is saying to others in the community of Christ's Church.

X. THE FORCE OPPOSED TO EVANGELISM

It is good to know who our friends are. It is also good to recognize those who may oppose us.

1. *What organized groups or agencies would be opposed to the proclamation of the gospel among this group?*

2. *What forces, spiritual or other, appear to be arrayed against the gospel? What forces hinder individuals or family*

*groups from committing themselves to Christ in an open active
way?*

*3. If some have become Christians and then turned away from
the Lord, what were the things that seemed important in drawing
them away from God?*

*4. If Christians are present in this group, what important
factors seem to keep them from active and effective witness?*

XI. EXAMINE MEANS AND METHODS

Each individual comes to know Jesus Christ as a personal
experience. The Person of our Lord meets the <u>person</u> in a
one-to-one relationship. However, within different cultures,
societies, situations, different means and methods of communicating the gospel have been found effective. There is a danger
that we will adopt one method and believe that this method is
uniformly applicable to all different peoples in all different
situations. This is obviously not so. We have an infinite
God. He is capable of an infinite variety of means and methods
to reach people. We need to be ready to accept this tremendous
diversity. At the same time, through the history of Christ's
Church, we have learned a great deal about how people come to
know Christ. There are "methods and means" of all types. We
should be expecting diversity rather than uniformity.

*1. In light of the needs of this people, where they seem to
be as a group in their understanding of the gospel, the available force for evangelism, what means and methods do you believe
are most likely to meet the need?*

*2. What methods would move people along the Engel Scale
toward Christ?*

*3. Are the suggested methods compatible with biblical
principles? Are they ethical?*

*4. Where could you learn more about possible means and
methods?*

*5. What organizations or individuals would probably
cooperate with you?*

XII. ASSUMPTIONS

How easy it is to move ahead without understanding our own
motivations, as well as the motivations of others. All of us
proceed into the future on the basis of our assumptions about
the present and the past, both spoken and unspoken.

1. What are your assumptions in all of this about yourself?

2. What are your assumptions about your organization?

3. What are your assumptions about other churches or missions?

4. What are your assumptions about the country within which these people live?

5. What are your assumptions about the culture of these people?

6. What other assumptions are you making other than those listed above?

XIII. DEFINE AN APPROACH

The analysis which these questions will develop are intended to first give us an understanding of the people group we are trying to reach, to identify the force for evangelism that might be available to reach them, to examine various means and methods that God might use. Now we are ready to attempt to discover God's strategy for them. We need to think about an overall strategy, where to begin, what we might expect God might be going to do with this particular people. We need a broad overall goal and a broad set of plans around which to start building constructive programs which will meet the perceived need of the people and at the same time give them a clear witness of the saving power of Jesus Christ.

1. Will your strategy be to try to reach the entire people group or a sub-group of the people? If a sub-group, which part?

2. Since it should be our approach to meet the perceived needs of the people to whom we go, with which perceived need will you begin?

3. Who should be mobilized to carry out the task of the reaching of this particular group?

4. What means and methods should you utilize to reach them?

XIV. ANTICIPATE OUTCOMES

So much for strategy. The next question we face is what will happen as a result of this strategy. No one can predict the future. God is still in control of the universe, and his will will be done. Evidently God expects us to exercise our

faith in deciding what he would have us to be, where he would
have us to go and what he would have us to do. He expects us
to think about the future to discover the direction our lives
should take. He expects us to think about the outcomes, or
goals of the activities in which we are going to become involved. We need to think about the outcome of our strategy:

  1. If your approach is successful, what do you expect God
to do? What do you think God will allow the force for evangelism to accomplish?

  2. How will these people move in terms of the Engel Scale?

  3. How will you know whether it happened or not so you can
build on the results?

  4. What problems will you encounter with this approach?
Can you minimize or overcome them?

  5. Are these satisfactory outcomes? Could they be improved?

XV.   DECIDE OUR ROLE

It does not necessarily follow that because an individual
Christian or a local body of Christians has a concern for
another individual or group that they are the ones who will be
most effective in reaching these people. We need to understand
where we fit in the total task of evangelization. Those with a
gift for planning are not necessarily leaders. Evangelists are
not always good coordinators. We may play different roles at
different times, a leader now, a follower later.

  1. What role, if any, can you and/or your agency best play
in carrying out this strategy?

  2. How will you and your agency have to change in order to
adopt this strategy?

XVI. MAKE PLANS

God's strategy is made up of the people to be evangelized,
the evangelist, the means of evangelism, and the possible outcomes, or goals, of evangelism. In other words, "It's best we
understand God's will for the people we want to reach, we
believe that this people (evangelists) should use these methods
(means) to bring these hoped-for results (outcomes)." Now we
need to move our prayers and our faith into action, and to the
extent that we believe that we are God's instruments of love to
this people, to decide what steps to take to be obedient servants, in other words, to make plans:

1. What do you believe are the goals or outcomes that God wants to see happen to this people?

2. For each of these major goals, what steps (sub-goals) should be taken to reach this major goal or goals?

3. When are these steps needed to be taken and who should be responsible for each one?

XVII. GATHER RESOURCES

The best plans are useless unless we have adequate resources to implement them:

1. What people will be needed to carry out these plans?

2. What finances will be needed to carry out these plans? From whence will they come?

3. What facilities or equipment will be needed to carry out these plans?

XVIII. ACT

The answers to these questions will represent a great investment in time and energy. We have identified the people to whom we believe God has called us. We have analyzed all those whom God might provide to try to reach them. We have tried to find our own role in God's plan and where we fit into his strategy. We have tried to set down plans to reach a given people we believe need the message of the gospel. We have taken into account where they are in their movement toward Christ and we have analyzed all the resources that might be needed. Before we begin we need to ask some final prayerful questions:

1. Is the plan practical? If not, what next? How should it be modified?

2. If the plan looks like God's best, what is our first step?

XIX. EVALUATE

Many programs of evangelism fail needlessly because no effort was made to make an early evaluation of progress. We evaluate in order to measure progress against our stated goals. Are we indeed involved in a series of steps that are taking us where we think God wants us to go? Evaluation enables us to be accountable and to hold others involved in evangelism account-

able to God and each other in carrying out the steps we feel
are God's will for this people. Through it we can gain awareness of where our goals need to be changed, our methods
re-thought, our resources and time redistributed so it will be
more effective for Christ:

1. *What is your plan for checking your progress during the
carrying out of your strategy?*

2. *When do you plan to have the first full review of your
strategy and effectiveness in reaching your goals? Who will
be involved?*

3. *What are the crucial things about which you will have
to have good information in order to evaluate how well your
strategy is doing?*

XX. REDEFINING THE MISSION

This then closes the circle and brings us back to where we
began.

XXI. CONCLUSION

In this brief paper we can only state the questions with very
little commentary. The important thing to remember is that the
discovery and asking of the right questions is the foundation
of effective Muslim evangelization.

SUMMARY OF PARTICIPANT'S RESPONSES

Most respondents found this to be a very valuable paper, though perhaps a bit overwhelming. They felt Mr. Dayton asked the right questions and that the questions provided a helpful model for initiating mission work. Those voicing concerns felt that there was somewhat of a mechanical or even manipulative tone which could lack the warmth of "personal encounters with people."

AUTHOR'S REJOINDER TO PARTICIPANT'S RESPONSES

The major difficulties experienced with this paper might be summed up as: 1) The format looks so mechanical, manipulative and lacks any mention of the need for "personal encounter with people." 2) The volume of the questions are overwhelming: How much time would it take to do this adequately? 3) Have we allowed enough scope for the intervention of the Holy Spirit to lead?

Most of these questions are dealt with in the larger workbook, Planning Strategies for Evangelism--Sixth Edition, from which this paper was drawn.

The mechanistic approach? If evangelism was carried out in such a mechanistic form that would be tragic. The thing to remember here is we are not spelling out steps to evangelism. Rather, we are enunciating the steps to planning. We are attempting to gather the experience of Christian men and women all over the world who have attempted the very difficult task of cross-cultural evangelism, and to summarize this experience in a way that will be useful to other faithful witnesses. Proverbs 16:9 says, "A man's mind plans his way, but the Lord directs his steps." Both are needed. Spirit-filled Christians should assume that the Spirit is just as much at work in the planning as he is in the doing. We are called to be good stewards of our resources and gifts, just as we are called to be responsible to reach the unreached people of the world.

Too many questions? Let us remember that it is usually the questions that are important, rather than the answers. Too often we come to situations with ready-made solutions rather than to discover God's strategy for a particular situation. We may not have the answers to all these questions. In fact, it would be the rare situation in which we had most of the answers. But it is in the asking that we discover not only answers, but new questions. The important thing is not data. The important thing is our response to the situation.

Can the Holy Spirit intervene? All plans are statements of faith. Any statement about the future is a statement of faith. When we attempt to write down our plans for the future, we are essentially offering to the Lord our understanding of what he would have us to do. Plans that have to do with people are quite different than plans that have to do with things, such as buildings. The mechanics of placing a man on the moon and returning him safely to earth are simple as compared to those of announcing the good news to three billion people who are outside of Christ. Rarely, if ever, will plans that have to do with people work themselves out as we intended over any long term period. Plans are like an arrow. They point direction to the future so that we can communicate with one another and so that the Holy Spirit can intervene. All of us have intentions. All of us pray that the Holy Spirit will lead us to the very best intentions. A written plan is nothing more than a statement of our intentions. We are depending upon the Holy Spirit to tell us when to rewrite them.

The methodology of this paper has been worked out over a period of 11 years of seeking to identify and reach unreached people. Those who find it difficult to identify specific unreached people may be helped by reading more about information on unreached people. The first of a proposed annual series of directories on unreached people was published by David C. Cook in January 1979, edited by the author and C. Peter Wagner. This first directory is entitled Unreached Peoples '79.

TENTMAKING MINISTRIES IN MUSLIM COUNTRIES

J. Christy Wilson Jr.

In the light of our Lord's clear command to take the gospel to all people everywhere (Matt. 28:18-20), how is the Islamic world to be evangelized with so many of its areas off limits to regular missionary work? "No land is closed to God," declared Mildred Cable who for years boldly witnessed for Christ among the Muslims of the Gobi Desert in Central Asia. "If we look around us, we shall see that even if the front door be shut a back door may be open. What we want is a new illumination of the Spirit of wisdom to see where there is an opening and how to seize it" (Cable 1946:3, 4). One of these God-given opportunities in Muslim countries today is the witness of tentmaking ministries which so far is a largely untapped source of evangelism.

When Don McCurry conducted a survey of priorities which needed to be studied relating to Muslim evangelization, the highest number of responses for the consideration of the prospects and problems dealing with self-supporting witness in Islamic nations. Waldron Scott, General Secretary of the World Evangelical Fellowship, in speaking about tentmaking ministries says: "I feel in my soul that this perhaps is the next great creative movement that God's Spirit is going to bring into existence in missionary efforts.... We are talking about a project that is at least as big in size as the total missionary movement today, and maybe much bigger" (Scott 1977). One reason for such a statement is the fact that even though there are more North American Protestant missionaries abroad than ever before (Dayton 1976:24), other Americans living overseas outnumber these by over 100 to 1 (U.S. State Department). This in no way lessens the importance of regular church supported missionaries in Muslim lands. Many

more of these are needed in areas where they are allowed to
enter. But tentmakers can and should complement the work of
Christian missionaries by working right alongside them for the
evangelization of the Muslim world.

I. SCRIPTURAL FOUNDATIONS

Some may view self-supporting witness in Muslim nations as a
novel approach. But is it new? From the Scriptures we see that
our Lord, before his fully supported ministry (Luke 8:2, 3), was
a carpenter (Mark 6:3) and the Apostle Paul was a tentmaker
(Acts 18:3). Also, the great men and women of faith in the Old
Testament were usually professionals in self-supporting positions.

In I Corinthians 9, the Apostle Paul shows that the two types
of witnesses, full-time Christian workers as well as tentmakers,
are legitimate. Both means for funding personnel to spread the
gospel are scriptural. He mentions that he decided to pay his
own way so that he might "win the more" (I Cor. 9:19b) for Christ.
On the other hand, he points out how Peter, the Lord's brothers
and other apostles, along with their wives, were quite rightfully
supported by the churches (I Cor. 9:5).

Paul testified to the Ephesian elders about his tentmaking
profession: "These hands of mine worked to pay my own way and
even to supply the needs of those who were with me" (Acts 20:34,
Living Bible). He also wrote to the Thessalonian Christians
mentioning that one reason he did this was to be a model for
them to emulate. "You ought to follow our example. We were not
idle when we were with you, nor did we eat anyone's food without
paying for it. On the contrary, we worked night and day,
laboring and toiling so that we would not be a burden to any of
you. We did this, not because we do not have the right to such
help, but in order to make ourselves a model for you to follow"
(II Thess. 3:7b-9, New International Version). Tentmaking
Christian witnesses abroad today can be living examples of the
way national believers in Muslim countries and indigenous churches
can and should be self-supporting, as well as self-governing and
self-propagating. In fact the scriptural teaching of the "priesthood of the believers" (Rev. 1:6, 5:10) involves a relation not
only to God but also a function to others, and therefore illustrates the principle that all Christians are to be witnesses
wherever they are whether they are fully supported by churches
or not.

II. HISTORICAL ILLUSTRATIONS

Throughout the history of Islam, it has been the self-
supporting witnesses such as soldiers, scholars, merchants, and
political administrators who have been largely responsible for

the spread of their religion. The calendar for 1978 of the Muslim Students' Association lists the names and addresses of 310 mosques and Islamic organizations in North America (M.S.A., P. O. Box 38, Plainfield, Indiana 46168). Even though there are fully-funded Muslim missionaries in the West today, the main thrust of Islamic work to establish mosques and Muslim student associations is in the hands of diplomats, business people, and self-supported adherents. If this is the case, why have we as evangelical Christians been so slow to adopt this scriptural method' in our evangelistic strategy?

God however has singularly blessed instances where this method has been employed. The following are illustrations of evangelical Christians who have served in the Muslim world as self-supporting witnesses.

A. SIR HERBERT EDWARDES, GENERAL OVER THE NORTHWEST FRONTIER

Sir Herbert Edwardes, who as a general in the British Army was Commissioner of Peshawar (1853-1859), was firstly "a good soldier of Jesus Christ" (II Tim. 2:3). He allowed missionaries to enter that previously closed Muslim Northwest Frontier area. When another officer challenged him saying this policy was sure to result in trouble, his answer was: "It is the primary duty of a Christian to preach the Gospel of Christ. In this crowded city we may hear the Brahman in his temple sound his 'sunkh' and gong; the Muezzin in his lofty minaret fill the air with the 'azawn'; and the Civil government which protects them both, will take upon itself the duty of protecting the Christian missionary who goes forth to preach the Gospel. He who has brought us here with His own right arm will shield and bless us, if in simple reliance upon Him we try to do His will" (Clark 1904:178, 179). Because of General Edwardes' rare faith and courage, this predominantly Muslim area today is dotted with little Christian churches. Also an institution for higher learning in Peshawar now bears the name of Edwardes College as a memorial to this man of God.

B. JENNY DE MAYER, RUSSIAN RED CROSS NURSE

Or again, Jenny de Mayer, an amazing Russian Christian, went into Siberia and Central Asia as a registered Red Cross nurse early in the 20th century, witnessing for her Lord and distributing Scriptures in those unreached Islamic areas. She also served as a Christian nurse on pilgrim ships, taking Muslims from the Russian Black Sea ports to Jidda. Furthermore, she courageously and lovingly established a medical clinic there, a short distance from the forbidden city of Mecca. She finally was arrested for her witness in Russia and spent eight years in communist prisons. But she felt that the time of her internment was the most fruitful of her whole life with the opportunitites it afforded to bear testimony to her living Lord to the guards, the authorities, and the other prisoners (de Mayer 1942).

C.   TENTMAKERS IN AFGHANISTAN

Faced with the fact that Afghanistan was closed to evangelistic workers from abroad, the only way Christians could first enter in 1948 and plant the Church there was in self-supporting capacities. After these tentmakers had worked there for some years as teachers, technicians, diplomats, and United Nations advisers, the opportunity opened for the entrance of missionary doctors, nurses, and others who had professional training that was needed in the country. (It should be noted that Afghans often have misunderstood the term "missionary." They have transposed the Islamic idea of forcing subjugated populations to become Muslims and have thought that Christian nations would also compel conversions. Thus to them the "missionaries" along Afghanistan's borders were considered as the religious branch of the British army and as such they believed they had a political connection.) Therefore, when these mission-supported workers from abroad were allowed entrance into Afghanistan they were openly referred to as "Christian" doctors, nurses, and workers; instead of "missionaries." Since most officials in Muslim countries do not understand the difference between an evangelical or a nominal Christian, these who had the qualifications needed were welcome for positions in this land.

D.   A FULBRIGHT MENNONITE SCHOLAR IN SWAT

While in Kabul, I met a man on the street who was completely out of context. At first I thought he was a Jewish rabbi since he was wearing a black hat and suit. I then found out that he was a Mennonite from Ohio who was teaching English in a government high school in the Swat area of northern Pakistan. He mentioned that he and his wife had been able to have Swati students in their home and were studying the Bible with these who had never seen the Christian Scripture before. Knowing that Swat was a Muslim state closed to missionary work, I asked him how he had been able to get in. He replied: "I never had heard of the place. I applied under a Fulbright Fellowship to teach English in Germany, and they sent me to Swat!" (Wilson 1974). This is an example of the amazing phenomenon which the Holy Spirit has brought about in our day of a modern Christian "diaspora" throughout the Muslim world.

E.   CHRISTIAN ENGINEERS IN MUSLIM COUNTRIES

A Christian engineer taught at a Muslim university abroad in a country closed to missionaries. Beside doing outstanding work

in his profession, he led some of his students to Christ, disci-
pled them in their faith, conducted prayer meetings and Bible
studies in his home and took an active part along with his
family in the local church for internationals. He also gave
away half of his salary to help support missionaries and Christian projects around the world (Wilson 1974). Another oil engineer in a "closed" Muslim country has given Arabic New Testaments to all the men working with him. He is valuable to this
nation economically and thus has not been expelled. We need to
recognize these people for what they are doing, recruit others to
help them, challenge them, equip them, pray for them and encourage them to report back.

F.   CHRISTIAN STUDENTS IN MUSLIM UNIVERSITIES

Another wonderful opportunity is that of evangelical Christian
students studying in Muslim universities around the world. The
few who have done this have found it a valuable experience in
cross-cultural research and a fruitful field for witness. Bruce
Nicholls with the Theological Commission of the World Evangelical Fellowship is looking for mature Christian students who can
enroll and engage in research at various Islamic universities
(W.E.F., 105 Savitri Building, Greater Kailash II, New Delhi-
110048, India). Along with their academic work they can be
living witnesses for Christ in the institutions where they study.
Since Muslim nations are sending many of their students to the
West, they are happy reciprocally to welcome Christian young people to their centers of learning.

G.   EXPATRIATE CHRISTIAN CHURCHES IN MUSLIM NATIONS

As born-again Christians are now living and working in all
Muslim countries of the world, more and more expatriate churches
and house fellowships are being started in these areas. Since
Islam according to the Quran allows "the People of the Book"
freedom of worship, these churches have usually been formed with
the full knowledge and approval of local Muslim authorities.
For example, 380 expatriates attended a Christian Christmas service in Riyadh, Saudi Arabia. There are also over 20,000 South
Koreans in this same country and they too have started a church
among their own people. Even though the Kabul Community Christian Church building was destroyed by an unfriendly regime during
the summer of 1973 mainly because of the conversions of Muslims
to Christ, nevertheless the congregation has continued to meet
and worship freely.

III. LOGICAL CONSIDERATIONS

Though in relation to the total missionary force comparatively few have been working with Muslims, nevertheless their effect has been felt enough for the International Islamic World Congress held in Karachi, Pakistan, in 1976 to call on the 44 countries represented to ban all foreign missionaries. We thank God for those fully supported witnesses who are faithfully working in Muslim nations. These missionaries can provide the wisdom, experience, orientation, and fellowship which tentmakers so desperately need. And thus in Islamic areas where fully supported Christian workers are allowed, self-supporting witnesses should be closely associated as "workers together" with them. One missionary medical couple who were forced out of North Africa were able to return as tentmakers and thus personified the way these two forms of service should be joined.

Self-supporting witnesses who are in Muslim countries fall into two main groups. The first is made up of those Christians who have found themselves assigned abroad by international companies, government agencies, private foundations, or educational institutions without necessarily seeking to go overseas for the purpose of evangelization. They need to be helped to make their testimony effective and to be grafted into the local church situation. Secondly, there is a much smaller number who go as tentmakers to various parts of the Muslim world in order to carry out Christ's commission. Many more need to be encouraged in this area and also assisted with preparation, orientation, and effective association with Christians on the field.

There are difficulties connected with this type of service. As Dr. Ted Ward points out, self-supporting witnesses must be missionaries in their spare time (Ward 1971). But they should live, work and witness discreetly for Christ all the time. Furthermore, they are often isolated from the local population and live in a "little America" ghetto type of situation. Also, with a full-time job it is difficult to master the local language and culture the way a missionary can who has a year or two to concentrate on this. But some tentmakers have learned languages well in spite of this, which has greatly enhanced their ability to witness.

On the other hand, there are advantages to having a regular position in the Muslim country. A tentmaker often can associate with a stratum of society that is unreached by missions. Also, such a Christian is not suspect in regard to being "paid to witness." Local people often find it hard to understand the system of support which comes from voluntary contributions of Christians abroad. They often imagine that such a person is paid to be in the secret service of his or her country.

There is a need to tie in these earnest Christian tentmakers more closely with mission boards. They thereby could receive good orientation and even be included in the mission prayer bulletin. Certain sending agencies have started programs whereby these self-supporting witnesses are linked as "field partners" or "mission associates." The Navigators also have initiated a program to recruit Christians and send them abroad as professionals in various positions. If the witness of tentmakers is to be effective and if the results are to be permanent, there must be a close association with cross-cultural mission agencies and national churches. Fine illustrations of such cooperation are the Christian teachers working in government schools in Indonesia under the Overseas Missionary Fellowship and in Nigeria under the Sudan Interior Mission.

Local congregations at home also need to be educated to the fact that these tentmakers in Muslim countries require prayer in the same way as those who are fully supported. Some churches already have short commissioning services for tentmakers before they go abroad.

Congregations at home also need to be alerted to the opportunities of reaching international Muslim visitors and students who are in our midst. They can be assisted in this by such organizations as International Students, Inc., The Inter-Varsity Christian Fellowship, Crusade's International Student Ministry. As these come to Christ, they too can be tentmakers in the Muslim lands to which they return as lay witnesses among their own people.

IV. PRACTICAL QUESTIONS

With the fact that born again Christians are now scattered throughout the Muslim world, the practical question arises as to how these can best be helped with proper orientation and prayer backing. There are now about 90 North American mission organizations which have work in Muslim lands. How can these assist self-supporting witnesses in the nations where they work? Also, how can churches be challenged to pray more effectively for these tentmakers? How can para-church organizations help in this strategic area of witness in Muslim nations? Furthermore, how can more literature be produced and distributed to these tentmakers in order to help them become more fruitful in their witness for Christ abroad? Also, should there be a new agency started to help recruit Christians for self-supporting positions, assist with their orientation, link them up with others on the field and help them with their specialized needs?

These questions need concrete answers if tentmaking ministries are to be an effective means of evangelizing closed Muslim
countries for Christ.

BIBLIOGRAPHY

Allen, Roland
  1960   The Ministry of the Spirit. London: World Dominion
           Press, pp. 63-86.

Arnold, T. W.
  1913   The Preaching of Islam. London: Constable, pp. 353,
           354.

Cable, Mildred
  1946   "Missions on the Borders of Afghanistan." Phila-
           delphia. January, pp. 3, 4.

Clark, Robert
  1904   The Missions of the CMS and CEZMS in the Punjab and
           Sindh. London: CMS, pp. 178, 179.

Cleveland, Harlan and Gerald Mangone
  1957   The Art of Overseasmanship. Syracuse: Syracuse
           University Press.

Dayton, Edward R., editor
  1976   Mission Handbook: North American Protestant Minis-
           tries Overseas. 11th edition. Monrovia: MARC,
           p. 24.

deMayer, Jenny
  1942   Adventures With God. New York: Evangelical Pub-
           lishers.

Grubb, Sir Kenneth
  1931   The Need For Non-Professional Missionaries. London:
           World Dominion Press. January.

Hopewell, James F.
  1966   "Training a Tent Making Ministry in Latin America,"
           International Review of Missions 219:333-339.

Kane Herbert
  1973   Winds of Change in the Christian Mission. Chicago:
           Moody Press, pp. 117-134.

Kroeker, Wally
  1974   "They Witness While They Work," Moody Monthly 75.

Kurtz, Robert
  1953   "The Lay-Worker As a New Type of Missionary," Inter-
            national Review of Missions 167:308-317.

Missionary Convention Compendium for Mutana
  1970

Phelps, Cathy
  1978   The Guide to Moving Overseas. Privately published.
            Box 236, Lemont, PA 16851.

Rosengrant, John, et al
  1960   Assignment Overseas. New York: Thomas Y. Crowell.

Scott, Waldron
  1977   "The Student Missions Movement." A message given at
            the Association of Church Missions Committees' Na-
            tional Conference, Wheaton College. August.

Voelkel, Jack W.
  1974   Student Evangelism in a World of Revolution. Grand
            Rapids: Zondervan.

Ward, Ted
  1971   "Options for Overseas Service in World Evangelism,"
            Christ the Liberator. Downers Grove: Inter-Varsity
            Press, pp. 133-143.

Wilson, J. Christy, Jr.
  1974   "Self-Supporting Witness Overseas," Jesus Christ:
            Lord of the Universe, Hope of the World. Downers
            Grove: Inter-Varsity Press, pp. 113-121.

  1974   "Witness While You Work Abroad," Interlit. Elgin:
            David C. Cook Foundation.

SUMMARY OF PARTICIPANT'S RESPONSES

Through an editorial oversight, the title, "Tentmaking Strategies for Closed Countries," was proposed by Dr. Wilson, while the printed title, under which the paper was distributed was simply "Strategies for Closed Countries." A number of respondents commented that Dr. Wilson had not dealt with other strategies which is, of course, the case. Our apologies to Dr. Wilson for the confusion this has caused.

The qualifications of the author to write the paper having worked for many years in a "closed" country, were well recognized by the readers. Their respect for Dr. Wilson, his work and his suggestions, was apparent in virtually every response.

Readers agreed with Dr. Wilson that there are really no "closed" countries, especially since a country which might be closed to a Westerner may be open to someone of another nationality. "We should encourage," they said, "the involvement of non-western expatriates in tentmaking or other ministries in these countries." To do so, more information is needed on the kinds of jobs that may be available for tentmaking ministries, as well as scholarships available for students who want to study in "closed" countries.

With respect to the potential for tentmakers in closed countries, some respondents asked how we can reconcile optimism for this strategy with the cautions of those who argue that it is a rare individual who has enough gifts and energy to do a good job of both working and witnessing. Further, they wondered why, if this is a good strategy, that "seculars" in closed countries haven't been more effective.

To the question posed by Dr. Wilson as to whether or not a new agency or center should be formed for the purpose of training tentmakers, the response was mixed. Among those who felt a new such center was not necessary were those who argued that it might be a hindrance to be trained and affiliated with such an institution. Nevertheless, it was suggested by one that the U.S. Center for World Mission and/or the Fuller School of World Mission be challenged to establish a training base for tentmaker missionaries.

A number of respondents questioned how the converts of tentmaker ministries were to be shepherded, especially since the tentmaker would probably be short-term, and, if he were very effective, would probably be asked to leave before long. The merits of starting new churches of affiliation with existing local churches (if any) was also discussed.

AUTHOR'S REJOINDER TO PARTICIPANT'S RESPONSES

"Without lay people involved in world evangelism," writes
William Kerr of the Christian and Missionary Alliance, "the
task will never be completed." But how is this to be done?
John Bennett of the Association of Church Missions Committees
states that there are "few ideas with greater potential than
the establishment of an agency to facilitate self-supporting
witness." Margaret Mitchell, who served in Iran, observes,
"The major problem of the tentmaker is that he/she has no
support structure. An agency or subagency under another organization would be fantastic."

Some respondents pointed out that certain organizations have
already initiated work in this area. Inter-Varsity Christian
Fellowship's Ruth Siemens is assisting Christian students and
graduates with assignments abroad. Campus Crusade for Christ
International, through its Agape Movement, is training and
locating dedicated workers. Missionary Internship, Inc. stands
ready to assist tentmakers with orientation and works with
Wayne Shabaz, who has set up a Christian placement service for
overseas positions. Many mission boards are also developing
programs to incorporate self-supporting witnesses into their
field strategies. But if, as Waldron Scott of World Evangelical
Fellowship (WEF) states, tentmaking ministries are to be "the
next great creative movement that God's spirit is going to
bring into existence in missionary efforts," participants felt
that there needed to be more coordination of efforts. It was
suggested that this could be a service ministry under an organization like World Vision or the U.S. Center for World Mission and
could cooperate with the above programs.

One respondent writes, "This organization would need some
degree of interface with Interdenominational Foreign Mission
Association, Evangelical Foreign Mission Association, associations of Third World sending agencies and organizations such
as WEF. At the same time, it would need a profile attractive
to international business and government."

What would be the function of such an organization?
Dr. Ray Windsor, General Director of Bible and Medical
Missionary Fellowship writes, "We have not sent tentmakers for
deputation ministry in churches and amongst university student
groups or people in the professions. Most missionaries are
inspired to offer for service mainly as a result of face-to-
face contact. I am a strong advocate for applying the same
standards to tentmakers as traditional missionaries. Surely
they need systematic Bible training and pre-field orientation."
Thus, such an agency could coordinate recruitment, provide
information, direct preparation and assist in placement. It

could link tentmakers with mission boards, sensitize local
congregations to appreciate the idea of self-supporting missionaries and encourage them to pray. It could help Christian
students enroll in universities around the world where they
could acquire language skills, become culturally oriented,
witness for Christ and prepare for possible future service in
that nation. This agency could also research countries and
peoples to discover needs for development and seek to provide
these through tentmakers. It could keep tabs on all known
self-supporting missionaries, put them in touch with expatriate
and national churches, provide training seminars on the field,
assist with language learning, prepare them for effective
evangelism, conserve their converts, tie in their work with
ongoing mission strategy, provide a publication with hints on
witnessing, testimonies of other tentmakers, etc., send roving
delegates to encourage and edify them, debrief them after their
service abroad and help them with their reentry adjustment.

"The opportunities opened by this are mind-boggling," writes
Ken Nolin who worked with the United Presbyterian Mission in
Egypt, "if only we can take advantage of it all quietly, without
undue publicity so that we do not jeopardize what's being done."

THE ROLE OF LOCAL CHURCHES IN GOD'S REDEMPTIVE PLAN FOR THE MUSLIM WORLD

Frank S. Khair Ullah

I firmly believe that if Pakistan is to be won for our Lord
Jesus Christ, it can and will be won through the Pakistani
Church. The aid from other churches abroad in money, personnel,
techniques and experience may be most helpful, but, in the
final analysis, it is primarily through the Christians of the
national Church that their fellow-countrymen will be evangelized
and formed into a strong local church in the country. But the
key is a "community of the faithful" doing this work in each
country. I cannot express this idea better than Bishop Hassan
Dehqani-Tafti has done in his short autobiography called Design
of My World. His final paragraphs are:

> "But words alone cannot bring Muslims to the foot of the
> Cross. No amount of interpretation in the abstract brings
> the Muslims to feel with those in the boat who 'worshipped
> him, saying, Truly you are the Son of God' (Matt. 14:33).
> Christians must show in their lives how Christianity is in
> truth the incarnation of the love of God. Most Muslims I
> know who have followed Christ have done so because of the
> sacrificial life and sustained love of some Christian
> friend. You cannot bring the Muslim to Christ unless you
> love him personally...

> "But there is more. No individual, however saintly, shows
> the love of God in Christ fully. Its interpretation needs
> the community of the faithful--the people of God. The
> Church where two or three are gathered together in His
> Name--this is the core of the matter. What a tremendous

role is theirs, not least when their gathering together
is in the midst of a world where for centuries Islam has
prevailed!" (1963:79-80).

It is only when we Pakistanis have realized our tremendous
role in this carrying out of the great commission, that we will
begin to communicate effectively with our Muslim brothers.

Communication means sharing--that is the etymological
meaning of the word--and sharing is much more than only giving,
it means receiving too. How can we give to our Muslim brothers
the message of salvation, if we do not try to understand their
mind and attitude towards life and their own faith? Therefore,
a preacher to the Muslims must know a great deal about their
beliefs and practices, their hopes and aspirations. I like
the English word "preaching." There is a hidden pre-aching in
it, a yearning pain to deliver the message and tc see his
brother safe and reconciled like Joseph for his brother
Benjamin: "...for his heart yearned for his brother" (Gen.
43:30). Unless we have that yearning too in us, we cannot
preach the gospel - "Woe unto me if I don't."

But seemingly, the Pakistani Church has no concern for its
Muslim brothers.

Recently, we were having an informal meeting of those who
are interested in Muslim evangelism. Two Pakistanis were also
present. The question under consideration was how to help the
new converts to become a part of the Church. A suggestion was
made that as a transitional step, there should be a fellowship
of other Muslim converts and sympathizers. Fear was expressed
spontaneously by one Pakistani, that such a step might give to
the new convert an undue sense of superiority and that one
should be careful about this.

This is a typical and symptomatic attitude of the Church
leaders. A certain unwillingness to share the good news with
our "unconsciously regarded enemy" neighbor. Most Christians
have an in-built hatred for the Muslim, which we, by God's
grace, need to overcome.

But why is this so? It is only a little over a century ago
that the Church was established in this part of the world,
among a group of people who were mostly drawn from a low-caste
Hindu background. The sub-culture evolved by this Church over
the years, was typically Hindu--its way of worship, its
religious music, many of the social customs, even the language
was influenced by Hinduism. To give you one interesting example
from the Anglican Communion which is rather conservative in

changing its order of worship, of how it was influenced by Hindu
practices: look up in the Book of Common Prayer the order of
service for "The Solemnization of Matrimony" where provision is
made for giving the bride, instead of, or in addition to, a
"ring," a western custom, a mangalasutra: a Hindu religious
custom of giving a wedding necklace (1963:640). Before the
creation of Pakistan, when we had a mixed population of Hindus
and Muslims, some of these customs could be accepted. Now in
the new situation, things are different and the Church should
accordingly adapt itself to its new environment.

This change is necessary, not only for evangelistic purposes,
but also for our own nationalistic reasons. This is a fine
point and needs to be carefully considered. We Pakistanis
achieved our independence a little over 30 years ago. We are
still struggling with some of our problems in which language,
culture and religion are all mixed up. What constitutes our
"nationality?" What is our identity? What kind of government
is suitable for Pakistan? These are some of the subjects that
pose a problem that needs to be resolved soon. Strong emotions
sometimes vitiate our thinking. But, as we have chosen to be
Pakistanis, it is our Christian duty to face these problems and
cooperate with our countrymen to find answers to them.

The fact is that the people of Pakistan are a mixture of
Hindu and Muslim cultures. Some Muslims, generations ago, were
Hindus. A great many of our social customs, including the
dowry system, have Hindu origins. Even our national language,
Urdu, shows this duality. Its syntax is based on Hindi grammar;
all the pronouns, prepositions and conjunctions are from Hindi.
But to show our identity with the Muslim world, and to break
away from India, we are moving, culturally and linguistically,
towards the neighboring West--"arabicizing" and "persianizing"
our vocabulary, avoiding all Sanskrit and Hindi words. There is
a deliberate effort to avoid all vestiges of Hindu culture, and
even things Indian. An interesting example of this came up
recently, when the Indian television station across the border
started telecasting programs connected with folk music and folk
dance and common Indo-Pakistan heritage. A crescendo of
protests went up from the Pakistani papers urging Pakistani
viewers not to see these programs. It was called a "cultural
invasion" of Pakistan. Please remember that 97 percent of people
of Pakistan are Muslims, and in their struggle have become very
culture-conscious. In this situation, we Christians should play
our part and help them to resolve their (and our) problems,
rather than aggravating them. Fraternal workers sometimes
cannot see this in the correct perspective. The Church which
is interested in evangelizing the Muslims must make all efforts
to be in reasonable harmony with the surrounding cultural milieu

234

as much as possible, and share in the just aspirations of its countrymen.

But instead of this healthy growth we have become an inward looking ghetto more concerned with preserving our hybrid culture than going all out with the message of the gospel to our Muslim brothers courageously. In our present Hindu-oriented pseudo-westernized Church, a convert from Islam hardly feels at home. But who cares?!

God certainly cares! But we his instruments are not quite ready. This will happen when the Church is renewed. The Church can only play its role in God's redemptive plan if and when it has redeemed itself. What is the image of the Church that we have presented to our countrymen: "Look! How these Christians hate one another, and run to the civil courts with their endless and senseless litigations." There are divisions in the Church over property and offices, encouraged by foreign funds, and "theological" controversies that have no bearing on our life here.

Our Euroamerican fraternal workers have a great responsibility towards this situation. Have they helped us to grow independently and naturally, or have they unconsciously forced their views on us? Is there a genuine "cooperation in evangelism" between the mother churches and the younger churches? And, are these "churches in evangelistic partnership" as envisaged in sections 7 and 8 of The Lausanne Covenant?

I fully agree with Bishop Stephen Neill's observation as given in his Christian Faith Today, though without seeing the heartening signs that he mentions in Pakistan. He writes:

"The Christianity of these younger Churches still tends to be imitative, and too much dependent on western ideas and categories of thought. But there are heartening and increasing signs that the Churches in each of the great regions of the world are becoming genuinely indigenous, and learning to impart to their understanding of the Christian faith a character of their own, not derivative from the experiences of the West. This process, as it goes forward, should both enable each particular Church to become genuinely at home in the country of which it is called to be the soul, and make of the universal Church a treasury which all nations can enrich by bringing into it the varied richness of their own inheritance" (1956:233).

Some well-intentioned but misguided para-church organizations in their unchecked zeal, have tried to transplant into Pakistan

a campaign that was very successful back home in some big city
in the States. They used the same techniques, the same gadgets
and electronic paraphernalia, the same language translated into
Urdu, and it was heavily backed by plentiful finance. Often
they little realize how much harm they have done without
achieving much real results. Remember, one man's meat may be
another man's poison.

Take another example of how much effort is wasted if proper
consultation and cooperation is not carried out between the
overseas keen campaigners and the local national churches in
the country. A "scripture distribution" program was launched
from Wheaton, Illinois. Every name listed in the telephone
directory of some city or cities in Pakistan was sent a copy
of the New Testament in Urdu by mail. Some addresses were
changed by the time the packets arrived, some people refused
to accept these unsolicited packets of the Christian Scriptures.
Tons of these got accummulated in the post office, which had to
be disposed of by auction as "waste paper." Some of us
discovered this when some small merchandise was purveyed to
people in envelopes made out of the pages of the Bible. Any one
who is familiar with our culture would have been horrified for
the greatest respect is accorded to all Scriptures in the East
whether it be the Quran or the Bible. You can imagine the
chagrin of our Muslim friends who could not understand why such
mass desecration of our Holy Book was carried out by the American
Christians.

Pakistan Bible Society, I am told, did make a protest. But
they were told that some letters of appreciation did arrive at
their office appreciating the distribution. How many? That we
were not told. This is just the type of situation where we all
should be engaged in constant self-examination and evaluation
of our effectiveness as part of the Church universal in cooperation with the local churches.

The quality of Christian life in the Church is very important
for evangelistic thrust. This we have observed earlier. We
should also have an intellectual preparedness for our work among
the Muslims. Our seminaries should provide that.

Courses in our seminaries need to be revised and brought in
line with our needs. Study of Islam, both classical and popular,
should be a must. Interpretation of Christianity to Muslims in
a language and thought form that can be understood by them
should be a course, which should be developed by an Islamicist
who knows the oriental schools of thought--an Al Azhar or
Deoband type of approach. Instead of taking over a whole block
of instructions from some western theological college, experts
should help us to devise courses which will be more relevant to

our past and present, sending roots back to the <u>Acts of the Apostles</u> or even further back, because the Semitic background of the Old Testament is more in harmony with our culture. Euro-american theology will be an interesting case study but not our entire preoccupation. There have been attempts in the recent past in Pakistan to form new seminaries, however small they may be. Why? Because we wish to preserve and strengthen one of our pet denominational "isms"--our Anglicanism, our Lutheranism or Presbyterianism. It is high time that we should break away from all this and develop our own theology--native to the soil, born out of the clash we have had with Islam and our under-standing of Islam, which may necessitate our modifying some of our views. A theology is never shaped in the comfortable armchairs of a seminary occupied by people trained only to think in western modes of thoughts. It is born in the every day life of the people, where ideas clash and minds wrestle to arrive at a solution under the guidance of the Holy Spirit.

We nearly had such a theology born. But history took a turn in a different direction and gave us another story.

Let me try to reclaim a bit of the first story. The West for a long time carried a dislike for Islam, until the begin-ning of the evangelical movement of the 19th century. Great missionaries came into the field to work among the Muslims; names which even today carry an aura of grandeur and glory: Henry Martyn, Bishop French, Pfander, Gairdner, Zwemer, and a host of others. They produced scholarly books, and won many converts. Some of these converts produced literature that the Church should have preserved as a rich heritage: commentaries and other theological books in our own language, by men like Dr. Imad-ud-Din, and works of true scholarship in the oriental style. Rev. Ahmad Shah produced a concordance of the <u>Quran</u>. Hughes' <u>Dictionary of Islam</u> is still available in a reprint by a Pakistani publisher. But something happened and all this wonderful work disappeared. The curtain was rung down on all this achievement. Limelight was stolen by another piece of missionary work in this country. A phenomenon in consequence of which the excellent work done among the Muslims was shelved, ignored and forgotten.

I am rather critical of the American Society of Missiology in what they call a "people movement," a euphemism for "mass movement." A true "people movement" causes a spontaneous and deep change in the whole people. We have a genuine example in Korea. An interesting account about this is found in Roy E. Shearer's book <u>Wildfire Church Growth in Korea - A Case Study of Missionary Activity in Korea</u>. Shearer writes:

"This great movement to Christ that we see in Pyongan Provinces of northwest was not a mass movement in the sense that mobs of unconverted people were taken into the Churches. It was rather a response of faith to the gospel, flowing unimpeded along the web of family relationships. A father became a Christian, led his wife, and then his sons and daughters and sons-in-law into conviction that Christ was the answer. This conversion was followed by a long period of training, and these new Christians then led others by the same method" (1966:148-149).

In this Korean "people movement" conversion not many ulterior motives were involved. The movement that occurred in India, and in what is now Pakistan, was not a pure spiritual phenomenon (of course, there are rarely ever pure and simple spiritual phenomena), but some of the motives were patently clear. Eugene Stock, the writer of the History of the Church Missionary Society comments (quoted in People Movements in the Punjab):

"Why had such people professed to become Christians at all? Simply because to them it was a rise in the social scale. Despised as the Christians were by the Hindus and Mohammadans, the Church as such was still more despised..." (Stock 1975:240).

Rev. Bateman of Church Missionary Society (CMS), when asked to take over these newly acquired Christians, described the process as "indiscriminant baptism" and wrote:

"When we received these people, together with a certificate of their baptism, there were not five in a hundred of them who knew anything distinctly Christian, though several hundred of them were registered as communicants. Many would tell you that they had become Christians 'mukti de waste' (to obtain salvation), but if you asked them what 'mukti' (salvation) meant, they could give you no answer at all" (Stock 1975:240).

One of the books that has been highly recommended by the leading missiologists, and from which I have quoted above, is People Movements in the Punjab by Fredrick and Margaret Stock. I have read the book carefully with great appreciation. Excellent research has gone into the making of this book. It gives sound advice on a number of matters. It is an honest book, but I would not recommend it for Muslim evangelism. It has hardly half a dozen pages devoted to that subject. But, someone may challenge me and counter my criticism by saying

that that is neither the subject nor the purpose of the book.
However, Dr. McGavran, the guiding spirit of that book, claims
in the foreword:

"The Stocks' brilliant book <u>People Movements in the
Punjab</u> is an essential reading for Christian leaders
concerned for world evangelism. It should be taught
in all Christian colleges and seminaries on the Indian
sub-continent, as well as in courses on Missions in
the homeland..." (Stock 1975:xvi).

And Dr. Warren Webster, General Director of the Conservative
Baptist Foreign Mission Society, adds on the blurb of the book:

"The Stocks provide a perceptive historical analysis
of Church growth in Pakistan, where a million
Protestants and Catholics comprise the country's
fastest growing religious minority. The study, based
on years of personal involvement, points the way to
continued growth for those who understand what the
Spirit is saying to the churches of the Punjab today."

I have a very great respect for all that the Stocks have
done. But I must sound a note of caution to all the readers of
the book, especially those interested in evangelistic work
among the Muslims. Pakistan is not yet ripe for a people
movement in the majority community. A hint seems to be given
in the preface of the book, that millions are knocking at the
door asking for teaching, but then the attention of the authors
is diverted to another mass movement in Sindh.

"Gradually we found our eyes lifted from the struggles
and tensions of the 1.4 percent in Pakistan who already
bear the name of Christ, and focused upon the 98.6
percent who as yet do not give Him allegiance. More
specifically our attention was drawn to the 'whitened
fields'--those ready for harvest <u>now</u>, the scheduled
Castes" (Stock 1975:xx).

Far be it for me to condemn a "people movement." Surely
God's hand is in it. We should be sensitive to see what the
Spirit is saying to the churches. But when all this is
reinforced with scientific, computer-aided research, with
multitudes of graphs and statistics, and various scales, I
feel that the promptings of the Holy Spirit are being squeezed
out. Even a professor of theology, a leading scholar of the
time, was warned by our Lord, "The wind blows where it wills,
and you hear the sound of it, but you do not know whence it

comes or whither it goes; so it is with every one who is born of the Spirit" (John 3:8).

What is happening in Sindh greatly appeals to the mind of the Euroamerican missionary societies because it shows tangible results. Field workers can file in reports backed with facts and figures. But remember, in Sindh we are only talking of 0.98 percent of the total population of Pakistan. No doubt, if these people join the Church, the numerical strength of the Church will be nearly doubled! Yes, we should certainly win them for our Lord, but that should not make us neglect the work that we should be doing among the other 97 percent of the population of our country.

Stocks, and for that matter the preoccupation of a great many foreign missionaries with the evangelism among the scheduled caste people is praiseworthy, but that should not make them condemn others who have a burden to work among the seemingly unresponsive people.

"Say not the struggle naught availeth. The labor and the wounds are vain..."

The point that I am laboring to make is this. The Stocks are such forceful and convincing writers, that the policies of church boards and sponsoring agencies are influenced by their book. Guidelines laid down by them carry a certain authority on subjects like church growth and priorities decided by them. Take this passage:

"How can the Church grow? Where can the effective outreach be made? We have seen that the Church is stymied in its efforts to win the majority community. There are too many theological, cultural and social barriers to be overcome. New approaches need to be explored in Muslim evangelism that may produce increased fruit. Nevertheless, let us not fail to learn the lessons it took so many years for God to teach the early missionaries. Let us not keep looking to the 'high and mighty' but open our hearts and doors to the 'weak and lowly,' the Scheduled Castes, who have shown ample evidence of spiritual hunger and potential responsiveness. If God has prepared their hearts, who are we to call them unworthy and unclean? Let us humble ourselves and reach out to them, having the mind of Christ who humbled Himself all the way from His throne in heaven to death on the cross in order to win us" (Stock 1975:216).

I certainly do not agree with what I have underlined in the above passage. Numerical increase is not God's only plan. I vehemently disagree with the idea expressed in the chapter entitled "Principles Essential for Church Planting Today" (chapter 16) and especially the passage that has the sub-heading "Recognize Numerical Church Growth as God's Will" (Stock 1975:218).

Maybe God wants us to win a whole group of people, but he certainly does not condemn a one-by-one approach. We had people movement in the Acts, but also a single convert, Paul who changed the whole complexion of the early Church. The Stocks and the whole group of American missiologists seem to regard this approach as utterly wrong:

"The tragedy is that this same faulty strategy was current in every Mission in the Punjab and many others in India. Most of the Missions persisted in concentrating on individual conversions from high castes for many years, thus remaining static and stunted, until they were willing to follow God's better plan...

"Even more tragic is the tendency today to return to this unproductive strategy in evangelism, failing to learn from the past that one-by-one conversions resulting in separation from family and social dislocation cannot produce a Church that will grow and multiply as God intends" (Stock 1975:32).

Some of the shortcomings of the present Church can be traced back to its origins. Even the Stocks are willing to admit that the present factionalism in the Church is due to a carry over from the caste system:

"Factionalism, an integral part of the caste system, permeates society on the Indian sub-continent. That it is found in the Church does not so much reveal sub-Christian behavior as it represents a true picture of the way culture operates" (Stock 1975:186).

This kind of behavior is discovered as part of one's social inheritance. John C. Heinrich in his book The Psychology of a Suppressed People confirms it. Other historians have questioned the wisdom of what happened in India in mass movement. R. Vidler, author of the 5th volume of the Pelican History of the Church called The Church in an Age of Revolution, writes:

"...in a country like India very few members of the ruling classes or higher castes were converted. This may have been natural and creditable, but missionary statesmen with longer view would have seen that the best way to

christianize a people is to christianize its natural
leaders. Here the narrow intellectual outlook of most
missionaries was a liability" (Vidler 1961:252).

When Eugene Stock questioned the wisdom of one particular
kind of mass movement, the Stocks lashed back at him in these
words:

"It is interesting to see Eugene Stock taken in by this
missiological error. The supposition that highly
subsidized, paternalistic, hot-house care, which a
Mission can give to a few one-by-one converts who
dribble into a well staffed mission station, is
normal and healthy, is one of the most pernicious and
damaging errors."

I wish somebody would write a book to set the balance right.
The achievements of some of the converts has been played down
in Stocks' book. They talk of a vigorous Church. Where was its
vigor and its strength? The greatest literary achievement of
the United Presbyterian (UP) Church is the Punjabi Psalter. And
who was responsible for it? It was a Muslim convert won by
CMS and passed on to the UP's.

The appendix of Stocks' book does no justice to other
missions. It simply tries to justify the UP Church's "people
movement!" What is missing in the book is any warm reference to
the achievements of the individual converts from Islam and
Hinduism: Imad-ud-Din, Safdar Ali, Bishop Subhan, Sultan Mohd,
Paul, Ghulam Masih, Talib-ud-Din, Ahmad Shah, Ahsan Ullah, Qazi
Khair Ullah, Barkat Ullah, who are just a few names whose
literary achievements should be proudly remembered by the
Pakistani Church. Where is their record?!

Only when the Pakistani Church discovers itself and takes
pride in the heritage that has almost been forgotten and turns
outwards in love and concern for the salvation of its countrymen
will the Church simultaneously revive and grow.

There are hopeful signs on the horizon. Radio ministry,
correspondence schools, and Pakistan Association Concerning
Theological Education by Extension (PACTEE) show great promises,
but there is need of more Pakistani participation. Under God's
guidance, in cooperation with the Church universal the Pakistani
Church with its "blood, sweat and tears" must carry out our
Lord's great commission! And that will be our role in God's
redemptive plan for Pakistan. Amen.

BIBLIOGRAPHY

The Book of Common Prayer
     1963   London: S.P.C.K.

Dehqani-Tafti, Hassan
     1963   Design of My World. London: Lutterworth Press.

Neill, Stephen
     1956   Christian Faith Today. New York: Penguins.

Shearer, Roy E.
     1966   Wildfire Church Growth in Korea - A Case Study of
                Missionary Activity in Korea. Grand Rapids:
                Eerdmans.

Stock, Frederick and Margaret Stock
     1975   People Movements in the Punjab. South Pasadena:
                William Carey Library.

Vidler, R.
     1961   The Church in an Age of Revolution. 5th volume.
                New York: Penguins.

SUMMARY OF PARTICIPANT'S RESPONSES

Response to this paper was about equal in praise and critique.
Interestingly enough this was often, though not exclusively,
divided along national lines: non-western respondents were very
favorable to the presentation, and Westerners found areas of
objection. Those reacting positively characterized it as
"a very challenging paper calling us back from a one-sided
position," and "a bold paper with much food for thought." The
readers particularly appreciated the author's description of
preaching as "pre-aching," and agreed that there must be this
intense yearning for the hearers to come to Christ, lest we be
trafficking in unfelt truth.

On the other hand, a number of readers felt that Dr. Khair
Ullah was too negative and might have therefore weakened his
argument. While they agreed with him that the evangelism of
Pakistan must be done by the Pakistani Church, they did not
see from the paper how this could be accomplished. The
author, they said, "is negative toward people movements, toward
tribal evangelism, toward foreign missions, and even toward
the existing church." Thus, while "we are apparently being
told to leave it to the existing church, we are also told that
it is essentially a Hindu church and not ready or able to do
evangelism."

Other readers felt that Dr. Khair Ullah may have misunderstood the point of the church growth movement or at least
presented it unfairly. And, some failed to see where the
author had really grappled with the subject indicated in the
title of his paper.

There were then differing opinions about the effectiveness
of the paper, but all agreed that it provided a very useful
gauge of underlying feelings and values and a most worthwhile
perspective.

AUTHOR'S REJOINDER TO PARTICIPANT'S RESPONSES

I enjoyed writing the paper as much as I enjoyed reading the responses that were elicited by it from the participants. I wrote the paper in a hurry. Frankly speaking, the commission to me to write this paper was a wise afterthought. It did not form part of the original well thought out plan of the foundation papers--a list of which appeared in the margin of the paper used for most of the conference correspondence. I think the director, Don McCurry, after receiving my rather strongly worded responses to the first few foundation papers, felt that my "Third Worldian" views should be heard and a paper on the above subject by a native would be useful. The canvas to be covered was too broad and so I covered only Pakistan, hoping that something similar would be felt by the other "local" churches and they could complete the picture themselves. I was not very much amiss, because some of the other "local" people did respond sympathetically.

In all, I received 29 responses. Four of these were strongly critical of my attitude. Sixteen were appreciative of my point of view. The rest, though favorably inclined, pleaded that a more balanced assessment of the situation would be helpful. Most of the critics were very kind and tactful. Here is one that started as follows: "At first I felt that here was a man with a 'chip on his shoulder' for some reason," but the writer tactfully qualified it by: "...And yet as I read further I found that some of the reservations which he expressed about 'the people movement' concepts, especially as they relate to the mission among the Muslims, were also thoughts I have had" (John Stelling).

Personally, my intention was only to remind the participants that we "easterns" do not always see eye-to-eye with our "western" brothers. My other intention was to generate enough heat to make people take part in an exciting discussion--in which I unexpectedly succeeded.

The comments of the people in the first group had a sobering effect on me. Here are a few examples: "Maybe I missed something, but I felt this paper misread the point and nature of the church growth argument about people movements.... Nor was I sure at the end of the paper what the title had to do with the actual content!!..." (no name on my sheet). "It seems to me that the author had a faulty understanding of McGoverns [sic] church growth, people movement principle.... The author ends the article by fomenting controversy and the very unity he called for in the outset! There are many valuable clues in the article, however, to underlying feelings and values" (Larry DeVilbiss). "This paper disappoints me. Despite many good statements and

sentiments, it appears altogether too negative.... My
conclusion? This is too negative: let's find a positive solution, at least a beginning..." (Roger E. Hedlund).

The remarks of the people in the second group were almost
"flattering:" "In my opinion, this is the best article I have
received of its nature" (Shaf Shafir). "I would like to commend
the author on his courage..." (A. J. Wiebe). "All I can say is
'Amen! Amen!' How _very_ important that we not lose sight of
Muslim/Christian problems as we move quickly with the Stocks into
their people movement..." (Ken Nolin). "A very challenging paper
to call back from a 'one-sided' position. It is healthy to read
such a presentation calling for a non-biased study..."
(Edward C. Pentecost).

The third group was the most helpful one. They found much
that was objectively stated in my paper, but wanted me to correct
some of the overstatements and so bring about a more balanced
appreciation of the situation. I wish I had space to quote from
many of them, but let me confine myself to just one. The writer
takes up my first rather bold statement that if Pakistan is to
be won for our Lord Jesus Christ it can and will be won through
the Pakistani Church. He tactfully begins: "It is a very well
written paper...." Then goes on, "I am sure the writer does
not mean that...The writer also emphasized the point that in
order to effectuate God's redemptive plan for Pakistan, the
Church of Pakistan itself has to be redeemed. This is vitally
true. There has to be a meaningful cooperation between the
committed missionaries and a committed church to be co-workers
in the Lord's harvest if the job is to be done. There cannot
be two opinions about it" (Theodore Manaen).

My thanks to all those who responded to my paper. I stand
for much correction, but I would hardly make any changes in my
basic assumptions! Even if they were wrong, they have served
their purpose of "stimulating thinking afresh."

THE CHRISTIAN APPROACH TO THE MUSLIM WOMAN AND FAMILY

Valerie Hoffman

The superiority of Christianity over Islam has been regarded by many evangelicals of the past as especially evident in the realm of morals and ethics, and the exploitation of the Muslim woman was contrasted with the superior status of the woman in Christian society. The logical outcome of such an attitude was that an important part of evangelism involved establishing schools and educating men and women according to the norms of western society. Today, while most of the world continues to acknowledge the technological superiority of western civilization, on the moral plane our superiority is highly questionable. In light of the disintegration of the family in our society, the high rate of crime and divorce, the increasing frequency of wife- and child-beatings, and the increasing acceptability of sexual perversion, we have little of which to boast. We must reevaluate our own attitudes toward Muslim society and the relationship of the gospel to the Muslim woman and family.

I. THE STATUS OF WOMAN IN ISLAM

The quranic basis for the subjection of women is found in Sura 4:34:

"Men have authority over women because Allah has made the one superior to the others, and because they spend their wealth to maintain them. Good women are obedient. They guard their unseen parts because Allah has guarded them. As for those from whom you fear disobedience, admonish them and send them to beds apart and beat them. Then if

246

they obey you, take no further action against them:
(Dawood 1974:370).

Men and women are regarded in the Quran as equal in spiritual
worth as evidenced by their origins (4:1) and by the promise to
both of reward in Paradise (9:72). Nonetheless, the testimony
of the woman is worth half that of the male witness in court
(2:282), in the house she is subject to corporal punishment by
her husband (4:34), and she may inherit only one share for every
two of her brother (4:11). Men have the unilateral right of
divorce (2:227-232), as well as the right of concubinage with
female slaves (4:3, 4:24). Women have the right to seek a
judicial separation.

Hadith literature expands on the theme of woman's inferiority
beyond the limitation of her legal rights. Believing women are
seen first of all not in the context of their relation to God,
but in their role as wives and mothers, and it is by virtue of
their faithfulness in fulfilling these roles that they attain
Paradise (Smith and Haddad 1975:43). The capacity of women to
do good is limited. There are several accounts in hadith of
Muhammad's vision of hellfire, in which the majority of the
tormented were women:

"I saw the Fire and I have not seen to this day a more
terrible sight. Most of the inhabitants are women. They
(those to whom the Prophet was talking) said, O Messenger of
God, why? He said, Because of their ingratitude (kufr).
They said, Are they ungrateful to the companion (i.e.,
husband) and ungrateful to the charity (shown by their husbands to them)? Even if you men continue to do good things
for them, and a woman sees one thing (bad) from you, she will
say, I never saw anything at all good from you" (Smith and
Haddad 1975:44).

Smith and Haddad comment:

"The two worst sins of Islam are shirk (association of
anything with God) and kufr (ingratitude or rejection of
God's signs). What these traditions seem to be saying is
that the worst things man can do in relation to God are
precisely those things which, if done by woman in relation
to man, earn her damnation. Specifically, this means the
shirk of giving herself to more than one man (or not safe-
guarding her honor) and the kufr of being ungrateful for the
charity and beneficence of her husband. We reach the
somewhat unnerving conclusion that in these traditions there
may be a real sense in which woman's sins are to man as man's
are to God" (ibid.:44).

Another hadith gives some reasons for the inferiority of women:

"O you women, I have not seen anyone more deficient in intelligence and in religion than you. . . As for the deficiency in your religion, it is your religion, it is your menstruation which befalls you and remains with you as long as God wills, so that you stay without prayer or fasting . . . As for what I said about the deficiency in your intelligence, it is because your witness is but half a witness" (ibid.:45).

On the level of modern perceptions of the woman, Richard Antoun found that in Arab villages:

". . . the ideology of women's inferiority finds its most intense expression neither in her legal nor ritual status, nor in beliefs about her rational capacity, but rather in views about her ethical capability. There is the firm belief that women are the initiators in any illicit relations. Women's propensity for sexual license is attributed to the animalistic impulses that move them" (Antoun 1968:678).

David Gordon also writes:

"Women in Islamic culture suffer from a deeply rooted suspicion that they are morally unreliable, that there is something demonic, even unclean, about them" (1968:12).

Women are considered in Moroccan folklore to be the depository of demonic forces (Doutte 1908:33).

The veil and seclusion of women may be seen in light of the dual notion of the woman as both vulnerable and sexually aggressive:

"Only the full observance of the modesty code can, at once, protect the fragile woman, for she is a mirror that a breath will cloud, and contain the lust that dwells within her" (Antoun 1968:691).

I am not attempting here to claim that this view of the nature of woman is universal throughout the Muslim world, and one cannot deny that Westernization and the desegregation of the sexes has in certain segments of society produced great changes in both the legal status of the woman and her relationships with men. Yet even there, things are not always very clear. Fatima Mernissi writes of modern Morocco:

"Relations between the sexes seem to be going through a
period of anomie, of deep confusion and absence of norms.
The traditional norms governing relations between the sexes
are violated every day by a growing majority of people
without incurring legal or social sanctions. The woman's
right to traditionally male spaces is far from being insti-
tutionalized or even accepted, whether at the level of the
laws or of the underlying ideology. The anomie stems from
the gap between the ideology and the reality" (1975:51).

Vast segments of Middle Eastern society have been influenced
by centuries of tradition that remain relatively untouched by
modernization. Religious leaders in Al-Azhar continue to argue
against women taking jobs in public life "because of their
femininity which makes them likely to quit the path of reason
and moderation" (Goode 1963), and Hajji Shaykh Yusuf of Iran
has argued for the veiling of women on the basis of their
stronger animality and their lesser capacity for vigilance,
faithfulness, and intelligence (1965:356-357). Yet to the Muslim woman Jesus Christ offers dignity and wholeness, complete
cleansing by his blood, and full membership in the priesthood
of believers. How can we convey this to her?

II. THE WORLDVIEW OF THE MUSLIM WOMAN

The majority of works written about Muslim women deal with
what men think of women and how men regulate women's lives; but
the worldview of the Muslim woman has remained largely an enigma
to Westerners and, not unlikely, to Muslim men.

C. R. Marsh wrote that there are three things which
characterize most Muslim women: first, a background of fear--
fear of being beaten, of evil spirits, of divorce, of the
authority of her mother-in-law, of gossip leading to loss of
honor; second, they are dominated by men or by a single man;
third, "whatever the outward veneer due to western influence,
there is always an underlying superstitious awe of the unseen
spirit world, a respect for the religious leaders of Islam, and
usually a deeply ingrained fear of God" (1975:69-70). Ethno-
graphic studies have proved this analysis to be close to the
truth.

Emmy Bos Kunst writes of the women of Azam Basti, a slum area
of Karachi:

"Expressions like 'the man is the king of the house,' 'the
husband is the second God,' or 'a husband is the crown on a
woman's head,' illustrate to a certain degree the relationship between husband and wife. . . In our presence humility
and obedience were indeed the external characteristics of the

social intercourse between husband and wife. As soon as the man came in, the woman kept quiet and faded into the background. She did not even take any initiative in making tea or food for us, but waited until her husband ordered it. The majority of women are firmly convinced that they cannot make one step without the permission of the man. The only influence of men in their absence seemed to be that the majority of the women were deeply concerned not to provoke the bad opinion of the neighborhood" (1970:26).

Much of the information the women receive about the outside world is received from their husbands. In this way, men exert a tremendous influence on the beliefs and prejudices of their wives (ibid.:28). The chief topics of conversation among women are pregnancies, births, and babies. Children are the pride of every mother. Women desire to have children who are respected and who in turn respect the family (ibid.:29-31).

Family honor and solidarity are major values in most Muslim societies, whether the traditional patriarchal type is adhered to or not. All that the individual does reflects back on the way the family is regarded. The family as a whole is responsible for the actions of any individual. Members of the family are bound together by strong ties of mutual obligations and responsibilities. This interdependence represents both security and a lack of individualistic expression. Muhammad Abdul-Rauf, a modern Muslim apologist who attempts to emphasize the independence and rights of family members as individuals, nevertheless admits this, particularly in relation to the religion of children:

"According to the Muslim law, a child of a Muslim parent is a Muslim at birth. A parent who allows his child to be of another faith is regarded to have rejected his own religion" (1977:103).

The woman, particularly the wife and mother, represent the family in its aspects as a moral corporation through her reputation for modesty. The family is the focus of security, and the woman of traditional segments of society prefers to stay within the familiar surroundings of neighborhood, friends and relations.

"By definition, a male outsider is considered a thief and a female outsider is considered a prostitute. It is not surprising then that a woman and her family consider it a great loss of prestige that she should leave her place of origin to go to get married in another village" (Abu-Zahra 1970:1085).

Mernissi adds:

"The fear of mistreatment and of beating is one of the
reasons why the girl and her family usually prefer marriage
to a husband who lives in the same neighborhood" (Mernissi
1975:61).

Elizabeth Fernea's experiences in southern Iraq confirm the fact
that the women were afraid of being beaten, divorced, or left
bereft of their wealth: her friends taught her to cook rice
so she would not be beaten by her husband, advised her to gain
weight so he would not divorce her, and to get much gold
jewelry from him and wear it at all times against possible
disaster (Fernea 1965:86,138,139).

The women of Azam Basti value respect more than love:
"Respect always comes first; there can only be love if there is
respect" (Kunst 1970:41). While on the one hand a husband's
love for his wife is considered a distraction from his worship
of God (Mernissi 1975:14), love for the mother is encouraged
to take the form of life-long gratitude (Abdul-Rauf 1977:24,25).
The figure of the mother-in-law is a powerful one in traditional
families where sexual segregation prevails; in more modern
families, the husband has become the most important person in
the woman's daily life (Mernissi 1975:46). She can be both a
safeguard for the woman against the injustices of her husband
and a hindrance to a close friendship between the spouses. It
is the mother, not the son, who initiates the marriage and
carries out the decisions concerning the creation of her son's
new family.

III. THE PARTICIPATION OF WOMEN IN ISLAM

The participation of women in Islam has usually been spoken
of with respect to the five pillars of Islam, duties which they
are also responsible to fulfill. Women are generally encouraged
or obliged to pray at home rather than in the mosques; attentiveness to prayer varies a great deal from place to place. "On
the whole," wrote Hilma Granquist, "it seems that both the men
and the women think that the Koran is something which does not
concern the women and this may account for their holding fast
to the ancient customs" (Granquist 1947:154). Maryam Jameelah,
an American convert to Islam living in Pakistan, wrote: "Too
many Muslim households keep their copy of the Quran wrapped up
in a beautiful silken cover on a high shelf merely to gather
dust" (1976:9). Lucy Wood Saunders wrote that in the rural
areas of the Egyptian Delta, the women:

"hear the Koran only during Ramadan when it is read in their
own houses, and that happens only in houses of women of

higher socio-economic position, or when they listen from
outside guest houses during funeral recitations or when they
go to tombs on days of special observance. On the other
hand, women are well informed about magical practices; they
go to the shaikh in a nearby village for cures, preventives
of harm, divining, and also for magically harmful objects.
Men also employ such means, but women are more open about
it while men are more likely to conceal it, especially if
they are somewhat more sophisticated" (Fernea and Fernea
1972:389).

Although regular mosques are sometimes inaccessible to
women, the many shrines are not subject to this restriction. On
occasions of mawlids and moussems (celebrations marking the
death or birth of a saint, shaykh, or holy man), men and women
often mix freely. In some countries there are female counter-
parts to the men's zawiyas (religious brotherhoods), which form
an important part of the social and religious life of the women.
A category of religious women--mullahs, shaykhas, nakibas, etc.--
play an important role in women's religious activities, and an
often financially important role in their own families as well.

Much of the religious life of the Muslim woman remains
elusive to us because of our tendency to focus on formal rather
than popular Islam. Robert and Elizabeth Fernea write:

"Perhaps Western Orientalists have considered Sufism in its
myriad forms to be the exhaustive popular response of the
formalities of orthodox Islam. Yet as anyone knows who has
been attentive to the patterns of behavior and belief in
Middle Eastern villages (or towns, or cities), these worlds
are full of holy men and women, shrines, incarnate forces of
good and evil, evil eyes, incantations, and ceremonies; all
of which help to make up a cosmological outlook in which
formal Islam plays an important but by no means exclusive
role. Thus, our ignorance of the special religious worlds of
Middle Eastern women is only a subcategory in our general
lack of knowledge of popular belief systems" (Fernea and
Fernea 1972:391).

Working in southern Iraq, this husband-wife team observed
the qrayas, or popular readings held during the month of
Ramadan. The qraya was one of the few occasions that allowed
women to meet together in groups that cut across ordinary kin
groupings and which included representatives from all segments
of the community. Perhaps because of this, the women were
observed to be more involved in the proceedings than the men,
who were more passive. Among the women also the community
leadership patterns were less clear, prompting more women to
take responsibility for sponsoring the qraya. Following the

qrayas there were quranic readings. Each woman present would
take a turn at reading the suras, which gave everyone an
opportunity to participate personally in the proceedings.

   Throughout the whole Muslim world there are millions of
shrines dedicated to holy men and women from whom blessing is
sought. In all parts of the Middle East, these shrines form
an important part of the lives of the women, who visit them and
make vows, looking for help in matters that closely concern
them. In many places other inhabitants of the Nile river are
often placated with food, prayers, vows, and sacrifices. The
exorcism ceremony called the zar is found among many social
classes in Egypt. Women's zars no doubt serve to release a
great deal of inner tension, as the women fall into trances,
dance wildly and grab at the long hair of the shaykh leading the
dance, and laugh and weep energetically. Although the zar is
illegal and is called un-Islamic by Muslim modernists, it
continues to be widely practiced, even by those who claim
not to really believe in its efficacy.

   Robert and Elizabeth Fernea conclude:

"However sexually segregated Middle Eastern communities have
been, religion has normally provided women with a legitimate
arena of activity outside the home; in many instances women
have utilized this freedom to develop meaningful rituals
that reflect their own needs and concerns. Their freedom
to do this has perhaps been enhanced by a greater distance
from the influence of the ulama, the learned men of Islam
who have defined and protected orthodoxy. In this regard,
the position of women may differ slightly from that of men"
(1972:401).

   Women like the 8th century mystic Rabica al-Adawiyya, or
the teacher of the theologian Ibn Taymiyya (d. 1328) are rare
in Islam. Very few women have been schooled in the Islamic
sciences or have claimed to love God and know him. Rabica, by
her celibate lifestyle and her association with men, can only
be seen as an eccentric in the history of Muslim womanhood.
The majority of women probably believe, as Fatima Mernissi
wrote, that Allah does not speak to women (1975:81). Most women
turn instead to saints, spirits, talismans, and magic. What
a contrast to see our Lord sitting at a well, telling a despised
Samaritan woman that he wishes to give her a spring of water
welling up to eternal life! Only in Christ will the Muslim
woman find dignity, wholeness, freedom from fear, and a new
life by the power of the Spirit of God.

IV.   THE FAMILY AND CHURCH PLANTING

In an article in the July 1978 issue of <u>Evangelical Missions Quarterly</u>, Dr. Terry Hulbert of the Columbia Graduate School of Bible and Missions wrote that:

> "The home is a key factor in evangelism and church growth
> . . . Household evangelism has strong biblical and strategic
> bonds with church growth principles. It involves two ideas:
> 1) The Christian home is a <u>means</u> of evangelizing the extended
> family and the community, and 2) the pagan family is the <u>goal</u>
> of evangelism " (p. 171).

The author relates how in Sierra Leone evangelists first went to the person in authority and received permission to teach the people.

> "They were exposed to the basics of the gospel in the process
> of determining if the message should be taught. When the
> village leader gives permission to preach, people feel freer
> to receive the message than if their leader had been bypassed.
> Even when the ruler is resistant to the gospel, he will often
> give permission to teach it, if he is approached with respect.
> What is true of a village situation usually applies also to
> penetrating a household unit. A respectful approach to the
> head is appropriate and potentially very productive" (p. 172).

God has certainly dealt with households as units in both Old and New Testaments, and this tactic has been cited as a factor in the effectiveness of Father Zacharia's ministry in Egypt. In light of all that we have said concerning the influence of men over women, most explicitly stated in Emmy Bos Kunst's study of the women of Azam Basti, it seems that to go directly to the women with the gospel, circumventing the authority of the man, could reduce our effectiveness and have harmful repercussions. Although we do not deny that Christ calls us each to individually follow him, the individualism of our culture may cause our evangelistic methods to be ill-adapted to Muslim culture. "Household evangelism respects the integrity of the home, moving <u>with</u> and not <u>against</u> the social unit created by God" (Hulbert 1978:175). Isn't this a biblical response to the problem of social ostracism?

Are there any limitations to the implementation of this plan in the Muslim world? For example, Peter and Paul both preached to whole households at a time. C. R. Marsh found himself reading from the Word to an entire Kabyle family; the women, though ignored, were present and listening (1970:57-58). Are there restrictions to applying this in a sex-segregated society?

The other side of household evangelism is the impact of Christian households. Dr. Hulbert writes that in South Africa, the witness of Christian families who invite Hindu families to spend time with them has resulted in entire families turning to Christ. "In this practical way, household evangelism reveals Jesus Christ to a whole Hindu family in a way they would never have seen by passing a church building, or by a brief individual contact" (Hulbert 1978:176). How much of an impact are Christian families making on the Muslim world?

V. THE IDEAL WOMAN IN ISLAMIC SOCIETY: WHAT THIS MEANS FOR US

Any western woman who has lived in the Muslim world has no doubt experienced the humiliation of offensive male behavior. But what is our offense to them? Do we refuse to abide by accepted norms of modesty in dress and behavior? Do we associate freely with men, walking with them in the streets, sitting next to them in worship services? We may excuse ourselves, knowing that they know that we are different, and do not expect us to conform to their standards. But as long as we abide in this difference, we will be considered as outsiders and strangers. The Muslim world knows of the sexual laxity of our society. The assumption is that we are immodest and unchaste until we prove ourselves otherwise. Although the Muslim woman is a mirror which a breath may cloud, we are already clouded and can only win trust and respect by patience and a willingness to do that which is honorable in their sight.

Emmy Bos Kunst wrote:

"When we got to know more about the customs and ways of the women, which takes quite a time for a foreigner, we felt more and more the need for conformity in behavior. We adopted, as far as possible, the external characteristics of the people, for instance their dress, language, and manners. This was appreciated to such an extent that the women even started insisting that we adapt ourselves completely to their ways. Still, we rarely had a feeling of being considered part of their number" (1970:8).

Had Ms. Kunst settled among them and involved herself in daily relationships with them, would she have felt more as one of them?

What really are the keys to acceptance? In southern Iraq, Elizabeth Fernea adopted the veil and adhered to the rules of purdah. Then she finally found acceptance into the society of the women when she learned Arabic well enough to reply to their sarcastic humor! "This repartee succeeded brilliantly where my former bland and accommodating manner had not" (Fernea 1965:140).

What is the ideal woman in Muslim society?

"Though the town and the country are worlds apart, a good
woman is the same in both spheres: her reputation for
fidelity is above reproach, she is hard-working, a devoted
wife and mother, a good cook and housekeeper, and a quiet,
obedient companion to her husband. Women did influence,
but without coercion, without publicity, and above all
without reproach" (Fernea 1965:65).

Our religion is a religion of love. "'All I learn here,' said
a Mohammedan woman in a missionary hospital, 'is of love. We
hear no mention of love in our religion.'" (Zwemer 1926:69). It
is the love of Christ that will speak most urgently to the
Muslim woman. Yet Muslim women also see that respect comes
before love (Kunst 1970:41-42). Surely our highest respect
to the Muslim woman can be seen in acknowledging the goodness
of her values, and accommodating ourselves to her ways.

VI. PROPOSALS

1. That we respect the code of modesty and sexual segregation
in classes and countries where this prevails.

2. That in addition to worship services for both sexes,
women's activities in their homes are important, that women
may feel at ease to participate and express themselves freely.

3. That we recognize and respect the authority of men who
are heads of households, and attempt to witness to entire
families at once.

4. That we attempt to find out what women are recognized as
religious or community leaders, and work through them.

5. A Christian alternative to demonic influence in the lives
of women must be presented in a demonstration of the power of
Christ.

I invite the participants in this conference to comment on
the extent and manner that these proposals are already being
acted out in the Muslim world, and to expand on the suggestions
here made.

BIBLIOGRAPHY

Abdul-Rauf, Muhammad
    1977   The Islamic View of Women and the Family. New York:
            Robert Speller & Sons, Inc.

Abu-Zahra, Nadia M.
    1970   "On the Modesty of Women in Arab Muslim Villages: A
            Reply," American Anthropologist 72:1079-1087.

Antoun, Richard T.
    1968   "On the Modesty of Women in Arab Muslim Villages,"
            American Anthropologist 70:671-697.

Dawood, N. J.
    1974   The Koran. Penguin Books.

Doutte, Edmund
    1908   Magie et Religion dans l'Afrique du Nord. Algiers:
            Societe Musulmane du Maghreb.

Fernea, Elizabeth W.
    1965   Guests of the Sheik. New York: Doubleday & Co.,
            Inc.

    1970   A View of the Nile. New York: Doubleday & Co., Inc.

    1975   A Street in Marrakech. New York: Doubleday & Co.,
            Inc.

Fernea, Robert A. and Elizabeth W. Fernea
    1972   "Variation in Religious Observance among Islamic
            Women," Scholars, Saints and Sufis: Muslim
            Religious Institutions Since 1500. Edited by
            Nikkie R. Keddie. University of California Press,
            pp. 385-401.

Goode, W. J.
    1963   World Revolution and Family Patterns. Glencoe: The
            Free Press.

Gordon, David C.
    1968   Women of Algeria: An Essay on Change. Harvard
            University.

Granquist, Hilma
    1947   Birth and Childhood Among the Arabs. Hilsingfors.

Hulbert, Terry C.
　　1978　　"Families are both the means and goal of evangelism,"
　　　　　　Evangelical Missions Quarterly 14:171-177.

Jameelah, Maryam
　　1976　　Islam and the Muslim Woman Today. Lahore: Mohammad
　　　　　　Yusuf Khan.

Kunst, Emmy Bos
　　1970　　Women of Azam Basti.

Marsh, C. R.
　　1970　　Too Hard for God? Bath: Echoes of Service.

　　1975　　Share Your Faith With A Muslim. Chicago: Moody
　　　　　　Bible Institute.

Mernissi, Fatima
　　1975　　Beyond the Veil. Cambridge, Mass.: Schenkman.

Smith, Jane I. and Yvonne Y. Haddad
　　1975　　"Women in the Afterlife: The Islamic View As Seen
　　　　　　From Quran and Tradition," Journal of the American
　　　　　　Academy of Religion 43:39-50.

Yonan, Isaac Malek
　　1898　　Persian Women. Nashville: Cumberland Presbyterian
　　　　　　Publishing House.

Yusuf, Hajji Shaykh
　　1965　　"In Defense of the Veil," The Contemporary Middle
　　　　　　East. Edited by B. Rivlin and J. S. Szyliowicz.

Zwemer, Dr. and Mrs. Samuel Zwemer
　　1926　　Moslem Women. West Medford, Mass.: The Central
　　　　　　Committee of the United Study of Foreign Missions.

SUMMARY OF PARTICIPANT'S RESPONSES

--"Generally satisfactory and thorough (though) perhaps
   emphasizing the closed societies of Islam rather than the
   modern Muslim world."

Our readers felt that the proposals suggested by Ms. Hoffman
were excellent starting points. Only a few readers were able
to respond to this "late-in-the-process" paper, but several
of those who did offered further suggestions as to how to
open doors to Muslim women and families. Among them were the
development and use of further memorization skills, especially
important since so many Muslim women are non-readers, and
exploration of ways to help Muslim women have a better experience of natural childbirth and home birth. This was noted
in light of the point made by Ms. Hoffman that pregnancy and
childbirth are such prominant topics among Muslim women, and
a feeling that the hospital approach to childbirth we have
offered has been a great mistake.

AUTHOR'S REJOINDER TO PARTICIPANT'S RESPONSES

The drawbacks of a paper of this type are obvious from the start.
It is just as naive to consider all Muslim women as a unity as
it is to consider all Muslims as a unity. I was not attempting
in this paper to draw a picture of "the Muslim woman," but to
assess the many factors that must be considered before we can
plan specific strategies to reach Muslim women with the gospel.
No one of these factors is solely responsible for the status
and outlook of the Muslim woman, but they all interact with one
another in varying degrees according to the situation. I quoted
the quranic basis for the subjection of women without making
any comment as to whether Islam is to be blamed for the status
of the woman in most Muslim societies, or whether the average
Muslim's notion of what is Islamic is really based on the Quran.
Due to the limitations imposed on the length of the paper, I was
unable to draw together all the implications of the data I
supplied, but had to leave it in a somewhat uncohesive state.

I also do not deny the great differences between women in
different Muslim countries, or that sexual segregation is
breaking down. I attempted to be as broad as possible in the
terminology I used. However, I believe the changes have often
been far more superficial than most people realize or would like
to believe. Fatima Mernissi's comments, quoted on the fourth
page of my paper, reveal the deep confusion resulting from superficial change that has not found its correspondence in the
mind-set of the people. Family honor, with or without

traditional family structure, continues to be a strong value. In Tunisia, I was continually confronted with the contradiction between what some people said was socially acceptable and what was actually accepted by the people. Men and women who could converse freely within the walls of 'the University parted company when they left. Women in the police force were subjected to ridicule. There were open assumptions about the virtue of any woman who entered a 'restaurant. Yet in outward appearances, Tunisian women are among the most liberated in the Arab world. I do not believe that what I said in my paper is out of date for the vast majority of Muslim women. Nonetheless, I agree with Mitchell that we must be prepared to give answers to women who are not bound by traditional roles and outlooks. Responsible, educated Muslim women are Muslim women too, and should not be ignored. One of the purposes of the research to be carried out by the task force on strategies to reach women and children is to reach a better understanding of the differences that do exist between women in different social classes and countries. My paper can only be the most general introduction; societies and classes must be treated separately.

Surat al-A'raf (VII): 11-17, referred to by Rev. Jadalla S. Ghrayyeb in his response to my paper, tells the story of Satan's refusal to bow before Adam, and the condemnation of Satan as a result of his disobedience to God's command. Although one may possibly infer from the fact that Adam was to be worshiped, but not Eve, that man is superior to woman, this is not stated in the verses. Adam represents mankind, and it is not even clear that Eve was created before this incident is said to take place.

Finally, I would like to thank David Owen for his proposals. I did think of the memorization and chanting of Bible verses as a possible activity for women's meetings. There needs to be more research and experimentation on how the ways that women participate in Islam could be meaningfully adapted for Muslim women seeking Christ.

GLOSSARY

abangan
    the name used to describe the less orthodox of soft-line
    Muslims of Indonesia.

adat
    the name applied to the indigenous system of customary law in
    Indonesia.

Ahmadiah
    a heretical sect of Islam. The name is taken from the founder,
    Ghulam Ahmad Mirza, who claimed to have superseded Muhammad.

Al-din
    religious faith in Islam, implies a complete way of life.

Allah
    literally it means "The God," the name of the Supreme Being of
    the Muslims.

ayat
    the signs of God; his mighty acts in nature; miracles.

baraka
    the blessing of God; that charisma that characterizes a person
    with special religious power.

buduh
    the name applied to a common numerical talisman in the Middle
    East.

262

caliph
> the anglicisized form of the word "khalifah."

dawah
> the act of calling men to the path of Allah; the Islamic
> equivalent of missionary activity.

din
> the term for religion in Islam; it is applied to religious
> duties, specifically, the five basic obligations of the Muslim.

Fatima
> the daughter of Muhammad, the hand of Fatima--a talisman used
> in the Middle East to ward off the evil eye.

Five Pillars of Islam
> 1. the witness or recitation of the creed.
> 2. the saying of prayers at the five specified times of day.
> 3. the keeping of the fast during the month of Ramadan.
> 4. the giving of 1/40th of one's income to the poor, or for
>   religious causes.
> 5. the pilgrimage to Mecca and its environs.

hadith
> "tradition" in Islam, with regard to the reporting and recording
> of it; that which is transmitted is called the sunnah.

hajj
> pilgrimage to Mecca and its environs during the sacred month of
> Ramadan; required of a Muslim once in his lifetime.

hidayah
> guidance or instruction.

hijrah
> the emigration of Muhammad and the Muslim community from Mecca
> to Medina in 622 A. D. The Muslim calendar commences with
> this date.

huda
> guidance; revelation which guides man.

'id al adha
> the major festival in Islam during which sheep, camels, or
> cattle are sacrificed; it is obligatory of any Muslim who can
> afford it.

imam
> the leader of the mosque prayers.

iman
the articles of faith in Islam; the act of faith as
distinguished from the practice of faith or din.

Injil
the quranic term applied to the New Testament, incorrectly
understood by Muslim to mean the book that God revealed to
and through Jesus.

Isa
the Arabic term for the name of Jesus.

Isawa
a sect of Islam in northern Nigeria which exalts Jesus.

Issawiyun
the word used to describe a Muslim who exalts Jesus; can be
translated as "Jesus-ite."

Ishmaeli
a person belonging to a branch of Shiite Islam; taken from the
name of the son of Abraham, Ishmael.

Islam
literally, submission or surrender; understood to mean
surrender to Allah; the faith and practice of Muslim people.

jihad
exertion or militancy in the cause of Islam; holy war.

jinn
supernatural or angelic type beings, thought to be made of
fire; generally understood to be more evil than good.

kafir
the person who blasphemes, who says "no" to God, hence one who
rejects revelation in the Islamic sense.

khalifah
understood as God's vice-regent on earth; politically, the
succession of Muslim rulers from the time of the first one after Muhammad, Abu Bakr, to 1924 when it was abolished in Turkey.

kufur, kufr
the act of blaspheming; disbelief in God; rejection of
revelation; whatever belies God.

"la ilaha illa Allah"
"There is no god except God."

Maghreb
Arabic for west; generally applied to North Africa.

Mahdi
the rightly guided one; Muslims believe such a one shall return or appear, particularly in Shiah Islam, to lead the whole world to embrace Islam.

marabout
North African religious saint; a charasmatic leader of a Muslim religious order.

masjid
the place of bowing down, hence, the mosque, the Muslim place of worship.

Masjid 'Issawi
a Jesus Mosque.

minbar
the pulpit in the mosque.

mosque
the anglicized word for masjid, the Muslim place of worship.

mullah
a term applied to a Muslim religious leader.

Muslim
one who has surrendered to God; a follower of the Islamic faith.

nakibas
plural form of the head of an Islamic religious brotherhood.

Nebi 'Isa
The Prophet Jesus.

"People of the Book"
the translation of the quranic phrase "ahl-i-kitab"; refers to Jews and Christians who have holy books.

Pillars of Islam
(see Five Pillars of Islam)

qadr
the decree or power of God in determining men's affairs; the Islamic understanding of predestination.

qarina
a familiar spirit; an offspring of Satan.

qraya
> popular reading of the Quran, especially during the sacred month of Ramadan.

Quran
> the name of the sacred Scriptures of Islam; the book of the revelations which Muhammad understood he was to recite.

ramadan, ramadhan
> the name of the sacred month in the Islamic (lunar) calendar, during which a Muslim is supposed to fast from sunrise to sunset.

salat
> ritual or liturgical prayer, performed five times a day.

santri
> applied to orthodox Muslims in Indonesia.

shahadah
> the witness or confession that "There is no god except God and Muhammad is the Messenger of God."

shariah
> the sacred law in Islam.

shaykhas
> plural of heads of religious brotherhoods in Islam.

shiah
> literally, "the sect," a minority sect of Islam that arose over the question of who should succeed Muhammad; the followers of Ali.

shirk
> association of anything with God; idolatry; the worse sin in Islam.

shukr
> gratitude, thankfulness.

sufi
> Muslim mystics; the word originally came from the word for "wool," because of the woolen garments worn by members of these orders.

sunnah
> the path of tradition; the traditions of Muhammad and the community of Islam.

sunni
> the major sect of Islam; those who follow the sunnah and the Quran.

sura, surah
> the word applied to describe a chapter of the Quran.

tauhid, tawhid
> the doctrine of divine unity; the oneness of God.

Towrah
> the Law which God gave to Moses.

ulama
> the learned and scholarly men of Islam; those who define and protect Islamic orthodoxy.

umma, ummah
> the community of Islam; the people of Islam.

waqf
> the system in Islam for the receiving and distribution of the alms, or the religious tax, called zakat.

Zabur
> the name applied to the Scriptures or the book God gave to David the Prophet.

zakat
> the word for alms, or the religious tax.

zar
> a ceremony connected with exorcism commonly practiced in Egypt.

BIOGRAPHIC INFORMATION

HARVIE M. CONN is Professor of Missions and Apologetics at Westminster Theological Seminary. He was a missionary to Korea under the Orthodox Presbyterian Church and the Reformed Church for 12 years. He has an Litt.D. from Geneva College and is the author of several books, including his forthcoming one Reaching the Unreached. He has also authored numerous journal articles and is editor of Theological Perspectives on Church Growth.

KENNETH A. CRAGG is Assistant Bishop of the Diocese of Wakefield, England. He has served as Assistant Bishop of Jerusalem and holds a D.Phil. from Jesus College, Oxford and an Honorary D.D. from Huron College in Ontario. He is a well known author of several books on Islam and the Christian understanding of Islam including The Call of the Minaret, The Mind of the Qu'ran and most recently Mohammed and the Christian: A Question of Response.

EDWARD R. DAYTON is Vice President of Mission and Evangelism at World Vision International. He has served on various church boards in the United States and holds a M.Div. from Fuller Theological Seminary. He has authored/co-authored five books focused on Christian management.

DAVID A. FRASER served in various overseas assignments with World Vision and has taught in several capacities. He has an M.A. from Harvard University and an M.Div. from Fuller Theological Seminary and is currently completing his Ph.D dissertation at Vanderbilt W. He has co-authored two books and has a number of journal articles published including a series on world mission with Dr. Ralph Winter.

ARTHUR F. GLASSER is Dean Emeritus of the School of world Mission at Fuller Theological Seminary. He served as a missionary...is the former editor of Missiology.

267

PAUL G. HIEBERT is Professor of Anthropology and Missions at Fuller Theological Seminary, School of World Mission...He is author of Cultural Anthropology as well as several other books and numerous articles.

VALERIE HOFFMAN teaches Arabic and Islamics, including Islam in Africa at the University of Illinois, Urbana from where she also received her Ph.D. in Islamics. She also studied for two years in Egypt and other Middle East locations.

CHARLES H. KRAFT is a Professor of Anthropology and African Studies at Fuller Theological Seminary, School of World Mission. He has been both a missionary and a field researcher in Northern Nigeria, and holds a Ph.D. in Anthropological Linguistics from Hartford Seminary Foundation. He is the author of several journal articles and the book Christianity in Culture.

DONALD N. LARSON is Chairman of the Department of Linguistics at Bethel College, as well as consultant to numerous mission boards on the subject of missionary orientation. He has a Ph.D. in Linguistics from the University of Chicago and has served as a missionary linguist in several capacities. He is the co-author of Becoming Bilingual: A Guide for Language Learning and A Barefoot Approach to Language Learning as well as other books and numerous journal articles.

BASHIR ABDOL MASSIH has served as an evangelist among Muslims in the Middle East for 20 years where he pioneered two fields and in which capacity he is presently serving. He is currently Home Director of Worldwide Evangelization Crusade. He has done postgraduate work in Islamics and Linguistics and is the author of several articles on witness to Islam and the cross-cultural communication of Christ.

DON M. McCURRY is Executive Director of the Samuel Zwemer Institute in Pasadena, California. He has a United Presbyterian missionary in Pakistan for 18 years. His post-graduate work has been in Urdu Literature at the Hartford Seminary Foundation and in English Education at Temple University. He is a Ph.D. candidate at Fuller Theological Seminary, School of World Mission. He is co-author of the Muslim Awareness Seminar Notebook and editor of Sharing the Gospel With Iranians: A Handbook and has articles published in several Christian periodicals.

BILL A. MUSK serves as Assistant Rector of All Saints Cathedral in Cairo. He as served as a short-term worker in Turkey and consultant for a publishing house in Lebanon and Turkey. He holds an M.A. in modern history from Oxford University and is a Ph.D. candidate at Fuller Theological Seminary, School of World Mission.

BRUCE J. NICHOLLS has worked in India for 30 years in several capacities. He is the former Secretary of the Theological Research and Communications Institute, New Delhi and is Chairman of the Theological Communications of WEF, as well. He has an M.Th. from Princeton Seminary and has contributed to several books as editor of <u>Evangelistic Theological Review</u> as well as numerous articles.

CHARLES R. TABER is Director of the Institute of World Studies/ Church Growth at Milligan College as well as an Associate Professor. He has 17 years experience as a missionary in France and French Equatorial Africa. He holds a Ph.D. in Anthropology/ Linguistics from the Hartford Seminary Foundation. He has edited several journals including **Gospel in Context** and had authored several books and numerous journal articles.

FRANK S. KHAIR ULLAH is Director of the Creative Writing Project of the Christian Publishing House in Lahore. He has 43 years of Christian work in Egypt and Pakistan and holds a Ph.D from Edinburgh University. He has done translation work in modern Urdu and contributed numerous articles to various Christian magazines.

WARREN W. WEBSTER is the General Director of the Conservative Baptist Foreign Missions Society. He served 15 years in Pakistan with CBFMS. He is a Summa Cum Laude graduate of Fuller Theological Seminary and holds an honorary doctorate from Denver Conservative Baptist Seminary. He is a contributor to several volumes on missions and the author of numerous articles.

J. CHRISTY WILSON, JR. is a Professor of Missions and Evangelism at Gordon-Conwell Theological Seminary. He ministered in various capacities in Afghanistan for 22 years and holds a Ph.D. from Edinburgh University. He has authored several books, the latest being <u>Today's Tentmakers. Self-support: An alternative model for worldwide witness</u>.